Children in conflict

Educational strategies for the emotionally disturbed
and behaviorally disordered

Children in conflict

Educational strategies for the emotionally disturbed
and behaviorally disordered

HENRY R. REINERT

Chairman, Department of Special Learning Problems,
University of Northern Colorado School of Special Education,
Greeley, Colorado

THE C. V. MOSBY COMPANY

Saint Louis   1976

Library of Congress Cataloging in Publication Data

Reinert, Henry R   1936-
    Children in conflict.

    Bibliography: p.
    Includes index.
    1. Mentally ill children—Education. I. Title.
LC4165.R44   371.9′4   75-22244
ISBN 0-8016-4105-5

Cover photograph by Norma Holt, New York, New York

GW/CB/B 9 8 7 6 5 4 3 2

To

Mary Ann, Brennan, Bernadette,
Kimberly, Kennan, and Becky

PREFACE

Children in Conflict is primarily a college level text for introductory or methods courses about emotionally disturbed and behaviorally disordered children. The text grew out of a need to acquaint students with a variety of theoretical approaches because not a single reference was available that adequately addressed itself to more than one or two approaches and then only in the form of readings.

This text is organized so that all the major theoretical approaches can be reviewed, compared, and contrasted without unnecessary expenditure of student or faculty time. For the student who wishes to pursue the study of emotional disturbance in more depth, extensive references and suggested readings are available.

The text is teacher and education directed. It is designed to give the teacher the necessary theoretical background, as well as the practical tools to implement programs for children in conflict. No single theoretical construct is held as the model for teachers to follow. Each is outlined, with strengths and weaknesses discussed briefly. I believe that teachers will select techniques that are effective in their classrooms once they are acquainted with a variety of tools.

The text is divided into three major sections. Section one deals with definitions, theoretical constructs, background information, and placement; section two covers classroom application and case studies; and section three outlines how theory can be integrated into practice. These major components correspond to those presented in our introductory and methods classes at the University of Northern Colorado. I hope others find them useful in support of their efforts.

I am sincerely grateful to all my students and colleagues who have helped to stimulate and direct my efforts. Special thanks go to Erik Blackhurst who did all the photographic work for the manuscript and to Jeanne Fuller, Dr. Tim Roberts, George Spitzmiller, and Mary Straw for their contributions to the text.

Additional thanks go to Mrs. Irma Anderson, Dr. James Bitter, and Dr. Bill Gearheart for reading the manuscript and for their helpful suggestions. Finally, my thanks to the administration of the University of Northern Colorado who granted a one-quarter sabbatical leave in the initial stages of manuscript preparation.

Henry R. Reinert

CONTENTS

Definitions, theoretical constructs, background information, and placement

CHAPTER 1

Emotional disturbance—an overview

Educational intervention with emotionally disturbed children has been a recent development in the public schools. John F. Kennedy, one of the most articulate presidents to speak on behalf of handicapped children, did much to stimulate this involvement. On February 5, 1963, President Kennedy (Public papers, 1963:137) made the following statement:

I have sent to the Congress today a series of proposals to help fight mental illness and mental retardation. These two afflictions have long been neglected. They occur more frequently, affect more people, require more prolonged treatment, cause more individual and family suffering than any other condition in American life.

It has been tolerated too long. It has troubled our national conscience, but only as a problem unpleasant to mention, easy to postpone, and despairing of solution. The time has come for a great national effort. New medical, scientific, and social tools and insights are now available.

The President was successful in securing a bill, Public Law 88-164, that included broad benefits for the handicapped. In addition to other provisions this law was aimed at increasing the number of professional personnel available to work with the handicapped, seriously emotionally disturbed, crippled, or other health impaired individuals (Martin, 1968).

The signing of Public Law 88-164 climaxed the efforts of dedicated professional and political leaders of the previous decade with ad-ditional legislative breakthroughs to follow.

John F. Kennedy, who had done so much to awaken America's conscience to the educational needs of handicapped children, died at the hand of an assassin who, as a child, was labeled "an emotionally, quite disturbed youngster" (The President's Commission, 1964:10). Whether the assassin could have been helped—and the destructive act avoided—is debatable; whether he was mentally ill at the time of the killing is unknown. What is known and important is the impetus supplied to education for the handicapped by the late President. His efforts on behalf of the handicapped were the catalyst for future growth, a foundation on which to build subsequent educational programs.

Educators have come a long way in building programs that were only dreams in the late 1950s and early 1960s, but many problems remain. Emotionally disturbed children pose many unanswered questions. How do educators best address themselves to the problems they present? What is the correct posture for the school in their regard? Where do educators go from here in their efforts to support mental health and a more productive future for all children? Section one will discuss these issues, beginning with a definition of children in conflict and proceeding to school placement alternatives.

Fig. 1-1. Children in conflict look much like other children, and they often do things that other children do. This boy looks "normal" and in most ways he is. However, his feelings often get in his way, and at times he is in conflict with himself and others.

DEFINING EMOTIONAL DISTURBANCE

Everyone is aware of terms like *problem behavior, emotional disturbance,* and *mental illness.* Although these phrases are in common usage, they appear to be vague when analyzed closely for exact meaning. The term most often used to describe children in conflict has been *emotionally disturbed.* Although this term suggests specific problems in children, its usefulness for teachers is questionable (Cumming and Cumming, 1968; Goffman, 1963; Szasz, 1961).

The term *emotionally disturbed* crept into the literature about seventy-five years ago without being defined (Reinert, 1972). Since then it has served a variety of needs for teachers, physicians, psychologists, and others interested in children's emotional problems, but it has no universally accepted definition.

Several commonly used definitions of the emotionally disturbed or behaviorally disordered child follow:

1. A moderate to marked reduction in behavioral freedom, which in turn reduces his ability to function effectively in learning or working with others. In the classroom, this loss of freedom affects the child's educative and social experiences and results in a noticeable susceptibility to one or more of these five patterns of behavior: (a) an inability to learn which cannot be adequately explained by intellectual, sensory, neurophysiological, or general health factors; (b) an inability to build or maintain satisfactory interpersonal relationships with peers and teachers; (c) inappropriate or immature types of behavior or feelings under normal conditions; (d) a general pervasive mood of unhappiness or depression; and (e) a tendency to develop physical symptoms, such as speech problems, pains, or fears, associated with personal or school problems. [Bower and Lambert, 1971: 142-143]

2. A child is disturbed when his behavior is so inappropriate that regular class attendance (a) would be dis-

rupting for the rest of the class, (b) would place undue pressure on the teacher, or (c) further the disturbance of the pupil. [Pate, 1963:242]

3. Behavioral disabilities are defined as a variety of excessive, chronic, deviant behaviors ranging from impulsive and aggressive to depressive and withdrawal acts (a) which violate the perceiver's expectations of appropriateness and (b) which the perceiver wishes to see stopped. [Graubard, 1973:246]

4. A behavior deviation is that behavior of a child which (a) has a detrimental effect on his development and adjustment and/or (b) interferes with the lives of other people. [Kirk, 1962:330]

5. One who because of organic and/or environmental influences, chronically displays: (a) inability to learn at a rate commensurate with his intellectual, sensory-motor and physical development, (b) inability to establish and maintain adequate social relationships, (c) inability to respond appropriately in day to day life situations, and (d) a variety of excessive behavior ranging from hyperactive, impulsive responses to depression and withdrawal. [Haring, 1963:291]

6. The child who cannot or will not adjust to the socially acceptable norms for behavior and consequently disrupts his own academic progress, the learning efforts of his classmates, and interpersonal relations. [Woody, 1969:7]

These six definitions of emotional disturbance and/or behavioral disorders indicate the wide interpretation given to this phenomenon. A large number of behavior deviations have been variously labeled and described by professionals. These terms represent a sincere effort to pinpoint deviance from a variety of viewpoints. The following terms point out the complexity of problems presented by children who are in conflict with themselves and/or those around them.

asocial Without apparent social values.
autistic Exhibiting severe withdrawal from reality.
behavior problem Any of the more severe behavior deviations.
character disorder Suffering from flaws in personal behavior.
delinquent Exhibiting unacceptable behavior in youth, which is in violation of the law.
disruptive Causing disorder that interferes with others, usually aggressive in nature.
emotionally disturbed Deviating from or interfering with normal emotional processes.
learning problem Any one of many behaviors that interferes with acquisition of knowledge.
nervous Excessively anxious.
neurotic Suffering from anxiety, fears, obsessions, and unusual behavior.
personality disorder Personality trait that interferes with social adjustment.

psychopathic Exhibiting lack of social feeling that allows social deviance without guilt.
psychotic Exhibiting extreme denial of reality through behavior.
schizophrenic Suffering from severely disorganized behavior.
sick Mentally ill.
socially maladjusted Deviating from socially accepted norms of behavior.
sociopathic Badly adjusted in regard to social relationships.
spoiled Excessively indulged.
uninhibited Acting without normal inhibitions.
unsocialized Lacking in social skills.
withdrawn or overinhibited Inhibited or restricted in behavior, which can negatively affect learning.

CHILDREN IN CONFLICT—AN ALTERNATIVE

In my opinion all of the preceding terms or labels are related to the problems that some children present to teachers, parents, and others with whom they come into contact. Some, such as autistic, schizophrenic, and psychotic, are labels of severe disorders seldom encountered in the regular classroom; others are references to relatively mild behavior problems that occur regularly throughout the school day. Most teachers have moved away from labels like *emotional disturbance* when referring to behavior problems in the classroom. The emerging pattern in special education programs is to abandon terms borrowed from other professions in favor of a more inclusive term like *behavioral disability* (Graubard, 1973). For the purposes of this text the term *behaviorally disordered* still fails to describe adequately the children served in public schools throughout the United States. This term implies that specific deviance or disorders are present *within the child.* Many children are encountering moderate to severe disorders in their daily activities, not because of *their* behavior but *because of the situation in which they find themselves.* The child whose mother recently died might well experience a serious problem which manifests itself in unusual behaviors (for that child) which require professional attention. This child, although experiencing behavior problems, certainly should not be labeled a behaviorally disordered child.

Labeling children as *emotionally disturbed,*

behaviorally disordered, or *mentally ill* will be avoided in this text whenever possible. These terms will only be used when the behaviors being considered can be more accurately described through their use rather than the more general term *children in conflict*. The main reason for choosing the term *children in conflict* is that it more adequately describes the children being served in school programs. These children are in conflict (nothing more or less) with their environment. They might be having a relationship problem with their teacher or a peer, they might be in conflict with themselves, or they may be the victims of uncontrollable circumstances in their homes.

The use of the term *children in conflict* offers several advantages for the child.

1. The sometimes traumatic impact of a term like *emotional disturbance* could be reduced significantly both for children and parents.

2. The self-fulfilling prophecy that often follows the labeling process could be minimized.

3. The term *children in conflict* more accurately describes the children being served than does the term *emotionally disturbed.*

4. The mystique surrounding mental illness could be diminished.

For this text the child in conflict is defined as follows: *the child whose manifest behavior has a deleterious effect on his personal or educational development and/or the personal or educational development of his peers. Negative effects may vary considerably from one child to another in terms of severity and prognosis.*

Several writers have tried to specify the deviant emotional behaviors typically found in the classroom (Bower, 1960; Dunn, 1973; Maes, 1966; Pate, 1963; Quay, Morse, and Cutler, 1966; Walker, 1970.) As a result of their efforts, my teaching experience, and observation of many classroom settings, four subcategories of children in conflict are proposed.

1. Acting-out behaviors (hitting, aggressive, disruptive behaviors)

2. Withdrawing behaviors (absence of

speech, thumbsucking, restricted behaviors)

3. Defensive behaviors (lying, cheating, avoiding tasks)

4. Disorganized behaviors (autistic behaviors, out of touch with reality)

These behaviors generally do not appear in isolation; often a child may exhibit combinations of these behaviors during a short period of time. For example, a child may act out feelings by hitting or other aggressive acts. When questioned by the teacher, the child may exhibit behavior such as lying or withdrawing into a shell of self-pity. The variety of behavior exhibited is often confusing to teachers. Classification of behaviors into meaningful systems is an attempt to simplify and increase teacher effectiveness in coping with deviance, but it will not, in itself, bring a change in a child's behavior; it will only help the teacher "get a handle" on deviance to facilitate educational programing.

The behaviors outlined as subcategories of children in conflict have one additional dimension that is important to teachers: the severity of the problem.

Kelly, Bullock, and Dykes (1974:10) have outlined three broad programs or service categories for behaviorally disordered children. These include the following broad classifications:

1. *Mild behavioral disorders*
   Children or youth with behavioral disorders who can be helped adequately by the regular classroom teacher and/or other school resource personnel through periodic counseling and/or short term individual attention and instruction

2. *Moderate behavioral disorders*
   Children or youth with behavioral disorders who can remain at their assigned school but require intensive help from one or more specialists (i.e., mental health clinics, diagnostic centers)

3. *Severe behavioral disorders*
   Children or youth with behavioral disorders who require assignment to a special class or special school

The impact of service categories outlined here will be discussed more fully in Chapter 3. For now it may be sufficient merely to outline the three program categories and to relate them briefly to children in conflict.

Marmor and Pumpian-Mindlin (1950) have

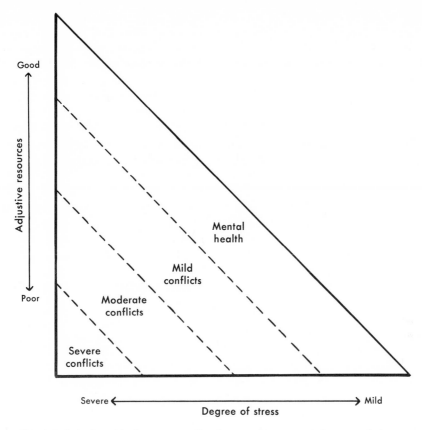

Fig. 1-2. Relationship between adjustive resources and degree of stress.

outlined the relationship that develops between the adjustive resources of an individual and the degree of stress under which he lives. Fig. 1-2 adapts this concept to children in conflict, describing their behavior as mild, moderate, and severe. Several important results of adjustive resources and degree of stress are shown in Fig. 1-2.

1. Most children are in the *mental health* portion of the diagram, whereas only a small portion of the total population fall into the *severe* category.

2. The conflict of each child is determined by two factors: the *degree of stress* and the child's *adjustive resources*. A child can have good mental health and still live under moderate to severe stress. Likewise a child can live with only mild stress and fall within the moderate to severe conflict portion of the diagram because of poor adjustive resources.

3. The *mental health* of an individual is not

statically categorized but a living interaction that changes with adjustive resources and stress.

Prevalence

The prevalence of children in conflict varies considerably from one study to another, depending on (1) the agency or individual making the prediction, (2) the definition used in each study, (3) the reason for estimating the population, and (4) the instrument used in evaluating deviance. The United States Office of Education, Bureau for the Education of the Handicapped, estimates that 2% of children are emotionally disturbed. Kirk (1972) in a review of several studies of emotional disturbance reports estimates of from 2% to 22%. Bower (1960) reports that approximately 10% of school-age children are handicapped by their emotions. Although studies of prevalence do not agree as to the specific number of disturbed children, they generally show that the number of children in conflict is high.

Boys who are identified as having emotional problems generally outnumber girls between six or seven to one and sometimes outnumber girls in special class placement by nine or ten to one. This is generally attributed to types of behaviors that boys exhibit (acting-out, aggressive behaviors), whereas girls often exhibit behavior (withdrawal) that is more acceptable in classrooms.

Chapter 2 will outline a theoretical construct for children in conflict, a construct that attends to deviance from five theoretical domains: biophysical, psychodynamic, behavioral, sociological/ecological, and counter theory.

Background information

It is important for teachers of children in conflict to develop a basic understanding of how human beings have evolved (educationally) to the point at which they now find themselves. An understanding of the background from which present educational prac-

tices have come should provide three advantages. First, it should put today's practices into perspective with what has gone before. Second, it should enable educators to avoid many of the errors of the past and capitalize on the positive approaches that have made an impact on children in conflict. Third, it should develop a basis of understanding that will serve as a "springboard" for acquiring new information and methods in teaching children.

Knowledge of mental illness and how to treat it has come slowly. New information evolved and then was rejected as society has repeatedly fallen backward into nonacceptance of new ideas concerning treatment of the mentally ill. Table 1 outlines several landmarks in the history of mental illness.

MENTAL ILLNESS BEFORE THE TWENTIETH CENTURY

In addition to these landmarks in treatment there were occurrences that have helped shape society's present attitude toward mental illness. One example is an apparent lack of concern for emotionally disturbed children.

Table 1. Landmarks in treatment of emotional problems prior to the twentieth century

Contribution	Era	Source
Hippocrates proposed that emotional disturbance was the result of natural causes rather than supernatural powers.	400 B.C.	Lewis, 1944
Plato postulated that mentally disturbed persons who committed criminal acts should not be held responsible for their deeds in the same manner as "normal persons."	375 B.C.	Plato, n.d.
Alexander the Great built temples, dedicated to Saturn, that were excellent sanatoriums for the mentally ill.	330 B.C.	Menninger, 1944
Asclepiades advocated humane treatment of mentally ill patients and made the first attempts at psychiatric classification of mental illness.	90 B.C.	Coleman, 1964
Aretaeus was the first to describe phases of mania and melancholia as expressions of the same illness.	100	Coleman, 1964
Death of Galen started the "Dark Ages" of psychiatry.	200	Coleman, 1964
Most difficult period in history for the mentally ill saw their persecution and a return to demonology and superstition.	1450-1700	Coleman, 1964
Anecdotal writings concerning deviant children began to appear.	1750	Kanner, 1962
Reform initiated for the mentally ill, including the work of William James, Emil Kraepelin, Benjamin Rush, Dorothea Dix, Ellen Key, and Clifford Beers.	1900	Felix, 1967; Beers, 1953; Kanner, 1962

Kanner (1962), a highly regarded practitioner and writer, reports that prior to the eighteenth century there was not so much as an allusion to emotional disorders in children. He says that "This does not warrant the assumption that infantile emotions always ran a smooth course in the past and that the occurrence of their disturbances is a relatively recent phenomenon."

It appears that "opinion setters" prior to the eighteenth century were preoccupied with matters other than children's emotional problems. Whether this was a gross indifference to children with emotional problems stemming from a lack of humanistic attitudes or a simple "setting of priorities" for survival is not known. A plausible explanation might be that children in conflict were more able to be molded into the more agrarian society prior to the nineteenth century. As society became more complex, children in conflict became a more serious problem for parents and for society in general.

In the years before the French and American revolutions the rights of the individual were becoming increasingly important. It was inevitable that the problems of the handicapped child would come into focus as people began to think about individual needs and rights. This does not mean, however, that techniques and materials were immediately available to those interested in helping children in need; an idea was begun, and people began to care and to speak up for those who would otherwise not be heard.

During the eighteenth century, various accounts or case reports of deviant children began to be published. These were generally in diary form rather than a scientific study and were written more for general informational value than for any other purpose. Kanner (1962) has translated a paragraph from a clergyman's diary that tells the story of Emerentia. The excerpt was taken from an autobiographical novel, *Der grüne Heinrich* by Gottfried Keller, in whose village the incident took place in 1713.

This 7-year-old girl, the offspring of an aristocratic family, whose father remarried after an unhappy first matrimony, offended her "noble and god-fearing" step-mother by her peculiar behavior. Worst of all, she would not join in the prayers and was panic-stricken when taken to the black-robed preacher in the dark and gloomy chapel. She avoided contact with people by hiding in closets or running away from home. The local physician had nothing to offer beyond declaring that she might be insane. She was placed in the custody of a minister known for his rigid orthodoxy. The minister, who saw in her ways the machinations of a "baneful and infernal" power, used a number of would-be therapeutic devices. He laid her on a bench and beat her with a cat-o'nine-tails. He locked her in a dark pantry. He subjected her to a period of starvation. He clothed her in a frock of burlap. Under these circumstances, the child did not last long. She died after a few months, and everybody felt relieved. The minister was amply rewarded for his efforts by Emerentia's parents.

By the middle of the nineteenth century a growing number of anecdotal writings began to be published. A few mental health professionals were not satisfied with simply reporting the accounts of deviant behavior—they wanted to study this behavior. In 1867 Maudsley wrote a chapter on "Insanity of Early Life," which he included in his text *Physiology and Pathology of Mind.* This work encouraged interest in children and the mental disorders that affected their lives.

In the final decades of the nineteenth century several texts were written concerning various mental and psychic disorders. In these texts there was a tendency toward fatalism. The authors described the disorders as the result of heredity, degeneracy, masturbation, overwork, preoccupation with religion, intestinal parasites, or sudden changes in temperature (Kanner, 1962).

Some of the ideas held by theorists of the nineteenth century were preliminary attempts at the much more sophisticated science of medicine that exists today. The lack of medical technology prevented these early attempts from reaching their full potential in answering questions being posed.

The conceptualization of mental illness as a definite sickness based on organic brain pathology is called the organic viewpoint, which represented the first great advance of modern science in the understanding and treatment of mental illness (Coleman, 1964). Several theorists, including Albrecht von Haller (1708-1777) and William Griesinger

(1817-1868), advocated the study of the brain as a basis of mental illness. However, it was Emil Kraepelin (1856-1926) who played the dominant role in the establishment of the organic viewpoint (Coleman, 1964). Kraepelin, whose textbook *Lehrbuch der Psychiatrie* (Theories of Psychology) was published in 1883, is generally credited with establishing the basis for the present psychiatric classification system, with the subsequent period in psychiatry often referred to as the "descriptive era." One of the finest hours of the organic approach was achieved with the discovery of the syphilitic basis of general paresis (syphilis of the brain). This was not accomplished as a shot in the dark but, rather, became a reality only after many years of research by the most able medical scientists in the world. The medical model also achieved significant success in uncovering the organic pathology of toxic psychosis and certain types of mental retardation.

Early efforts to study the individual child were being made in education toward the end of the nineteenth century. These early writers were undoubtedly influenced by such giants as Rousseau and Pestalozzi and by the teachings of William James and John Dewey. The change from looking at the individual as one who should fit into the mold of society to one who should grow as an individual was revolutionary at the turn of the century.

Two of the earliest writings that deal with the descriptive aspects of mental diseases in children were published in Paris in the latter part of the nineteenth century. One by Paul Moreau, *La folie chez les enfants*, 1888 (Madness in Children) indicates that little was done before the nineteenth century either to understand mentally ill children or to grasp the phenomena that caused the mental illness (Crutcher, 1943). A second early work was Marcel Manheimer's *Les troubles mentaux de l'enfance*, 1899 (Childhood Mental Problems). This text was similar to Moreau's work but was more complete. Both Moreau and Manheimer emphasized the importance of treatment; preventive treatment was stressed for parents and teachers, such as setting a good example and loving and showing affection to the child.

THE TWENTIETH CENTURY

At about the turn of the twentieth century, child psychiatry had its beginning. Although there were many theorists who paved the road for child psychiatry, no formal attempts to study children and their unique psychiatric problems were made prior to 1900 (Kanner, 1957). This same era saw dramatic changes for the child in need of special help for emotional problems. In 1900 Ellen Key (1909), the now famous Swedish sociologist, made her often-quoted announcement that the twentieth century would become "the century of the child." The diaries written by Darwin, Pestalozzi, and others cleared the way for a new science called *developmental psychology*.

Biogenetic theorists believed that pathology of mental illness would soon be as easily defined and the course of illness as predictable as a case of measles. The basis for their optimistic predictions originated during the eighteenth century, when medical science was slowly finding answers to the pathology underlying problems in physical health. It was only natural that proponents of this system would quickly develop confidence that medical science was about to solve many of the questions related to mental illness. Unfortunately this has not proved to be true, since more than one half of the patients studied during this period failed to show any organic pathology (Coleman, 1964).

Early in the twentieth century the organic viewpoint lost some of its earlier popularity as a new psychological viewpoint began to take hold. Those advocating the medical model, however, were not ready to capitulate. With the discovery of phenylketonuria (PKU) in 1934 new life was breathed into the organic movement. This metabolic disorder is found in infants who are void of an enzyme that is needed to properly assimilate phenylalanine, an amino acid found in foods containing protein. With early detection through relatively simple urine or blood tests and subsequent dietary treatment the course of the disease can be materially altered, if not eliminated altogether. PKU is only one of more than twenty relatively rare biochemical diseases that are directly related to mental retardation. Its discovery marked one of the dramatic successes of medical science (Lyman, 1963; Weinberg et al., 1962). Whereas there is some indication that medical breakthroughs for the mentally ill are imminent, none of proven validity has occurred within the last decade.

The conscience of America was touched in the first decade of the twentieth century by Clifford Beers, a young law student who had earlier been hospitalized for a depressive condition. Beers, in his now famous book *A Mind That Found Itself*, published in 1908, told of his mental collapse and how he recovered at the home of a friendly attendant after being in three different institutions. In describing his treatment in the institution, Beers aroused the interest of many public-minded citizens as well as understanding professionals, including the eminent psychologist William James and the psychiatrist Adolph Meyer. It was Meyer (1957) who is credited with suggesting the term *mental hygiene*, intended as a corollary to the concept of mental illness. The first Society for Mental Hygiene was formed in 1908, and this local society later developed into the National Committee for Mental Hygiene (Coleman, 1964).

The development of testing instruments for children paralleled medical advances of the twentieth century. Among these advances were formalized psychological testing, including the initial work done by Alfred Binet and Theodore Simon on intelligence scales, which first appeared in print in 1905 and was later revised into what is now called the Stanford-Binet individual intelligence test. The Stanford-Binet test, and later the Wechsler Intelligence Scale for Children (WISC), were to have a dramatic impact on the evaluation of children in conflict. These two instruments continued to provide valuable information to clinicians who must differentiate between children who are mentally retarded and those who are mentally ill.

After the development of individual intelligence tests came tests to measure certain personality variables. The study of a person's "inner life" has become known as projective testing. The best known of the projective techniques is undoubtedly the Rorschach, developed by the Swiss psychiatrist, Hermann Rorschach. This test, first described in 1921, attempts to predict from the subject's associations to inkblots how he will react to others in his environment in both specific and more complex situations (Anastasi, 1968).

Sociological thought was a counterpart of both medical theory and test development at the turn of the twentieth century. Through vigorous efforts of professionals in sociology and anthropology, a reservoir of evidence began to accumulate which suggested that a relationship between sociocultural factors and mental illness did exist (Becker, 1963; Benedict, 1934). The importance of the child's home and community, the values of society, and the technology of the world in which a child lives are representative factors. Gradually these sociocultural findings began to permeate psychology and psychiatry, giving these two disciplines a more socially oriented appearance. Among the psychiatrists who recognized these findings by adding sociological thought to their own theoretical framework were Alfred Adler, Karen Horney, Harry Stack Sullivan, and Erich Fromm. The inclusion of parents, siblings, peers, and significant others in the study of childhood deviance was a significant milestone for children in conflict. It was a unifying force that contributed to the fusion of organic, psychological, and sociological viewpoints into a holistic approach (Rhodes and Sagor, 1974).

One recent adaptation of sociological and biological thought was that of ecological theory. Although ecology is closely allied to sociological thought, it is actually an outgrowth of the biological sciences. Interest in this theoretical construct has helped guide practitioners to a new realization that children are not only affected by their environment, as suggested in sociological theory, but they in turn modify the environment into which they enter.

Twentieth century educational thought was molded to a great extent by psychodynamic thought. When special education programs were initiated, they often followed an analytical or introspective bent. In 1907 the Public Education Association in New York City employed several workers called visiting teachers who had a combined knowledge of social work and classroom teaching (Krugman, 1948). The development of the visiting teacher concept was uncertain, with little recognition or success. With the growth of the mental hygiene movement of the 1920s the visiting teacher program began to develop some stature in educational and psychological circles. In 1921 there were approximately ninety visiting teachers in thirteen states; by 1927 this number had increased to over two hundred. After World War II the growth of visiting teachers paralleled other educational growth so that almost every community of any size had one or more visiting teachers employed. The visiting teacher movement undoubtedly stimulated interest in special education techniques, individual diagnostics, and prescriptive educational programing. The two have become mutually supportive, since many teachers working as visiting teachers received some or all of their training in special education. Working with psychologists and psychiatrists either through direct consultation or as a referring agent, the visiting teacher did much to promote trust and a spirit of cooperation between professional mental health workers and the school (Nudd, 1925).

Another parallel movement of the twentieth century that cannot be overlooked is the dramatic work of Sigmund Freud (1856-1939) and those who have modeled their theories from his. No other man has made such a dramatic impact on the study of the human personality. The study of human emotions that surround children in conflict would undoubtedly be considerably different if it were not for his pioneer work.

MIDDLE TWENTIETH CENTURY

During the 1940s two antithetical trends began to develop. One group of theorists indicated an interest in returning to the pre-Kraepelinian period of indefiniteness in labeling. Rank (1949), who supported moving away from specific classification, introduced the idea of the "atypical child," with determined disregard for the specific classifications of what is "atypical." Under Rank's system no difference would be noted between childhood psychosis, mental retardation, or any other forms of childhood disturbance. Szurek (1956:522) adequately stated the position held by those who wished to return to the pre-Kraepelinian period: "We are beginning to consider it clinically fruitless, and even unnecessary . . . to draw any sharp dividing lines between a condition that one could consider psychoneurotic and another that one could call psychosis, autism, atypical development, or schizophrenia."

In contrast, there were several theorists who held that differences in etiology (causation) did exist and that these differences had direct implications for treatment. Kanner (1949) graphically outlined the syndrome called early infantile autism, Mahler (1952) described a condition she called symbiotic infantile psychosis, and Bergman and Escalona (1949) made note of what they termed children with unusual sensitivity to sensory stimulation. About this same time Bender (1955) was observing children with a retarded and otherwise irregular development. Seeing that schizophrenic children exhibited specific behaviors, she began to classify the condition into specific clinical types. As Kanner (1962) has effectively pointed out, the field had occupied itself almost exclusively with psychosis in early childhood or, more specifically, with schizophrenia.

Although Kanner's statement of emphasis is true of medical and psychodynamic thought, it failed to recognize the emerging field of behavioral theory that was getting a strong hold in education during the late part of the 1950s. Behaviorism was really not a new concept in the 1950s, but its impact on schools was initially felt at that time. Previous to the introduction of behavioral research, the major technique for obtaining data concerning mental processes had been the introspective or projective method. By applying the conditioning techniques developed by Pavlov to human subjects, Watson was able to demonstrate that children's behavior could be conditioned. His classic demonstration of how children who have no fear of small animals can be conditioned to experience this fear is representative. By presenting an unpleasant shock (striking a steel bar with a hammer behind a boy's head) at the same time that a small animal was shown, the child was taught to fear the animal (Watson and Rayner, 1920). However, it is probably not Watson's theoretical genius that places him in his unique position in American psychology. Rather, it was his willingness to advance a radically new theoretical construct in opposition to the German tradition of psychoanalysis that had been articulated (Hill, 1963). Watson was supported in much of his theory by his professors at the University of Chicago where he had been awarded that institution's first doctorate of philosophy. Although his professors agreed with many of his objections to traditional analytical psychology, they generally believed his approach to be too radical. Watson disappointed those who thought that age would help to modify and mellow his radical approach to psychology. He never retreated from his original position taken in 1913, when he published his first formal statement, *Psychology as a Behaviorist Views It* (Hill, 1963). The American psychological revolution was on.

Just as Freud had been such a dynamic force in the realm of the subconscious, Watson became the torchbearer for those who were seeking a theoretical construct based on conscious thought processes. Watson's behaviorism marked the beginning of a system that was to have greater theoretical and practical impact on programing for children in conflict than any other theorist of our time (Woody, 1969). Theorists and practitioners who were stimulated by the pioneer work of Watson soon grew to new levels of understanding and practical application with behavioral tools. The principles of contiguity and reinforcement eventually led to practical

application within classroom settings, often with children in conflict.

One of the most recent developments in education has been the attention being paid to countertheorists' attacks on school programs and programing. These critics have been challenging various components of the educational system for many years. They have criticized the system of labeling, systems of grading, segregation encouraged by special programs, categorization by grades, leadership of schools, use of intelligence as a descriptive tool, and role of teacher training institutions on the educational system (Tracy, 1972).

It should be evident from this discussion that the study of children in conflict has been anything but a logical, uninterrupted, well-directed attack on childhood deviance. It should also be clear that the term *emotional disturbance*, although allegedly intended to be a specific descriptive term, has not been used with any measure of precision.

The theory that supports much of the program development for children in conflict will be presented in Chapter 2. Theoretical development will be outlined using basic constructs similar to those used by Rhodes and Tracy (1972).

SUMMARY

The term *emotionally disturbed* has been used to label a variety of behavioral problems in schools. It first appeared in the literature seventy-five years ago without being defined. Emotionally disturbed children have not been a homogeneous group in incidence, causation, or remediation. It would seem appropriate to avoid labeling children as emotionally disturbed for three reasons. First, the stigma now attached to children who are labeled emotionally disturbed would be significantly decreased. Second, most teachers would feel less threatened by describing inappropriate behavior rather than labeling it. Third, the self-fulfilling prophecy that is often encouraged through labeling could be minimized. As an alternative to the label emotional disturbance I propose a more comprehensive and educationally practical term, *children in conflict.*

Children in conflict can be defined as those whose manifest behavior has a deleterious effect on their personal or educational development and/or the personal or educational development of their peers. Negative effects may vary considerably from one child to another in terms of severity and prognosis. Deviant behaviors are divided into four basic types, which can be delineated through observation. These include acting-out behaviors, withdrawing behaviors, defensive behaviors, and disorganized behaviors.

The history of children in conflict outlines several significant features of the treatment of children. The historical development indicates that progression in treatment has been anything but logical, sequential, or predictable.

Background information for children in conflict is important for three basic reasons:

1. It should put today's practices into perspective with what has gone before.

2. It should help educators to avoid many of the errors of the past and capitalize on the positive approaches that have made an impact on children in conflict.

3. It should develop a basis of understanding that will serve as a springboard for acquiring new information and methods in teaching children.

The status of emotional disturbance in children before the twentieth century was uncertain because opinion setters were preoccupied with other matters. As society became more complex, children in conflict presented a more serious problem for parents. With the Industrial Revolution came a new awareness of children and a role that they were to play in society. As the rights of individuals of this society became more pronounced, it was inevitable that the problems of handicapped children would come into sharper focus. The fact that little seemed to be done for emotionally disturbed children prior to the twentieth century is an indication that people's attention was not focused on the needs of children rather than the idea that children's problems were nonexistent.

Before the twentieth century much study of the handicapped child evolved around the case study approach or diary approach. Scientific instruments of measurement were not available at that time so that in-depth research was not forthcoming. The work of Kraepelin at the turn of the twentieth century stimulated the development of psychiatric classification. The discovery of the syphilitic basis of general paresis is generally considered a milestone in the "descriptive era." Twentieth century biogenetic theorists believed that the pathology of mental illness would soon be defined and the course of illness as easily predicted as a case of measles. The development of a theoretical understanding of organic pathology, toxic psychosis, and certain types of mental retardation such as phenylketonuria are examples.

Early in the twentieth century the Stanford-Binet test and later the Wechsler Intelligence Scale for Children were developed. A major breakthrough during the twentieth century included individual projective tests designed to pinpoint various forms of mental illness. The rapid growth of child psychiatry and the establishment of the visiting teacher concept are all significant occurrences during the early part of the twentieth century. A parallel movement at this time was the dramatic work of Sigmund Freud and his associates. It is difficult to establish theoretical constructs from any other viewpoint without referring to Freud. A sharp contrast to the analytical approach espoused by German psychologists was put forth by John Watson and other behavioral researchers. Just as Freud had been such a dynamic force in the realm of the subconscious, Watson became the torch bearer for those who were seeking a theoretical construct based on conscious thought.

During the twentieth century, sociological/ecological thought stimulated new perspectives in the theories of Adler, Horney, Sullivan, and Fromm. The holistic approach of child study was becoming a reality. Faris and Dunham applied social disorganization to the study of mental illness, whereas Merton formulated a theory of anomie that attempted to explain mental illness from a sociological viewpoint.

Countertheorists of the twentieth century have caused many educators to reconsider their former positions in terms of educating children in conflict. Four common assumptions that have been attacked by countertheorists include the following:

1. Opposition to the idea that education possesses a quantifiable set of knowledge that should be passed on to a generation of children
2. The role of the teacher as a reservoir knowledge to be siphoned to each student
3. The question of literacy as a value system that is used as a political tool
4. The destruction of an individual personality that often results from schools

BIBLIOGRAPHY AND SELECTED READINGS

Adler, A.: Social interest, a challenge to mankind, New York, 1964, Capricorn Books, Division of G. P. Putnam's Sons.

Anastasi, A.: Psychological testing, New York, 1968, The Macmillan Co.

Bandura, A.: Principles of behavior modification, New York, 1969, Holt, Rinehart & Winston, Inc.

Becker, H.: Outsiders: studies in the sociology of deviance, New York, 1963, The Free Press.

Beers, C.: A mind that found itself; an autobiography, Garden City, N. Y., 1953, Doubleday & Co., Inc.

Bender, L.: Twenty years of clinical research on schizophrenic children, with special reference to those under six years of age. In Capian, G., editor: Emotional problems of early childhood, New York, 1955, Basic Books, Inc., Publishers.

Benedict, R.: Anthropology and the abnormal, Journal of General Psychology 10:59:80, 1934.

Bergman, P., and Escalona, S.: Unusual sensitivities in very young children. In Psychoanalytic study of the child, vols. 3 and 4, New York, 1949, International Universities Press, Inc.

Bower, E.: Early identification of emotionally handicapped children in school, Springfield, Ill., 1960, Charles C Thomas, Publisher.

Bower, E., and Lambert, N.: In-school screening of children with emotional handicaps. In Long, N., Morse, W., and Newman, R., editors: Conflict in the classroom, Belmont, Calif., 1971, Wadsworth Publishing Co., Inc.

Bron, A.: Some strands of counter psychology. In Rhodes, W. C.: A study of child variance, Ann Arbor, Mich., 1972, The University of Michigan Press.

Buckley, N., and Walker, H.: Modifying classroom behavior, Champaign, Ill., 1970, Research Press Co.

Cleaver, E.: Soul on ice, New York, 1970, Dell Publishing Co., Inc.

Coleman, J. C.: Abnormal psychology and modern life, Glenview, Ill., 1964, Scott, Foresman and Co.

Crutcher, R.: Child psychiatry, a history of its development, Psychiatry 6:191-201, 1943.

Cumming, J., and Cumming, E.: On the stigma of mental illness. In Spitzer, S. P., and Denzin, N. K., editors: The mental patient: studies in the sociology of deviance, New York, 1968, McGraw-Hill Book Co.

Dunn, L. M.: Exceptional children in the schools, New York, 1973, Holt, Rinehart & Winston, Inc.

Erikson, E.: Identity, youth, and crisis, New York, 1968, W. W. Norton & Co., Inc.

Erikson, K.: Patient role and social uncertainty, Psychiatry; Journal for the Study of Interpersonal Processes 20:263-268, 1957.

Erikson, K.: Notes on the sociology of deviance, Social Problems 1:307-314, 1964.

Farber, J.: The student as nigger, New York, 1970, Pocket Books.

Faris, R. E. L., and Dunham, H. W.: Mental disorders in urban areas, Chicago, 1939, University of Chicago Press.

Feagans, L.: Ecological theory as a model for constructing a theory of emotional disturbance. In Rhodes, W. C.: A study of child variance, Ann Arbor, Mich., 1972, The University of Michigan Press.

Felix, R.: Mental illness: progress and prospects, New York, 1967, Columbia University Press.

Gagne, R. M.: The conditions of learning, New York, 1965, Holt, Rinehart & Winston, Inc.

Glasser, W.: Schools without failure, New York, 1969, Harper & Row, Publishers.

Goffman, E.: Stigma: notes on the management of spoiled identity, Englewood Cliffs, N. J., 1963, Prentice-Hall, Inc.

Goodman, P.: High school is too much, Psychology Today, p. 25, Oct., 1970.

Graubard, P. S.: Children with behavioral disabilities. In Dunn, L., editor: Exceptional children in the schools, New York, 1973, Holt, Rinehart & Winston, Inc.

Hall, C. S.: A primer of Freudian psychology, New York, 1954, The New American Library, Inc.

Hall, R., Lund, D., and Jackson, D.: Effects of teacher attention on study behavior, Journal of Applied Behavioral Analysis 1:1-12, 1968.

Haring, N.: The emotionally disturbed. In Kirk, S., and Weiner, B., editors: Behavioral research on exceptional children, Washington, D. C., 1963, The Council for Exceptional Children.

Haring, N., and Phillips, E.: Educating emotionally disturbed children, New York, 1962, McGraw-Hill Book Co.

Hewett, F.: The emotionally disturbed child in the classroom, Boston, 1968, Allyn & Bacon, Inc.

Hill, W.: Learning: a survey of psychological interpretations, San Francisco, 1963, Chandler Publishing Co.

Hoffer, W.: Psychoanalytic education, Psychoanalytic Study of the Child 1:293-306, 1945.

Jarlais, D.: Mental illness as social deviance. In Rhodes, W. C.: A study of child variance, Ann Arbor, Mich., 1972, The University of Michigan Press.

Kanner, L.: Problems of nosology and psychodynamics of early infantile autism, American Journal Orthopsychiatry 19:416-426, 1949.

Kanner, L.: Child psychiatry, ed 3, Springfield, Ill., 1957, Charles C Thomas, Publisher.

Kanner, L.: Emotionally disturbed children: a historical review, Child Development 33:97-102, 1962.

Kelly, T., Bullock, L., and Dykes, M.: Teacher's perceptions of behavioral disorders in children, May, 1974, Florida Educational Research and Development Council.

Kirk, S. A.: Educating exceptional children, ed. 2, Boston, 1972, Houghton Mifflin Co.

Krasner, L., and Ullmann, L.: Research in behavior modification: new developments and implications, New York, 1965, Holt, Rinehart & Winston, Inc.

Krugman, M.: Orthopsychiatry and education. In Lowrey, L. G., and Sloan, V., editors: Orthopsychiatry, 1923-1948, New York, 1948, American Orthopsychiatric Association.

Lewis, N.: A short history of psychiatric achievement, New York, 1941, W. W. Norton & Co., Inc.

Long, N., Morse, W., and Newman, R.: Conflict in the classroom; the education of children with problems, Belmont, Calif., 1972, Wadsworth Publishing Co., Inc.

Lovaas, O., Schaeffer, B., and Simmons, J.: Building social behavior in autistic children by use of electric shock, Journal of Experimental Research Personality 1:99-109, 1965.

Lyman, F.: Phenylketonuria, Springfield, Ill., 1963, Charles C Thomas, Publisher.

MacMillan, D.: Behavior modification in education, New York, 1973, The Macmillan Co.

Maes, W.: The identification of emotionally disturbed elementary school children, Exceptional Children 32:607-609, 1966.

Mahler, M.: On child psychosis and schizophrenia, Psychoanalytic Study of the Child 7:286-305, 1952.

Marmor, J., and Pumpian-Mindlin, E.: Toward an integrative conception of mental disorder, Journal of Nervous Mental Disorders 3:19-29, 1950.

Martin, E.: Breakthrough for the handicapped, legislative history, Exceptional Children 34:493-503, 1968.

McCarthy, J., and Paraskevopoulos, J.: Behavior patterns of learning disabled, emotionally disturbed, and average children, Exceptional Children 36:69-74, 1969.

Menninger, R.: The history of psychiatry, Disabilities of the Nervous System 5:52-55, 1944.

Merton, R.: Social structure and social theory, New York, 1957, The Free Press.

Meyer, A.: Psychobiology, Springfield, Ill., 1957, Charles C Thomas, Publisher.

Nudd, H.: The purpose and scope of visiting teacher work. In Sayles, M. B.: The problem child in school, New York, 1925, Joint Committee on Methods of Preventing Delinquency.

O'Leary, K., and Drabman, R.: Token reinforcement programs in the classroom: a review, Psychology Bulletin 75:379-398, 1971.

Orme, M., and Purnell, R.: Behavior modification and transfer in an out-of-control classroom. In Fargo, G., et al.: Behavior modification in the classroom, Belmont, Calif., 1970, Wadsworth Publishing Co., Inc.

Parsons, T.: The social system, Glencoe, Ill., 1951, The Free Press.

Pate, J.: Emotionally disturbed and socially maladjusted children, In Dunn, L.,: Exceptional children in the schools, New York, 1963, Holt, Rinehart & Winston, Inc.

Plato: The laws, vol. 5. Translated by G. Burges, London, George Bell & Sons.

Public papers of the Presidents of the United States, John F. Kennedy, January 1 to November 22, 1963, Government Printing Office.

Quay, H., Morse, W., and Cutler, R.: Personality patterns of pupils in special classes for the emotionally disturbed, Exceptional Children 32:297-301, 1966.

Rank, B.: Adaptation of the psychoanalytic techniques for the treatment of young children with atypical development, American Journal of Orthopsychiatry 19:130-139, 1949.

Reimer, E.: Unusual ideas in education. In Rhodes, W. C.: A study of child variance, Ann Arbor, Mich., 1972, The University of Michigan Press.

Reinert, H.: The emotionally disturbed, In Gearheart, B. R., editor: Education of the exceptional child, San Francisco, 1972, Intext Educational Publishers.

Rezmierski, V., and Kotre, J.: A limited literature review of theory of psychodynamic model. In Rhodes, W. C.: A study of child variance, Ann Arbor, Mich., 1972, The University of Michigan Press.

Rhodes, W. C.: The disturbing child: a problem in ecological management, Exceptional Children 33:449-455, 1967.

Rhodes, W. C., and Sagor, M.: A study of child variance: the future, Ann Arbor, Mich., 1974, The University of Michigan Press.

Rhodes, W. C., and Tracy, M.: A study of child variance, Ann Arbor, Mich., 1972, The University of Michigan Press.

Rimland, B.: Psychogenesis versus biogenesis: the issues and evidence. In Plog, S. C., and Edgerton, R. B., editors: Changing perspectives in mental illness, New York, 1969, Holt, Rinehart & Winston, Inc.

Rogers, C.: The clinical treatment of the problem child, New York, 1939, Houghton Mifflin Co.

Rogers, C.: A theory of therapy, personality and interpersonal relationships, as developed in the client-centered framework, In Kock, S., editor: Psychology, a study of a science, New York, 1959, McGraw-Hill Book Co., vol. 3.

Rosenthal, D., editor: The Genain quadruplets: a case study and theoretical analysis of heredity and environment in schizophrenia, New York, 1963, Basic Books, Inc., Publishers.

Sagor, M.: Biological bases of childhood behavior disorders. In Rhodes, W. C.: A study of child variance, Ann Arbor, Mich., 1972, The University of Michigan Press.

Silberman, C.: Crisis in the classroom, New York, 1970, Random House, Inc.

Skinner, B.: Science and human behavior, New York, 1953, The Macmillan Co.

Szasz, T.: The myth of mental illness, New York, 1961, Dell Publishing Co., Inc.

Szasz, T.: Ideology and insanity, Garden City, N. Y., 1970, Doubleday & Co., Inc.

Szurek, S.: Psychotic episodes and psychic maldevelopment, American Journal of Orthopsychiatry **26:**519-543, 1956.

The President's Commission on the Assassination of President Kennedy, Washington, D. C., 1964, Government Printing Office.

Tracy, M.: Conceptual models of emotional disturbance: some other thoughts, In Rhodes, W. C.: A study of child variance, Ann Arbor, Mich., 1972, The University of Michigan Press.

Ulman, C.: Identification of maladjusted school children, Public Health Monogr. no. 7, Washington, D. C., 1952, Federal Security Agency, United States Public Health Service.

Ullmann, L., and Krasner, L., editors: Case studies in behavior modification, New York, 1965, Holt, Rinehart & Winston, Inc.

Walker, H.: Walker problem behavior identification checklist, Los Angeles, 1970, Western Psychological Services.

Watson, J.: Psychology, Philadelphia, 1924, J. B. Lippincott Co.

Watson, J. B., and Rayner, R.: Conditioned emotional reactions, Journal of Experimental Psychology **3:**1-14, 1920.

Weinberg, S., Costello, M., and Rotchford, J.: Inborn errors of amino acid metabolism, New York State Journal of Medicine **62:**43-52, 1962.

Whelan, R. J., and Haring, N. G.: Modification and maintenance of behavior through systematic application of consequences, Exceptional Children **32:**281-289, 1966.

Woody, R. H.: Behavioral problem children in the schools, New York, 1969, Appleton-Century-Crofts.

CHAPTER 2

A theoretical construct for children in conflict

The idea of children in conflict has been shown to be a highly divergent concept. Although some children deviate greatly from what might be called "normal" behavior, most deviate only to a degree. Children in conflict can be described as being *too precise, too worried, too angry,* or *too happy;* they are *too easily* disappointed, and manipulate others *too much.*

Most of the behaviors attributed to children in conflict are normal behaviors; at least they are normal if one considers that normal children will sometimes cheat, or lie, or act out aggressive feelings by hitting other children. What often makes these behaviors deviant, and the children who exhibit them in conflict, is the fact that the behaviors are exhibited *in the wrong places, at the wrong time, in the presence of the wrong people,* and *to an inappropriate degree.*

Developing a theoretical basis for understanding these children is a rather involved but necessary process. It is apparent to me that no one group has a "corner" on the theoretical market. For teachers to interpret behaviors from a variety of viewpoints they must have a clear vision of the entire scope of the problem; they must know what various players of the game are doing, not just their job as third basemen. The five theoretical constructs: biophysical, psychodynamic, behavioral, sociological/ecological, and countertheoretical are presented in an effort to show the big picture and to avoid tunnel vision in viewing, analyzing, and treating deviance.

BIOPHYSICAL VIEWPOINT

From a biophysical point of view behavioral deviation is interpreted as having many of the same characteristics as physical illness. From this perspective there exists a direct cause-effect relationship. Inappropriate behavior is not a result of environmental influences, as suggested by behaviorists (Ullmann and Krasner, 1965), or is it a result of a society that labels behavior as deviant and therefore covertly encourages such behavior, as might be suggested by a sociological interpretation (Erikson, 1964).

A child who has a rare biochemical disorder such as phenylketonuria (PKU) will begin to act in ways different from a normal child if treatment for the disease is not initiated. However, with dietary controls the child identified as having PKU can grow to be a normal child.

Rimland, an eminent spokesman for the biophysical position, defines a biogenic disorder as ". . . a severe behavior disorder that results solely from the effects of the physical-chemical environment. Biological factors may exert their effects pre-natally, during labor and birth, and at any subsequent time" (1969:706). Rimland's theoretical approach suggests a finality in the cause-effect relationship that is generally not shared by other more moderate theorists in the biogenetic movement. Rosenthal (1963) has supported the diathesis-stress (i.e., inherited predisposition—environmental stimulation) theory. This postulates that an overactive thyroid, for example, would be *necessary* for emotional outbreaks to occur; however, in itself the hyperactive thyroid would not be *sufficient* to cause biting and hitting behavior. An environmental catalyst would be needed to "complete the circuit." Rimland has expressed concern that the "biogenetic cause and environmental catalyst" position may be "set in concrete" before evidence to the contrary is available.

Biophysical behavioral problems usually can be divided into two general categories: the genetic and the environmental (Rhodes and Sagor, 1974). The concept of biogenetic "triggering" of an inherited predisposition or weakness for deviance has been supported by several studies (Pollin, 1972) of childhood schizophrenia. Other studies (Rimland, 1969) point to the role of environmentally based deviance such as poor nutrition, injury, and stress that affects diet or sleep habits.

Rimland asks two questions of those who are hesitant to accept the biophysical model: "Why do psychiatrists and psychologists believe there are people whose mental disorder is functional rather than organic? Why do they reject the plausible premise that the 'functional' cases differ from the organic cases only in that our knowledge is at present too limited to identify the 'organic' defect in the 'functional' cases?" (1969:703). Rimland goes on to make a specific prediction regarding his theories: "I predict that research will ultimately show psycho-social factors to have minor if any relevance in causing a severe disorder known as psychosis" (1969:704).

Biogenetic theorists have become increas-

ingly concerned with the apparent weaknesses of psychotherapy as demonstrated in research, the tendency to blame parents for the psychopathology of their children, and the sweeping generalizations of a theory that tries to explain everything with one model (Sagor, 1972). In an effort to demonstrate the tunnel vision of psychoanalytical interpretation Rimland discussed a case formerly reviewed by Bettelheim (1959). In his review, Bettelheim attributed the pathology of a psychotic Jewish girl to a lack of maternal affection. The girl was conceived and raised in a small, cramped, dark hole beneath a farm building in Poland during World War II. German soldiers were nearby and had even fired shots into the building. Bettelheim emphasized psychological factors such as the mother's dislike for the father and the "unplanned" nature of the pregnancy. Rimland suggested that four possible causes of the deviance had been overlooked in the analytical evaluation: (1) faulty endocrine development due to maternal stress during pregnancy, (2) an absence of adequate sanitary facilities, both prenatal and postnatal, (3) poor prenatal and postnatal nutritional factors, and (4) postnatal sensory deprivation.

Most individuals who have experienced anxiety in their lives know well its effect on bodily functions. Sleeping, eating, and emotional stability can all be adversely affected as a result of this internal anxiety. One can easily believe that the fear of captivity and death for a pregnant mother could have a negative impact on the unborn child. When this deprivation and fear continue after birth the problems are compounded.

The study of genetic problems in children presents three major drawbacks for the researcher. First, genetic study is a time-consuming task, often taking the entire lifetime of the researcher to complete. A reluctance to this time commitment is understandable. Second, there is the inability of the researcher to control future relationships in the child's life. Life-styles change and with them research implications. Genetic counseling is tenuous, and the results are questionable. Third, permission to research the genetic components of a child's life is often not available. In an area where subjects are limited, a lack of research permission can prove discouraging. In spite of these difficulties, several productive efforts have been made.

Studies in genetics of schizophrenia, infantile autism, and related mental problems have generally been made through the study of twins. By comparing the concordance (agreement) between the behavior of monozygotic (identical) and dizygotic (fraternal) twins, researchers have tried to establish a relationship between serious mental illness in children and factors of heredity. The assumption is that if all factors are controlled except the twin relationship, the results will show the contribution of genetics to mental illness.

The studies indicate that a genetic relationship has probably been shown, but the evidence is not conclusive. Meehl (1969) has described the ability to diagnose schizophrenia without having any behavioral data from the patient or those who may observe the patient's behaviors. His belief is based on studies that show that identical twins are likely to exhibit similar affliction to schizophrenia. If one identical twin is schizophrenic, the other is also likely to be schizophrenic. This relationship is not perfect, but various studies suggest this relationship to be as high as 85% (Karlson, 1966).

Buss (1966) presented a summary of studies, the findings of which are outlined in Table 2.

Table 2. Rates of occurrence of schizophrenia*

General population	1%
Grandchildren, cousins, nephews, and neices	3%-4%
Half siblings	7%
Siblings	5%-14%
Children with one schizophrenic parent	16%
Children with two schizophrenic parents	39%-68%
Dizygotic twins (fraternal)	3%-17%
Monozygotic twins (identical)	67%-86%

*Adapted from Buss, 1966.

It can be seen that, in general, the closer the genetic relationship of a child to someone who has schizophrenia the more likely it is that sickness will occur. A child whose fraternal twin has schizophrenia will be three to seventeen times as likely to be affected as a child who has no history of schizophrenia in the family. Buss lists two conclusions that he believes are supported by the studies cited: (1) an inherited component of schizophrenia does exist and (2) environmental factors are necessary for schizophrenia to develop.

As suggested by Table 2, there is a positive correlation between the occurrence of schizophrenia and biological relationship. The closer the biological relationship the more likely for schizophrenia to be transmitted genetically. The dramatic difference between identical and fraternal twins suggests that factors other than environment are important in the transmission of schizophrenia. If the environmental factors were the major ingredient in this transmission, one would expect twins to show similar prevalence whether they were identical or fraternal. The studies cited indicate that identical twins have approximately four times the prevalence of schizophrenia in both individuals. The prevalence for fraternal twins is approximately the same as that expected between siblings, an unusual relationship if environmental factors are most important in the transmission process.

It should be pointed out that cases do exist where identical twins are not both schizophrenic even though one is afflicted. Various genetic theories are applied to explain this phenomenon, but conclusive evidence is still not available.

A review of twin studies made by Pollin (1972) indicates that concordance in twins is not as high as that reported by Buss. A summary of his findings appears in Table 3.

The review of these twin studies raises several questions. Is the concordance indicated by the research a result of genetic factors? What role does the intrauterine position play in future events? Is the life space of the identical twin essentially dif-

Table 3. Concordance rates of schizophrenia in twins*

Investigator		Number of MZ pairs	Percent of MZ concordance	Number of DZ pairs	Percent of DZ concordance
Luxenberger	1928	17	60-76	33	0
Luxenberger	1930	21	67	37	
Luxenberger	1934	27	33		
Rosanoff	1934	41	61	101	10
Moller	1941	11	55-64	27	15
Kallmann	1946	174	69-86	517	10-15
Slater	1953	41	68-76	115	11-14
Inouye	1961	55	36-60	17	22
Tienari	1963	16	6	21	5
Harvald and Hauge	1965	9	44	62	10
Gottesman and Shields	1966	24	42-65	33	9-17
Kringlen	1967	55	25-38	172	4-10
Pollin et al.	1969	80	14-16	146	4-4

*Adapted from Pollin, 1972.
MZ = monozygotic (identical twins); DZ = dizygotic (fraternal twins).

ferent from that of the fraternal twin? Pollin suggests that these factors are probably more important than once believed and that differences in concordance cannot be assumed as only genetic. As indicated by Table 2, the more recent studies show a percentage of monozygotic concordance to be less than 50%. The fact that these twin studies report findings that are not in total agreement raises some doubts concerning the genetic causation of schizophrenia. In his discussion of genetics and schizophrenia Sagor (1972) postulates that prenatal and postnatal physical environment and psychosocial interpretation may both be responsible in cases where schizophrenia exists.

Rimland (1969:731) said it another way:

> Actually, genetic familiar data on known physical disorders, such as tuberculosis and diabetes, give results very similar to those reported above for schizophrenia. . . . Some critics claim the data do not show genetic causation. By this they mean that the percentages do not follow the simple Mendelian model for dominant and recessive genes. Genetic disorders do not necessarily follow the Mendelian model.

A few studies appear to separate environmental factors of schizophrenia from genetic factors by studying specific target groups that were freed of the environmental factors that might contribute to the illness. Through these studies it has been found that children with one schizophrenic parent who were reared apart from the sick parent experienced substantial schizophrenic problems (Wender, 1969). Higgins (1966) compared the development of twenty-five children raised by their schizophrenic mothers with a control group of children raised apart from their schizophrenic mothers. The study indicated that no significant differences in maladjustment were noted between these two groups.

In a complex and interesting study of children with schizophrenic mothers Mednick (1971) found a solid relationship between heredity and environment.

Bender (1968) has contributed significant research efforts to schizophrenia in children. She has summarized her concept of childhood schizophrenia as follows:

> It is a total organismic disorder of the organism as a whole. It is inherited, according to Kallman's dictates, as a vulnerability and an inability to compensate. It is characterized by a lag in maturation at the embryonic level and, therefore, carries with it embryonic plasticity in all areas of bodily function, particularly that which is integrated by the central nervous system. This plasticity means both a lack of differentiation

into patterns and boundaries of every function, and a failure of determination. The individual can accelerate, maturate, regress, stand still, or move in almost any direction as he gets older because this plasticity is retained throughout the individual's lifetime.

The maturational or developmental lag suggested by Bender has been indicated in a number of studies on schizophrenic and autistic children (Fowle, 1968; Kennard, 1965; Ritvo et al., 1970). In these studies the deviant child is more like a normal infant than a child of his own mental age. Some of the developmental factors that have been studied and found to be immature in development include sleep patterns, white blood cell development, and blood and platelet studies. In most of these studies there is no attempt to differentiate between childhood schizophrenia and autism. Fowle specifically indicates that no attempt to separate these groups was made.

In studying the concordance of identical twins for schizophrenia one must add a bit of caution before assigning causation totally to developmental factors. In the studies cited little has been done to separate biogenetic factors from prenatal factors that influence the psychological development of the child. Research is complicated further by a lack of a common objective tool for diagnosis of schizophrenia. Each study relies on one or more definitions of this disease, none of which is totally in agreement with the others. Often studies have been done with chronic patients in psychiatric hospitals, which tend to raise concordance figures. In addition, many studies have been done with female subjects, which tend to show a higher concordance than do studies of male twins. As Buss (1966) indicates, a lowering of the concordance rate with twin studies does not raise the probability that environmental factors are the key to schizophrenia.

Pollin (1972) lists five major conclusions that have emerged from studies of pathogenesis of schizophrenia. In summary these are as follows:

1. A genetic predisposition to schizophrenia exists that may be nonspecific for this particular psychosis.

2. Genetic predisposition does not take the form of a single, major dominant gene as in Mendel's law.

3. The genetic predisposition may be expressed, in part, as an abnormality in one or both of two interrelated systems of biogenic amines.

4. Additional pathogenic determinants include familiar experiences and constitutional factors such as intrauterine experience of the unborn child.

5. Conceptual integration of biogenetic and experiential factors through the use of a construct that emphasizes weak ego boundaries cannot be validated empirically.

From Pollin's conclusions one can see that an easy pathological determinant of schizophrenia is not presently available. Pollin's summary suggests that a genetic weakness exists for schizophrenia which cannot be specifically predicted. The summary also suggests that environmental factors are important in determining the eventual outcome of the illness.

Theorists support a variety of biogenetic causal factors in describing serious mental illness. Some lean toward perceptual causation (McGhie and Chapman, 1961), others take an arousal approach (Deslauriers and Carlson, 1969), some indicate neurological impairment (Strauss and Kephart, 1955), whereas others suggest biochemical factors (Thompson, 1967). Other theorists group biophysical problems into two broad categories, genetic and environmental (Rhodes and Sagor, 1974). For teachers and other professionals who relate to the biophysical orientation only on a superficial level this grouping appears useful. The genetic component provides a base of general understanding for issues such as genetic counseling in family living or health courses, whereas environmental explanations should underscore the importance of nutrition, stress, accidents, classroom noise levels, and the quality of air that children breathe. Some caution is needed in the environmental area, however. Although it is logical to assume that noise level, the quality of air in the classroom, and diet are variables that make a difference in classroom performance of children, research evidence is still equivocal. Rimland (1969) has predicted that most neurotic behaviors would eventually be determined to have a biophysical basis, but presently this interpretation is not possible.

Meehl (1969) sets limits on the implications often drawn by those who oppose a medical interpretation of schizophrenia.

1. The etiological factor does not always, or even usually, produce clinical illness.

2. If illness occurs, the particular form and content of symptoms are not derivable by reference to the specific etiology alone.

3. The course of the illness can be materially influenced by procedures directed against factors other than the specific etiology.

4. All persons who share the specific etiology will not have closely similar histories, symptoms, and course of illness.

5. The largest single contributor to symptom variance is generally not the specific etiology (cause).

Meehl's position makes it clear that education has a place, along with other systems of intervention, in the process of changing the behaviors of children in conflict. If the five statements made by Meehl could be accepted and practiced by the various professionals working with children, many of the defensive barriers that now persist between theorists could be lowered.

Ritvo et al. (1970) make a strong case for biophysical interpretation of deviance by pointing out that these children are found all over the world, at all levels of socioeconomic background, with a variety of ethnic background, and living in homes with a variety of psychological types of parents.

The biophysical or medical model is one of the oldest theoretical systems being applied to children in conflict. Its followers are among the most positive and energetic in their belief that mental illness is caused by one of several biophysical factors. This enthusiasm is healthy for professional growth. It is an attitude that can lead to a new cooperation between professional groups that strive to answer difficult questions from a medical point of view.

PSYCHODYNAMIC VIEWPOINT

From a psychodynamic point of view the child in conflict has not negotiated, at a successful level, the various intrapsychic and external conflicts that he faced in the process of psychological and/or physiological maturity. As an example, the child whose transition from the oral stage of development (feeding, learning to make appropriate sounds) to the anal stage (toilet training) has been too severe may have problems at the latter stage of development. Likewise a child whose progression through the oedipal phase (sexual identification) has been unsatisfactory may have difficulty in establishing appropriate relations with those of the opposite sex at a later time in life (Rezmierski and Kotre, 1972). More socially oriented psychodynamic theorists emphasize the importance of "significant others" in the child's environment, thus diminishing the relative importance of conflicts in early years of life (Erikson, 1964).

This section was added to the text only after careful consideration and much personal debate. I am well aware of the concerns of many practitioners regarding the theoretical constructs on which analytical thought is based. I am also aware of the dissolution of practitioners who have abandoned all forms of analytical thought in favor of systems that offered observable answers to highly complex behavioral questions. It is my impression that a growing number of teachers are turning to systems that are more in the "middle of the road," somewhere between what may be termed *hard behaviorists* and those referred to as *analytical theorists*. Fine (1973) briefly describes nine theoretical systems that he believes have direct relationships to Freudian thought. These include Rogerian client-centered theory (Rogers, 1951), the rational-emotive system of Ellis (1970), the encounter movement developed by Schultz (1967) and Burton (1969), the eclectic system of Thorne (1967), the gestalt therapy of Perls et al. (1951), reality therapy of Glasser (1965), Jungian analysis (Jung, 1959), Adlerian therapy (Ansbacher and Ansbacher, 1956), and behavior therapy (Wolpe,

1958). Although Fine's attack on each of these theoretical approaches is debatable, in terms of objectivity, his thesis is well stated. There seems to be little theory that is actually new; it is just put together in different ways and with new emphasis and labels. The point being made, hopefully, is that the easiest way to understand the many theoretical constructs being offered is through study of the Freudian model of psychoanalysis. It has been my observation that even behaviorists who apply their skills effectively often have been trained in one of the psychodynamic theories.

Psychodynamic theory is not restricted to any one theorist or approach. Essentially, psychodynamic theory is a combination of several levels of psychological thought. Whereas psychoanalysis is concerned with the inner dynamics of personality, there are other constructs that, even though their philosophical basis was developed from psychoanalysis, espouse a more comprehensive view of behavior. These theorists might include the impact of experience, socialization, or other learning processes on the ultimate behavior of the child.

It seems logical to begin the study of psychodynamic thought by reviewing the basic theory of Sigmund Freud. His theory is still the basis of many theoretical constructs and indeed is the heart of most theories that approach behavior from a dynamic point of view. Even Skinner, the avowed behaviorist, suggests that Freud would, if he were alive, support his theoretical position (Skinner, 1972).

Freud is to psychology what Darwin is to genetics. He not only influenced those who have studied the human personality in a direct way, but his ideas are evident from novels, poetry, and even the jokes that enliven various social gatherings. Freud was born in Freiberg, Moravia, in 1856 and died in London, England, in 1939. However, Freud considered himself a son of Vienna, Austria, where he lived for almost eighty years.

Although Freud studied medicine and graduated from the University of Vienna in 1881, he never intended to practice medicine. However, a research scientist's income provided insufficient financial support for a wife and six children, so he was forced to practice his medical skills to support his family. Two people who probably affected Freud's work more than any others were Jean Charcot, with whom he studied for one year (1885-1886), and Joseph Breuer, a Viennese physician. From Charcot he learned the science of hypnosis in treating various mental disorders, particularly hysteria. From Breuer he learned the cathartic or "talking-out-your-problems" form of therapy (Hall, 1954). As Freud began to probe deeply into the minds of his patients, he gradually put physiology and neurology aside and became a psychological investigator.

By modern terminology Freud would be considered a psychiatrist, a physician who specialized in treatment of mental disorders, but by his admitted preference Freud was a scientist. He learned the scientific method as a medical student studying various physiological phenomena. In addition to these skills Freud was a philosopher. The ability to analyze, to probe, and to discover the intimate details of man's subconscious led Freud to be pessimistic and critical toward human nature. He believed that humans resist knowing the truth about themselves and that society reflected the irrationality of the human being (Hall, 1954). Freud was a philosopher, a psychologist, a scientist, a critic, and a psychoanalyst. His theoretical constructs were truly the catalyst for future psychological thought.

THE BASIS OF PSYCHOANALYTICAL THOUGHT

The personality of the child is made up of three major systems—the id, ego, and superego. In the mentally healthy child these three systems work in relative harmony with one another, supporting the function of meeting the individual's basic needs and desires. If, on the other hand, the three systems are in conflict with one another, the child is said to be maladjusted.

The *id* is the only system that is present at birth. It is the total inherited system of instinctual energy that supplies the power for the entire personality. The id operates on the pleasure principle (the reduction or elimination of tension from the person). Tension is seen as pain or discomfort, whereas pleasure or satisfaction is achieved when this pain or discomfort is eased. The goal of the id or pleasure principle is to avoid pain and achieve pleasure.

The *ego* is the mediating system between the demands of the id and the constraints of the world in which the child lives. The ego derives its power from the id; however, in the course of interacting with the external world the ego often must subdue the demands made by the id. When this occurs, a conflict inevitably arises between these two systems of the personality. In procuring objects of gratification for the id the ego must follow a logical and rational process, which is known as the reality principle.

The third system of personality is called the *superego*, which develops from the ego. The superego represents the norms and values of society that are taught to the child by his parents and significant others. The superego can be thought of as punishing or controlling (conscience) or as a positive ego-ideal, which are actually opposite sides of the same moral coin (Hall, 1954). The superego manipulates the ego by use of rewards and punishments. For example, appropriate responses to the demands of the id are rewarded by a satisfied feeling, whereas inappropriate responses might be followed by feelings of guilt.

Psychic energy, which allows the total personality system to function, is supplied by the id and is called the libido. This energy is sexual in nature, fluid, and displaceable. Being fluid and displaceable, it can be invested in any number of object or activity cathexis (Rezmierski and Kotre, 1972). This energy can be invested in a wide variety of objects either singly or together. Object cathexis is the process of investing psychic energy to satisfy an instinct. At times the ego

must use its libido (psychic energy) to control the id. This is called anticathexis, an example of which might be a child trying to control his temper. The temper is motivated by the needs of the id, whereas control is apparent in the efforts of the ego to calm the temper. If the anticathexis is not strong enough, the impulsive desires of the id may break through and the child has a temper tantrum.

In addition to the three systems of personality developed by Freud it seems appropriate to outline his five stages of development. It should be pointed out that Karl Abraham, an associate of Freud, elaborated the psychosexual stages of development that were later accepted by Freud (Hall, 1954). These include the oral, anal, phallic, latency, and genital stages. Each stage will be discussed in terms of children in conflict.

The five stages of development are all centered around the three erogenous zones: the area around the mouth, the anal area, and the genital area. As the child passes through the various developmental stages, one of the three erotic zones becomes the focal point of gratification for the child. There is much overlapping between stages, but normal development does follow a fairly systematized pattern. Even "normal" progression through the psychosexual stages is fraught with problems. The child may have feeding problems with various formulas being tried, the child may have difficulty at the time of weaning, may have difficulty adjusting to toileting routines, or may have an array of similar conflicts.

The *oral stage* begins at birth and usually continues until the child is about 2 years of age. During this psychological stage, the mouth is the center of gratification. At this stage the child begins to differentiate between the mother's breast and himself. This is the beginning of ego development, which will continue through the phallic stage. As anyone who has raised children knows, the oral stage seems to encourage nearly everything to enter the mouth. The child ostensibly is trying to "swallow the world." Karl Abraham (Rezmierski and Kotre, 1972) has divided this stage into two substages: the oral dependent, which extends over the first few months of a child's life, and the oral aggressive, which develops at the time that teeth become an effective tool. During the oral dependent stage, the child is seemingly much like a bird, swallowing whatever is presented. If the child becomes fixated (attached) to this substage, he will likely be overdependent on the world or too optimistic. This child feels the world will take care of him and is therefore easily disappointed. When the teeth erupt, the child has the tools to become much more aggressive; therefore the child who fixates at this substage may be orally aggressive, verbally attacking, and sarcastic. The child might also use oral means to get the love and attention necessary to function. Whether such a clear division between oral substages is evident in the classroom is debatable, although fixation at the oral stage is often evident with children who are in conflict. The exact substage is relatively unimportant in treatment, at least in an educational setting.

During the second year of life, the anal area of the body becomes the principal region for gratification. Two substages are again delineated—the *anal-expulsive substage* when the child derives much gratification from expelling of feces, and the *anal-retentive substage* when gratification is obtained by holding in and controlling the feces. The anal stage of development is usually consummated by the fourth year of life. Problems during the anal stage of development can lead to one of several conflicts. Children may become too orderly, with every pencil and every book in their desks having an exact spot, or the opposite behavior might develop with no apparent order. Children whose behavior is defiant, obstinate, cruel, and destructive have been associated with inappropriate progression through the anal stage of development.

Beginning at about 4 years of age and continuing until approximately 6 years of age the *phallic stage* becomes dominant. During this stage, children are preoccupied with the genital area of the body. Masturbation, look-

ing at the genitals (the child's own and others), and sex play with other children are common. At this stage children are extremely interested in knowing all about sex, where babies come from, the difference between boys and girls, and the sexual activities of parents. Children are trying to work out their sexual identity, a task beset with difficulty.

The Oedipus complex (attachment of the child for the parent of the opposite sex) was originally used to describe behaviors of both boys and girls. This rather complicated stage begins with the boy feeling very close to the mother. This closeness finally develops into a desire for more intimate contact with the mother, a thought that produces much fear and anxiety for the child. His father, whose role he would like to have, is seen as much more powerful and therefore a real threat to the boy. In fact the child feels his father may harm him severely for harboring such desires. The ultimate harm a boy could experience would likely be castration, a fear that is called castration anxiety. This anxiety causes the boy to repress both his sexual impulses for his mother and his anger and hostility for his father. To cope with feelings toward his father the son identifies with him (identification with the aggressor). Through the process of identification the boy incorporates much of the father's personality by a process called introjection. As the son incorporates the values of his father, he develops a superego in both its positive (ego-ideal) and negative (conscience) connotations.

It is less easy to explain the Oedipus complex as it relates to girls (Electra complex). Although it develops as a parallel to boys, it has some notable differences. As the girl recognizes that she does not have a penis, she feels cheated and angry, with her feelings being directed toward her mother. This leads to a "cooling off" of her relationship to her mother. To achieve what she does not possess she turns to her father. From this point the Electra complex follows a parallel course for girls as does the Oedipus complex for boys, with guilt and fear of the mother becoming evident. This leads the girl to identify with the mother and to replace the desire of the father with the desire for a baby. Most theorists believe that describing the Electra complex is extremely difficult. Apparently this resolution is more difficult for girls and less clearly made, suggesting that the superego of girls is not as strong as that developed by boys (Hall, 1954; Rezmierski and Kotre, 1972).

By the time the child successfully completes the phallic stage, the id, ego, and superego should be intact and the basic components of personality established.

Problems that occur during the phallic stage of development are apparent with children in conflict. Attitudes concerning the opposite sex that are not resolved at this stage will continue to cause problems in later life. Exaggerated masculinity, including boastfulness, extreme aggressiveness, and other behaviors that bring the child into conflict with peers and authority, may be the result of inappropriate resolution of the phallic stage.

The *latency stage* comes between the phallic and genital stages. It is really not a stage of development but a rest period between the tumultuous phallic and genital stages. During this period, sex interest is dormant, the conflicts of the phallic stage are resolved, and identification with the parent of the same sex has been accomplished. These are relatively calm years. Boys belong to boys' groups and play boys' games, whereas girls pursue activities of a feminine nature and establish relationships with girls. Learning seems to come quickly at this stage, since other conflicts are now put aside.

The *genital stage* begins with puberty and leads to the mature adult. During this stage the earlier conflicts of the phallic stage emerge once again. Partial solutions to the oedipal complex now become unacceptable during the more advanced genital stage. It should be pointed out that three basic differences exist between the phallic and genital stages. Although both are concerned with the genital areas as the center of gratification, the focus of this gratification is significantly different. During the phallic stage the child's

focus of sexual interest is incestuous or within the family, whereas sexual interest during the genital stage is external to the family. In addition, during the phallic stage the child was seeking satisfaction only for himself whereas during the genital stage the child seeks to bring satisfaction not only to himself but to the object of his love. Finally, the child now has the physiological capability to act out feelings toward the opposite sex.

In the Freudian view there is little in the way of pathology that cannot be traced to one of the prelatency stages. If the resolution of problems has been successfully completed at the first three psychosexual stages, there appear to be few later concerns.

There are several reasons for problem behaviors developing during the psychosexual stages of development. First, too much psychic energy might have been invested at any one of the various stages. With too much psychic energy expended there might be too little remaining to negotiate successive stages of development. Second, there is a problem of regression to an earlier stage. For example, a child who encounters problems adjusting to puberty might regress to the oral stage and fixate his behavior at that level. When the prospect of moving from one stage to the next is too threatening, the child might choose to remain at a more comfortable stage, thus creating further conflict as immature behavior is exhibited.

Freudian theory is not the "end all" in psychological thought. Although it has opened many avenues of thought for theorists and clinicians, it is admittedly sexist, with women being valued less than men; it is pessimistic in its attitude toward the goodness of man (Horney, 1951), and it looks for causation that is often seen as a waste of time (Mosak and Dreikurs, 1973). For all of these problem areas it still is the foundation on which other theories were built (Fine, 1973).

I have chosen not to review neo-Freudian theorists but to move on to the humanistic psychologists. Although the neo-Freudians depart from the strict Freudian interpretation of personality development, they are still very analytical in their approach to child study. For the teacher interested in the neo-Freudian viewpoint the works of Anna Freud, Melanie Klein, and Otto Rank or the more socially oriented analytical theorists Harry Sullivan, Karen Horney, and Erich Fromm are suggested.

Humanistic psychology

Adler is considered by many theorists to be among the first of the humanistic psychologists (Ellis, 1970; Mosak and Dreikurs, 1973), a group of psychologists who search for truth without using mechanistic and dehumanizing methods (Maslow, 1965). Adler (1870-1937) was born in Vienna, where he was awarded his M.D. degree in 1893. After working as a general practitioner for several years he turned his interest to psychiatry. At Freud's invitation in 1902 he joined his circle of closest associates to study the human personality from a Freudian perspective (Mosak and Dreikurs, 1973). In 1911 he separated from Freud's group to start his own school. Adler accepted a professorship at Columbia University in 1926, and from that point in his life he spent most of his time in the United States (Adler, 1970). The influence of the people and culture of this country undoubtedly influenced his theoretical approach, particularly his latest writings.

Adler follows the lead of Freud in his insistence of the importance of childhood as the foundation of a healthy personality. His attitude was not as severe as Freud's, however, and he leaned toward a social explanation of acceptable and unacceptable behavior. Adler departed from Freud on many issues, including the importance of sexual energy. Adler (1964) believed that all questions of life could be related to three major problems—that of communal life (community life), of work (occupation), and of love (Adler, 1963, 1970). He repeatedly stressed the problems of the spoiled child and the difficulty of using any system to overcome this basic undermining of the child's ability to function. Adler had an extreme dislike for oversimplification and easy answers, and he recommends leaving no stone unturned in an effort to secure understanding.

Several basic theoretical assumptions separate Adlerian theory from Freudian theory. These are outlined by Mosak and Dreikurs (1973) as follows: Adler, in relation to Freud, is (1) more subjective, (2) more socially oriented, (3) more holistic in his approach, (4) less fatalistic regarding the "goodness of man," and (5) less sexist.

In his review of humanistic psychology Bugental (1963) outlines eight major parameters of psychology undergoing change in a humanistic approach. These include the following:

1. Man is a composite of part functions rather than a catalog of individual parts.

2. The original model of science that was borrowed from physics is changing.

3. The medical model that has guided psychological thought is changing toward client involvement in the change process.

4. Changes are occurring in the role of graduate schools as training agencies from isolated theorists to practical application.

5. There is a moving away from statistical analysis as the way to find the truth.

6. A change is occurring in the belief that research must precede practice.

7. The clinical team has often been a myth, which has in many cases been a smoke screen for domination by a single professional.

8. The fallacy that diagnosis (a medical term) is necessary for treatment to proceed or be effective.

The extent to which these changes have taken place varies; however, movement away from clinical observation and dissection is apparent if one reads the works of Maslow, Allport, Combs, Rogers, and other humanist psychologists. Only one of these theorists, Rogers, will be reviewed. Although Rogers cannot be considered the torchbearer for humanistic psychology, his theoretical approach generally supports the general direction of humanism as outlined by Bugental (1963). In his early writing on clinical treatment of the problem child Rogers stated his position toward behavior change. He said that "In this book we shall deal with the child, not with behavior symptoms" (1939:3).

Rogers goes on to describe symptoms of behavior such as stealing, truancy, and thumbsucking, which are not problems and therefore cannot be treated. He concludes that "There are children—boys and girls—with very different backgrounds and personalities, and some of these children steal, and some of them run away from school, and others find satisfaction in sucking their thumbs, or in saying obscene words, or in defying their parents; but in each instance it is the child with whom we must deal, not the generalization we make about his behavior" (1959:3-4).

Rogers' theory is phenomenological (the way in which a child perceives reality at any given moment; the incongruence that develops between the child's self and his experiences). More precisely, psychological conflict, according to Rogers "exists when the organism denies to awareness, significant experiences, which consequently are not accurately symbolized and organized into the gestalt of the self-structure, thus creating an incongruence between self and experience" (1959:204). Rogers prefers the term *defensive behaviors* for symptoms commonly called neuroses and the term *disorganized behavior* to what has generally been called psychosis.

For the classroom teacher Rogers (1969) offers a conceptualization of relationships, a modern approach to the value system held in education and plan for self-directed change. For many practitioners in the classroom who must deal with behaviors as the behaviors occur, the impact of the phenomenological approach as espoused by Rogers has not been fully realized. Many teachers believe the approach to be more applicable to clinically oriented situations of one-to-one encounters rather than classroom application. Others believe the theory to be more attuned to adults than to children, a belief supported by Rogers (1959). It is my personal observation that Rogers has much to offer teachers who are able to use the mirroring techniques of counseling, adapt teaching to include "facilitation of change," develop an attitude of acceptance and trust, and cultivate empathetic understanding.

BEHAVIORAL THEORY

A significant contrast to psychodynamic theory is presented by those who espouse the behavioral model. It is unlikely that one definition of emotional disturbance will be acceptable to all behaviorists; however, most will accept something like the following: Behavioral deviance is essentially maladaptive behavior that has been learned. This maladaptive behavior has developed and is maintained just like other behaviors—through positive and negative reinforcement and punishment (Buckley and Walker, 1970). If patterns of behavior deviate sufficiently from accepted behavioral norms, the child might be recommended for special intervention techniques or even excluded from regular classroom activities. Behaviorists generally avoid labeling children emotionally disturbed, preferring instead to describe the behavior.

Several theoretical constructs of behavioral theory have been operationalized (MacMillan, 1973). From these models seven common assumptions can be drawn as follows:

1. Most inappropriate behavior is learned just like appropriate behavior (Ullmann and Krasner, 1965).

2. A relationship exists between the behavior a child exhibits and his environment. This relationship can be described as well as predicted if various components of the environment are known (Hill, 1963; Krasner and Ullmann, 1965).

3. Deviant behavior can be changed through the use of appropriate reinforcement techniques (Gagne, 1965; Haring and Phillips, 1962; Ullmann and Krasner, 1965).

4. Looking for causes of deviant behavior is counterproductive, since the original cause of a given behavior is unlikely to be what is maintaining the behavior at the present time (Ullmann and Krasner, 1965).

5. Behavioral theory is a "black box" theory with environmental inputs (stimuli) to the black box (individual) and outputs (responses) from the black box both observed (Rhodes and Sagor, 1974).

6. The relative goodness of any theory

rests on its demonstrability and predictive ability (Rhodes and Sagor, 1974).

7. Behaviorists are reductionists, imposing severe limitations on observation techniques, intervention specifications, and interpretation of data.

It is important to note that behaviorists generally acknowledge that some deviant behaviors are biologically motivated; however, their concerns are directed toward the response that society makes to the deviant behavior. For example, most behaviorists acknowledge that a child may exhibit deviant behaviors after an accident in which severe brain damage was incurred. The simple fact that brain damage occurred is not the central issue, however. The teacher, parents, peers, and others in the child's environment are also important to the behaviorist, since their reactions to the child will likely shape many behaviors of the injured child. It is not that the behaviorist is uninterested in what caused the deviant behavior. The important thing is what is *maintaining* the behavior at the present time (MacMillan, 1973).

Since behavior modification techniques have generally taken their strength from what behaviorists term the *failure of the medical model*, it is well to cite some of the common weaknesses attributed to the medical model (Ullmann and Krasner, 1965).

1. The original cause of a behavior is not what is maintaining behavior later in a child's life. A good example of this might be smoking. A child might begin smoking at 10 years of age because of peer pressure. At 17 years of age the young person is still smoking but for a variety of different reasons. Peer pressure may or may not be a factor. The reinforcers *maintaining* the smoking behavior may center around the taste acquired for tobacco during seven or eight years of smoking. Taking away or changing the peer pressure for smoking would likely have little or no affect on the smoking behavior once other reinforcers are acquired.

2. Finding the original cause of behavior is improbable. In trying to identify good reasons or causes of a child's reading failure the teacher might identify the following causes:

First, reading is not all that important in this particular home. The parents seldom read, and little stimulation for the child to read is apparent. Second, two languages are spoken in the home, with English being used only sparingly. Third, the child has not developed an attention span that will allow any in-depth focus on the reading task. The child is in and out of his seat on the average of ten times every five minutes. Fourth, the child's peer relationships are significant. The child is in constant conflict with other boys and girls, both during and outside of school. The teacher reports that he gets into fights on the average of three times each school day. Fifth, the child has a vision problem; his eyes do not track properly. Given the proposition that all five factors are *probable causes* of the reading failure, what are the odds of finding the one cause or the correct combination of causes? By a simple mathematical process one can determine that given five variables that might *cause* a given behavior to occur, there are 120 possible combinations of these variables. The point is that the odds of finding the cause of any one behavior are relatively slight. Most behaviorists believe that looking for causes is a guessing game that takes a great deal of time with few results.

3. Suppose for a minute that a teacher is fortunate enough to find *the cause* of the specific problem just outlined. The teacher determines that two languages spoken in the home is very confusing to the child, and this can be identified as *the problem* that causes the child's reading failure. What can the teacher do to alter this real problem? Can the language structure of the home be manipulated? Should the child be removed from the home? Both of these solutions would likely be a waste of effort on the teacher's part. Therefore behaviorists believe that finding *the cause* is no assurance that the teacher, or anyone else, can change the behavior.

4. Finally, what indications are there that gaining insight will help change behaviors? Consider again the example given earlier— the child who has been smoking from 10 years until 17 years of age. Will the young

person want to quit smoking after he gains insight into his smoking behavior? Many behaviorists believe that insight alone will not change the behavior but, in fact, may contribute to the continuance of inappropriate behavior by giving the person a reason or an excuse for continuing.

In general, behaviorists tend to believe that it is a waste of time to search for causation of inappropriate behaviors. It is difficult for teachers who have observed the process of referral, testing, conferencing, and placement for several years to remain completely objective in the matter. Even when causes for deviant behaviors are found, teachers are generally unable to change the behavior pattern effectively by other than behavioral manipulation of the symptoms. Many children have been victimized by referral, testing, conferencing, and placement with little or no effective teaching taking place. By the time the child is evaluated and placed the school year is over and the process begins again the following year. Most behaviorists believe a more efficient system is available; a behavioral system that tries to determine what is supporting or maintaining behaviors rather than finding the original cause.

Critical issues in behavior modification

Positive reinforcement, negative reinforcement, and punishment. Three terms common to the various behavior modification systems and critical to the modification process include *positive reinforcement, negative reinforcement,* and *punishment.* Reinforcement (in behavioral terms) is defined by the effects it has on behavior. For example, ice cream can be positive or negative as a reinforcer; it all depends on whether the person being reinforced responds or does not respond as a result of ice cream. Whether ice cream is good or not is irrelevant. A reinforcer like ice cream is positive if the behavior it follows is maintained at a high level or strengthened. If a child gets a perfect paper and the teacher says, "That's great!" will the child get more perfect papers or fewer? If the child aspires to achieve more perfect work, the teacher's words are said to be positive.

A reinforcer is negative if its *removal* increases the strength of a behavior. Negative reinforcement appears to have a more limited applicability to the teaching process than does positive reinforcement; however, its effective use is often critical in the solution of specific problems. Suppose a child is taken to a time-out room (a room away from the classroom where no positive reinforcement is likely) during a temper tantrum. As soon as the tantrum subsides the child is allowed to return to the classroom, where reinforcement can again be earned. The child is relieved of the sterile atmosphere of the time-out room by exhibiting the desired behavior. Being permitted to leave the time-out room is therefore the negative reinforcement. Its removal increases the probability that appropriate behavior will be repeated in the future. Examples of negative reinforcers in the everyday world include buzzers on seat belts and warning lights in automobiles. Although more severe negative reinforcers like bright lights and shock are generally not employed, their use has been demonstrated with severely disturbed children (Lovaas et al., 1965).

Punishment contrasts sharply with positive and negative reinforcement. Whereas reinforcement aims at *increasing* behavior, punishment has as its goal to *decrease* specific behaviors. Punishment, as used in this test, means the removal of positive reinforcement or the presentation of a negative reinforcer. As with positive reinforcers, the determination of punishment can only be made by the results. If the behavior decreases, the stimulus is said to be punishment.

Schedules of reinforcement. The rate at which positive reinforcers are delivered may follow a variety of patterns, called schedules of reinforcement. Reinforcement is generally scheduled according to time intervals (one reinforcer for every 10 seconds, one for every 15 minutes) or according to a ratio of acts to reinforcers (one reinforcer every three acts, one every ten acts). Both interval and ratio reinforcement may be fixed (one reinforcer given after each three acts or one reinforcer given every 15 minutes) or variable (random reinforcement after a various number of acts or after a varying number of minutes). Although fixed ratio and fixed interval reinforcement are generally considered to be best for learning new behaviors, variable and/or intermittent reinforcement is generally considered to be best for maintaining behaviors at a high rate and is more resistant to extinction over time (Skinner, 1971).

Types of reinforcers. The continuum of reinforcements used is often a concern of teachers who must work with a number of children at one time. Behaviorists generally believe that whatever works should be used as reinforcers. It seems, however, that caution should be employed within a school setting to avoid intrastaff and intrastudent conflicts, which are debilitating to student growth. The determination of types of reinforcers employed should be considered a staff responsibility in the same way as establishment of other teaching procedures that concern children. Honest disagreements concerning the kinds of reinforcements that should be made available to children must be debated openly, and acceptable agreements should be reached if a harmonious and efficient school operation is to be maintained. The comments that teachers and aids frequently make concerning the use of reinforcers indicate that basic disagreements plague the efforts of energetic and capable teachers and cut the learning efficiency of children. Giving dollar bills in school as reinforcers is one example of a reinforcement practice that is likely to create many staff problems.

There are two general guidelines for selection of reinforcers. First, the reinforcer used should not be stronger than is needed to effect changes in behavior. Everyone has heard the saying, "Let the punishment fit the crime." In terms of reinforcement one could say, "Let the reinforcer fit the behavior." The right kind of reinforcement is needed to ensure progress toward goal achievement. Second, the *right kind* of reinforcer can be determined by assessing the age of the child, the problem involved, and the relative strength of competing reinforcers. Two common errors of reinforcement include not giving a reinforcement that is sufficiently strong or giving reinforcement that is more potent than necessary. The concern often raised in reinforcement is the assumption that tangible reinforcers are better than social reinforcers. Children are given tokens, candy, and trinkets—often in lieu of more acceptable social reinforcers (at least to teachers) like praise and attention. Research in this sensitive area appears to be inconclusive. Although educators have a well-known aversion to extrinsic motivators (Hewett, 1968), there appears to be significant research that supports the use of primary rewards (food and water), toys, and tokens with a small percentage of deviant children (Birnbrauer and Lawler, 1964; Ferster and DeMyer, 1962; Levin and Simmons, 1962).

In deciding which reinforcers to use, the teacher should consider both long- and short-term goals. For example, candy might serve the immediate needs of the child effectively but pose a real problem for the future. Candy will need to be phased out and replaced with a social reinforcer that is more acceptable in the school situation. If the child will perform efficiently without candy, one step in the modification sequence is avoided by the teacher. In addition, a whole host of paltry problems that drive teachers to an early retirement are subsequently eluded. Complaints of staff members who do not approve of primary reinforcers, parents who believe the reinforcer to be a bribe, and other children who feel they are "left out" by the teacher's actions are only a few of the possible pitfalls that must concern teachers.

Behaviorism—a critical review. Any system that grows in popularity quickly is likely to be subjected to severe scrutiny at a later time. Such is the case with behavior modification. Even though behavior modification techniques were used as early as Roman times, their use in education did not have significant impact until the 1960s (Forness and MacMillan, 1970). During the 1960s, behavior modification techniques emerged from the laboratory and into the classroom with an impact unparalleled in education (Goldstein, 1973). Colleges and universities that had never accepted principles of behavior modification hired "behavior mod men" to bolster their staffs. Federal grants written with a behavioral bent suddenly became "the way to get money." In-service education for teachers stressing the importance of behavior modification proliferated. The day of accountability was just around the corner.

Many charges and countercharges have been leveled for and against behavior modification techniques (MacMillan, 1973). Raising theoretical issues serves a worthwhile purpose in bringing legitimate concerns to the attention of all professionals. It would appear profitable to consider some of the questions being raised by those who are skeptical about the modification process to establish a middle ground for using a technique that has demonstrated promise for boys and girls in conflict.

Behavior modification has given a tremendous lift to teachers who needed a technique that could restore confidence in their own ability to solve problems. After a period in which teachers were often considered second-rate citizens as contributing members to various "team efforts," behavior modification offers new hope for meaningful involvement with children. Teachers have attributed the rapid growth of behavior modification to the positive attitude of those who used modification techniques and to the antilabeling position taken by behaviorists.

This brief review of a field as complex as behavior modification could, justifiably, be seen as superficial or an oversimplification. With behavior modification being discussed in so many texts and journals and with educational programs in every conceivable setting using the technique, it seems appropriate to limit this presentation to those theoretical issues that will relate to methods of behavior modification discussed in Chapter 5.

SOCIOLOGICAL/ECOLOGICAL VIEWPOINTS

The sociological and ecological systems have so many commonalities that it appears

logical to develop their relative components in one section to emphasize these similarities. In situations where specific differences do exist these will be pointed out.

Sociological theory

Social theory has studied deviance from a broad social context including (1) the socially created role of labeling individuals as deviant (Rhodes and Sagor, 1974), (2) the process of rule breaking and rule following, and (3) the effects that social forces bring to the individual. Each of these related positions will be discussed independently.

Labeling. Labeling theorists suggest the cause of deviance to be the focusing of attention onto specific behaviors that a child exhibits. The model developed during the 1960s, and is variously called symbolic interactionist, societal reaction, and labeling theory (Jarlais, 1972). The labeling process is the most distinctive feature of this theory. Societies tend to distinguish between those who follow the rules (conformists) and those who break the rules (deviants). Labeling theorists hold to the premise that labeling alone is a powerful inducement toward deviance or conformity. Children do not become deviant by breaking the established rules; in fact a child can be labeled deviant without breaking any rules.

Lemert (1962) discusses deviance in terms of primary deviance (initial rule breaking) and secondary deviance (rule breaking that occurs after one is perceived as a rule breaker). Lemert points out that secondary deviance is more debilitating because it evolves around stigmatization, punishment, segregation, and social control.

The child who establishes an identity of deviance does so in the same manner as the child who forms a nondeviant identity (Jarlais, 1972). In both cases the child conforms to the expectations of others. Usually the deviance is given a specific label, such as emotionally disturbed, behavior problem, spoiled, socially maladjusted, or retarded. At times the child is even rewarded for playing out the deviant role in an acceptable manner.

Much criticism has been leveled against

special education programs for their labeling aspects. Charges have been made that special programs actually create problems for handicapped children by setting them apart and pointing out their differences (Sye, 1971). Present efforts toward mainstreaming exceptional children are partially a result of efforts to avoid labeling children who have been previously classified deviant. Others contend that deviant children label themselves without any effort from society. When a child violates the rules of society, he in effect sets himself apart. A number of theorists believe that the individual is responsible for most of his behaviors and that blaming an individual's inappropriate behavior on an anonymous society will do little to solve the problem (Matza, 1969).

There appear to be two practical reasons for labeling children in conflict. The first reason is to capitalize on resources available for adequate funding for programs. Funds frequently are not allowed unless labels are attached so as to provide funding agencies with some knowledge of where monies are being expended. Alternatives of accepting labeling for this purpose might include having less adequate funds or spending an inordinate effort in securing funding through other sources.

A second reason for labeling, which has much practical merit, is to facilitate programing for children. A label often acts as a signal for special techniques such as play therapy or reality therapy to be initiated. It provides the encouragement for specially trained professionals to become involved with the child and encourages the use of specialized materials. As children are labeled, three ingredients (specialized techniques, special teachers, and special materials) often become available to the children. If applying labels helps to facilitate evaluation and placement into viable programs that secure help for children, labeling will not have been in vain. If, however, labeling only allows expedient disregard for the needs of children, it cannot be tolerated.

Rule breaking and rule following. Rule breaking and rule following are often sug-gested as major ways in which the deviance or normalcy of an individual is established. From a sociological viewpoint deviance includes breaking the rules that society has set. The child is labeled according to the types of rules broken and the conditions under which rules are broken. If a child breaks the more clearly defined rules such as taking things that belong to others or telling lies, he might be labeled as a thief or a dishonest child. However, if the child violates rules that are less obvious such as making eye contact during conversation, using appropriate facial expression or proper voice inflection, the child might be given a less specific label such as withdrawn or emotionally disturbed.

Social agencies that enforce the rules and label rule breakers may include parents, police, courts, and teachers. From the vast number in society who break the rules only a few are chosen to be labeled deviant. The agencies mentioned often play an initial and continuing role in this process. It is important to note that social rules are broken by most individuals, even though they are labeled conformists. And most of those who are labeled deviant follow the rules much of the time. The child who is labeled deviant might, in fact, capitulate to the rules set down by the school in all areas except one in which his behavior is so nonconforming that a deviant label is attached. An otherwise normal child who exhibits himself or masturbates in the classroom would be one example.

Erikson (1957) suggests that the uncertainty of mental illness often leads individuals who are ill to exaggerate their symptoms so as to erase any doubt concerning their condition. In that way individuals can be legitimate in their claims of illness.

In general, children who are in conflict with their environment are treated differently from children who have physical illnesses. Children in conflict are expected to attend school and are generally given some responsibilities to perform. Except for extremely serious emotional disturbances, children are held responsible for the problems they present to society. This is probably true because there are no good or reliable indicators of the disturbance. If a child has a broken arm, there is a cast for all to see. In the case of emotional problems or other conflicts there are only the external components of the conflict to observe. Since the cause of the problem cannot be seen, people tend not to believe that a cause exists and therefore blame the child for the deviant behavior.

In comparing the role of the child who is physically ill with the child who breaks the rules society has established, one realizes that physical illness is a different role. The child who is physically ill is generally compliant, whereas the child in conflict is usually not attentive to socially acceptable standards of behavior. The physically ill child is treated with compassion, whereas the child in conflict may get no attention until he comes into serious conflict with the law. Finally, there is a definite stigma attached to emotional and social conflict that generally is not attached to physical illness. It would seem that physical illness and social and emotional disturbance are not comparable ideas when one considers their affect on children (Jarlais, 1972).

Social forces. Other theorists (Durkheim, 1951; Merton, 1957) propose that mental illness results from social forces that exert themselves on the individual. Anomie is the predictable result of social change that occurs at a rate faster than society can establish appropriate group norms (Jarlais, 1972).

Durkheim's theory of anomie is similar to Freud's theory. Both describe the human being as having potential needs that are inexhaustible (Jarlais, 1972). Whereas Freud used the id to describe the needs of an individual, Durkheim used the individual as a total entity. Both theories emphasize the controls that are placed on the individual. Freud used the concept of the ego, whereas Durkheim describes society as the controlling agent.

An example of anomie would be the Industrial Revolution. The rapid social changes brought about by industrialization encourage disruptive human relations and anomie. Society placed a high value on wealth and then limited the individual's ability to achieve

this end. The resultant conflict is called anomie. Wealth was desired, but limitations were placed on its achievement.

Although Durkheim's theory was developed with adult society in mind, its principles seem to have specific relevance to children who are products of that same society. When rapid change occurs within a child's life without the attending social structure to guide his needs, frustration results. The child's needs are infinitely expandable and require external points of reference the same as those required by adults. As the needs of the child expand beyond any reasonable level of fulfillment, conflicts are inevitable.

Anomie also appears to be a plausible way of looking at children in conflict. In a society where rapid change is occurring the role and function of children are often unclear. Change that occurs in the home, school, and community all contribute to this lack of clarity and resulting frustration for the child. As the child's needs expand and find a mixed structure of guidance for growth, this frustration may change to hate, distrust, withdrawal, or other forms of coping that may lead to deviance.

Anomie was designed to explain a social pathology rather than an individual pathology. If many people in a society suffer from severe emotional disintegration, one can utilize the theory of anomie to understand possible causation. Although anomie generally is less helpful in describing the behavior of one individual, this construct will be explored.

Table 4. Comparison of personality development and anomie

Personality organization (Freud)	Anomie (Durkheim)
Needs of id (unlimited)	Needs of individual (unlimited)
Restrictions of ego	Restrictions of society
Intrapersonality conflicts (id-ego)	Intrasociety conflicts (individual-society)

Durkheim's theory, although logical, suffers from the same problem as does Freud's theory. It is difficult, if not impossible, to test operationally (Jarlais, 1972). Table 4 compares the basic components of anomie with Freud's theory of personality organization.

Both anomie and personality organization are control theories, the id being controlled by the ego and the individual being controlled by society. If society fails to exercise its role of setting limits on the individual, deviance results. This theoretical approach was a product of Durkheim's theory of suicide, the ultimate of escape and personal pathology.

Merton (1949) set forth his concept of anomie as an example of social interaction produced by conflict between culturally approved goals and institutionally provided means to achieve these goals. Merton's formulation was made with adults in mind; however, there seems to be real application to children as well. An effort is made to make generalizations from adults to children while keeping Merton's basic theory intact. Table 5 outlines the various interactions envisioned by Merton. Five types of adaptation are shown schematically. The + signifies "acceptance," the − signifies "rejection," and ± signifies "rejection of values as they now stand and the desire to substitute new values."

Merton's conceptualization refers to role behavior of society in specific situations, not to the personality of one individual. A person does and probably should take different roles in different situations. A child may re-

Table 5. Modes of individual adaptation*

Modes of adaptation	Culture goals	Institutionalized means
I. Conformity	+	+
II. Innovation	+	−
III. Ritualism	−	+
IV. Retreatism	−	−
V. Rebellion	±	±

*Adapted from Merton, 1949.

ject specific goals without any warning of a change in attitude. Merton was considering the economic structure when he formulated his theory and, as such, considered wealth as a worthwhile goal. In making a generalization to children, other goals must replace the overall "economic goal" considered by Merton. "Doing well in school" or "school achievement" might be considered as an acceptable goal for children. Each of the five modes of adaptation will be considered using this goal as an example.

1. Conformity (acceptance of cultural goals and institutional means) is the basis of the goals of "school achievement." If school achievement were not generally accepted as a logical goal and its institutional means, "study," was not an accepted route to achievement, schools would be considerably different in their structure. Conformity to this goal and to the institutional means of achieving this goal exist in most schools. This is considered normal behavior for boys and girls of school age.

2. Innovation (acceptance of cultural goals but not the institutional means) is a source of many problems for teachers at all levels of education. School achievement is an acceptable goal, but study to achieve is not the only route to achievement. Cheating on exams, copying school work, or other unacceptable behaviors may be a few of the innovative efforts of children whose behavior falls into this second mode.

3. Ritualism (the rejection of cultural goals but the acceptance of institutional means) appears to be a problem for children who see no way to succeed in the system of education but who do not have the security to break completely with the system. Children who are of low ability or whose background has not prepared them for the rigorous competition they face in school are examples. These children may reject the possibility that the goals established by society are possible to achieve. School achievement is therefore rejected as a personal goal; however, they might continue to go through the ritual of study without any hope of achievement.

Schools that put a great deal of emphasis

on achievement or more specifically "signs of success," such as grades, run a risk of ritualism developing among students. The competitive struggle for grades is exhilarating for those who are able to achieve, but it is extremely debilitating to those who fail to achieve. There is still hope for ritualistic children if they do not break ties with the school, but ritualism is risky because it is difficult to determine what the problem really is. Does the child suffer from a learning disability, a physical problem, or low ability? It is a difficult task to identify the child who is "going through the motions" in ritualistic fashion and even more difficult to remediate this behavior.

4. Retreatism (the rejection of both cultural goals and institutional means) is probably the least common of all the modes of adaptation discussed. When retreatism does occur, the child is extremely difficult to reach. The child may withdraw into his own shell or may drop out of school if old enough to do so legally.

Severe forms of retreatism could include autistic behaviors, psychotic tendencies, and addiction to drugs (Jarlais, 1972). They have "retreated" from the real world to one more acceptable to themselves.

Children who retreat from the world of school are often ignored by the school, get few if any of the rewards of school, but also have few of the problems of school. In their world of retreat they may find a solitude stimulating unto themselves without regard for others and the strife that others impose.

5. Rebellion (rejection of both cultural goals and institutional means and the substitution of new goals and means) is a severe departure from other modes of adjustment that have been discussed. Children who rebel are not only rejecting that which is generally accepted, achievement and study, but replace this goal and means to the goal with their own goals. This presents the teacher with a most serious challenge, since the behavior is now tainted with distrust, rebellion, and often hate. Children in rebellion have been classified variously as socially maladjusted, personality disordered, and delinquent.

Anomie occurs as the child becomes alienated from society and develops a feeling of not belonging. Retreatism can be the ultimate result of not establishing meaningful connections between the goals of society and acceptable means of reaching those goals. Merton's theory of anomie has not been highly successful in describing the causes of mental illness from a scientific base, since establishing proof of a system that depends on a complex social interaction is difficult. For the teacher who is more interested in everyday interaction with children than scientific proofs, this theory offers a way of looking at children in conflict that may provide direction for intervention not offered by other systems.

Ecological system

William Rhodes is perhaps the most eloquent spokesman for ecological intervention with children in conflict. The term *ecological* perhaps conjures up a variety of interpretations, but to Rhodes (1970:310) a specific meaning is attached. Ecological intervention

. . . attempts to shift the locus of the disturbance from the child to an encounter point between the child and the micro-community or communities which surround him. It addresses itself to the ecological exchange nature of the disturbance. It searches for an intervention which will address itself to the shared process which is occurring between the child and the micro-communities he is encountering.

Rhodes does not advocate doing away with other modes of intervention such as psychotherapy or behavioral intervention; however, he suggests the simultaneous intervention on the conditions of the child and the surroundings of the child. Intervention on the behavior of the child is not enough, since the child's behavior is only one part of the problem. As the child acts on and reacts to his surroundings, a relationship is established that contributes to the child's emotional stability. If this interaction is detrimental to the child's development, the entire constellation must become a part of the intervention process. When a satisfactory relationship is not established, the child must continually return to an environment that is hostile to continued emotional stability, and any growth is probably lost. Rhodes (1970) discusses several basic tenants of ecological theory.

1. Ecological theory sees the conflict as one that encompasses both the child and his community rather than only as a pathology of the child or the community.

2. It is generally easier to intervene only with the child or with the community.

3. The ideal intervention would trace problems to their "cultural source" during treatment.

4. Intervention of an ecological type recognizes the totality of the problem.

The basic premise of ecological systems just described has implications for intervention that, in the view of those espousing this theory, must be considered in planned change. This theoretical approach would frown on any system that attempts to modify behavior of the child or change his environment without attending to the quality and nature of the interactive process between child and environment.

COUNTER THEORY

An individual who spends a few minutes browsing at a book store will probably be surprised to see the number of books that bring teachers, psychologists, schools, and various child-rearing practices under attack. Titles such as *Growing Up Absurd, The Myth of Mental Illness, The Student Is a Nigger, Death at an Early Age, Our Children Are Dying, The Way It Spozed To Be*, and *Stranger in His Native Land* are often found among the collection.

Countertheorists include those who abhor the status quo of traditional theory. They refuse to be put into a theoretical straight-jacket in which "the way it has been" is "the way it should be."

Countertheorists have several things in common. A major commonality seems to be the need to oversell their ideas. The "'hard-sell" approach often gives these theorists the appearance of having all the answers, of hav-

ing a new panacea for all children. If one looks critically, however, this usually is not the case. Countertheorists believe they must push hard or go unnoticed by better organized and accepted traditional theorists. Professionals who are frustrated by an apparent lack of progress with children often are ready consumers of a new approach that promises easy answers to difficult questions. Often the countertheorist's position is not complete; in fact many approaches appear only to be a prescription for practical application, not a theory at all.

Since counter theory generally springs from discontent with more traditional approaches, from a sense of frustration, or from a desire to solve problems in ways never before attempted, countertheorists generally support a freer concept of education (Goodman, 1962; Gross and Gross, 1969; Kohl, 1969; Neill, 1960). Most countertheorists have a humanistic bent toward children and education, reject the extreme views of Freudian theory, and will not accept the behaviorists' belief in behavior manipulation (Tracy, 1972). Countertheorists generally attack the school curriculum as not being relevant, do not approve of labeling handicapped children, and would like children to have a bigger say in their educational destiny (Glasser, 1969; Goodman, 1962; Henthoff, 1966; Holt, 1972; Reimer, 1971).

It is impossible to present the theoretical views of countertheorists in the same manner used to describe behavioral theory or psychodynamic theory. Countertheorists have no common approach to children in conflict. (Some, in fact, would deny the existence of such children.) To give the reader a flavor of counter theory I have chosen to outline the theoretical approaches of three countertheorists, Glasser, Neill, and Shapiro, who will be discussed in Chapter 6.

SUMMARY

The student of emotional disorders in children should be aware that disorders often occur for a variety of reasons. The reasons have been divided into five categories: (1) biophysical, (2) psychodynamic, (3) behavioral, (4) sociological/ecological, and (5) counter theories.

The biophysical model considers the pathology to be a part of the child. These theorists take one of two positions. The more strict position is taken by those theorists who believe that deviance can occur solely as a result of one or more biophysical problems. The less structured biophysical position indicates that biophysical predisposition is necessary for deviance to occur, but it must be stimulated by an environmental catalyst before deviance occurs.

The psychodynamic viewpoint postulates that psychological problems or conflicts can cause children to act in deviant ways. These theorists generally believe in looking for the causes of the problem and treating the causes rather than the symptoms of the deviance.

The psychodynamic viewpoint suggests that the child in conflict has not negotiated, at a successful level, the various intrapsychic and external conflicts faced in the process of psychological and/or physiological maturity. More contemporary theorists believe in looking at surface-level causation rather than in-depth psychological analysis.

From a behavioral viewpoint a child in conflict might be viewed as exhibiting deviant behavior learned through a process of interaction with an environment that gives inappropriate feedback. Rather than label a child as an acting-out or hostile child, the behaviorist would like to describe the behavior that indicates hostility or acting-out behavior. Generally, behaviorists hold four common assumptions regarding children in conflict.

1. Most inappropriate behavior is learned.
2. A relationship exists between the behavior the child exhibits and his environment.
3. Deviant behavior can be changed through the use of appropriate reinforcement techniques.
4. Looking for causes of deviant behaviors is counterproductive.

Sociologists have studied deviance from both medical and deviance perspectives. From a medical viewpoint the illness can be studied much as one would study physical illnesses. Emphasis would be placed on finding medical causes of the disease, who has it, and under what condition the illness appears. From a deviance perspective, emotional problems center around the concept of rule breaking and rule following. Through the process of rule setting by society and rule breaking by the child the label deviant may be used. From a sociological viewpoint the child is considered deviant because of inappropriate societal influence on the child.

Ecology as applied to children in conflict is a study of the dynamic interaction between the child and the environment. A child's emotional well-being is established on the basis of this interaction. This theory has significance for teachers who believe in treating the whole child.

Countertheorists have contributed educational strategies that have dared to be different. Although countertheorists have generally established approaches from a basis of more traditionally oriented theories, such as psychoanalytical or behavioral thought, they have added some of their own originality to develop a significant direction in working with children. Three countertheorists, Neill, Shapiro, and Glasser, are given as examples.

BIBLIOGRAPHY AND SELECTED READINGS

Adler, A.: The problem child, New York, 1963, Capricorn Books, Division of G. P. Putnam's Sons.

Adler, A.: Social interest, a challenge to mankind, New York, 1964, Capricorn Books, Division of G. P. Putnam's Sons.

Adler, A.: Depression in light of individual psychology, In Werner, H., editor: New understandings of human behavior, New York, 1970, Association Press.

Adler, A.: Sex, personality and the establishment—guidelines for social reeducation, limited edition, 1970.

Ansbacher, H., and Ansbacher, R., editors: The individual psychology of Alfred Adler, New York, 1956, Basic Books, Inc., Publishers.

Bandura, A.: Principles of behavior modification, New York, 1969, Holt, Rinehart & Winston, Inc.

Bender, L.: Childhood schizophrenia: a review, International Journal of Psychiatry 5:211-220, 1968.

Bettelheim, B.: Feral children and autistic children, American Journal of Sociology 64:455-467, 1959.

Birnbrauer, J., and Lawler, J.: Token reinforcement for learning, Mental Retardation 2:275-279, 1964.

Buckley, N., and Walker, H.: Modifying classroom behavior, Champaign, Ill., 1970, Research Press Co.

Bugental, J.: Humanistic psychology: a new breakthrough, American Psychologist 18:563-567, 1963.

Burton, A., editor: Encounter, San Francisco, 1969, Jossey-Bass, Inc., Publishers.

Buss, A.: Psychopathology, New York, 1966, John Wiley & Sons, Inc.

Deslauriers, A., and Carlson, C.: Your child is asleep: early infantile autism, Homewood, Ill., 1969, Dorsey Press.

Durkheim, E.: Suicide, a study in sociology. Translated by John Spaulding and George Simpson, Glencoe, Ill., 1951, The Free Press.

Ellis, A.: Reason and emotion in psychotherapy, New York, 1970, Lyle Stuart, Inc.

Erickson, E.: Identity, youth, and crisis, New York, 1968, W. W. Norton & Co., Inc.

Erikson, K.: Patient role and social uncertainty, Psychiatry; Journal for the Study Interpersonal Processes 20:263-268, 1957.

Erikson, K.: Notes on the sociology of deviance, Social Problems 1:307-314, 1964.

Felix, R.: Mental illness: progress and prospects, New York, 1967, Columbia University Press.

Ferster, C., and DeMyer, M.: A method for the experimental analysis of the behavior of autistic children, American Journal of Orthopsychiatry 32:89-98, 1962.

Fine, R.: Psychoanalysis. In Corsini, R., editor: Current psychotherapies, Itasca, Ill., 1973, F. E. Peacock Publishers, Inc.

Forness, S., and MacMillan, D.: The origins of behavior modification with exceptional children, Exceptional Children 37:93-100, 1970.

Fowle, A.: A typical leucocyte pattern of schizophrenic children, Archives of General Psychiatry 18:666-680, 1968.

Gagne, R. M.: The conditions of learning, New York, 1965, Holt, Rinehart & Winston, Inc.

Glasser, W.: Reality therapy, New York, 1965, Harper & Row, Publishers.

Glasser, W.: Schools without failure, New York, 1969, Harper & Row, Publishers.

Goldstein, A.: Behavior therapy. In Corsini, R., editor: Current psychotherapies, Itasca, Ill., 1973, F. E. Peacock Publishers, Inc.

Gross, B., and Gross, R.: Radical school reform, New York, 1969, Simon & Schuster, Inc.

Hall, C.: A primer of Freudian psychology, New York, 1954, The New American Library, Inc.

Haring, N., and Phillips, E.: Educating emotionally disturbed children, New York, 1962, McGraw-Hill Book Co.

Henthoff, N.: Our children are dying, New York, 1966, The Viking Press, Inc.

Hewett, F.: The emotionally disturbed child in the classroom, Boston, 1968, Allyn & Bacon, Inc.

Higgins, J.: Effects of child rearing by schizophrenic mothers, Journal of Psychiatric Research 4:153-167, 1966.

Hill, W.: Learning: a survey of psychological interpretations, San Francisco, 1963, Chandler Publishing Co.

Holt, J.: Freedom and beyond, New York, 1972, E. P. Dutton & Co., Inc.

Horney, K.: Neurosis and human growth, London, 1951, Routledge and Kegan Paul, Ltd.

Jarlais, D.: Mental illness as social deviance. In Rhodes, W. C.: A study of child variance, Ann Arbor, Mich., 1972, The University of Michigan Press.

Jung, C.: Basic writings, New York, 1959, Modern Library, Inc., Division of Random House, Inc.

Karlson, J.: The biological basis of schizophrenia, Springfield, Ill., 1966, Charles C Thomas, Publisher.

Kennard, M.: Application of EEG to psychiatry. In Wilson, W., editor: Applications of electroencephalography in psychiatry, Durham, N. C., 1965, Duke University Press.

Kohl, H.: The open classroom; a practical guide to a new way of teaching, New York, 1969, Vintage Books, Inc., Division of Random House, Inc.

Krasner, L., and Ullmann, L.: Research in behavior modification: new developments and implications, New York, 1965, Holt, Rinehart & Winston, Inc.

Lemert, E.: Paranoia and the dynamics of exclusion, Sociometry 25:2-20, 1962.

Levin, G., and Simmons, J.: Response to praise by emotionally disturbed boys, Psychological Reports 11:10, 1962.

Lovaas, O., Schaeffer, B., and Simmons, J.: Building social behavior in autistic children by use of electric shock, 1:99-109, 1965.

MacMillan, D.: Behavior modification in education, New York, 1973, The Macmillan Co.

McGhie, A., and Chapman, J.: Disorders of attention and perception in early schizophrenia, British Journal of Medical Psychology, 34:105-116, 1961.

Maslow, A.: Toward a psychology of being, Princeton, N. J., 1962, D. Van Nostrand Co., Inc.

Maslow, A.: Eupsychian management; a journal, Homewood, Ill. 1965, Richard D. Irwin, Inc.

Matza, D.: Becoming deviant, Englewood Cliffs, N. J., 1969, Prentice-Hall, Inc.

Mednick, S.: Birth defects and schizophrenia, Psychology Today 4:48-50, 80-81, 1971.

Meehl, P.: Schizotaxia, schizotypy, schizophrenia. In Buss, A. H., and Buss, E. H., editors: Theories of schizophrenia, New York, 1969, Atherton Press.

Merton, R.: Social theory and social structure: toward a codification of theory and research, Glencoe, Ill., 1949, The Free Press.

Merton, R., Reader, G., and Kendall, P., editors: The student physician; introductory studies in the sociology of medical education, Cambridge, Mass., 1957, Harvard University Press.

Mosak, H., and Dreikurs, R.: Adlerian psychotherapy. In Corsini, R., editor: Current psychotherapies, Itasca, Ill., 1973, F. E. Peacock Publishers, Inc.

Neill, A.: Summerhill: a radical approach to child rearing, New York, 1960, Hart Publishing Co., Inc.

Perls, F., Hefferline, R., and Goodman, P.: Gestalt therapy, New York, 1951, Julian Press, Inc.

Pollin, W.: The pathogenesis of schizophrenia, Archives of General Psychiatry **27**:29-37, 1972.

Reimer, E.: School is dead: Alternatives in education, Garden City, N. Y., 1971, Doubleday & Co., Inc.

Rezmierski, V., and Kotre, J.: A limited literature review of theory of the psychodynamic model. In Rhodes, W. C., director: A study of child variance, Ann Arbor, Mich., 1972, University of Michigan Press.

Rhodes, W. C.: The disturbing child: a problem in ecological management, Exceptional Children **00**:449-455, 1967.

Rhodes, W. C., and Sagor, M.: A study of child variance: the future, Ann Arbor, Mich., 1974, The University of Michigan Press.

Rimland, B.: Psychogenesis versus biogenesis: the issues and evidence. In Plog, S. C., and Edgerton, R. B., editors: Changing perspectives in mental illness, New York, 1969, Holt, Rinehart & Winston, Inc.

Ritvo, E., Yuwiler, A., Geller, E., Ornitz, E., Saeger, K., and Plotkin, S.: Increased blood serotonin and platelets in early infantile autism, Archives of General Psychiatry **23**:566-572, 1970.

Rogers, C.: The clinical treatment of the problem child, Boston, 1939, Houghton Mifflin Co.

Rogers, C.: Client-centered therapy, Boston, 1951, Houghton Mifflin Co.

Rogers, C.: A theory of therapy, personality, and interpersonal relationships, as developed in the client-centered framework. In Kock, S., editor: Psychology, a study of a science, New York, 1959, McGraw-Hill Book Co., vol. 3.

Rogers, C.: Freedom to learn; a view of what education might become, Columbus, Ohio, 1969, Charles E. Merrill Publishing Co.

Rosenthal, D., editor: The Genain quadruplets: a case study and theoretical analysis of heredity and environment in schizophrenia, New York, 1963, Basic Books, Inc., Publishers.

Sagor, M.: Biological bases of childhood behavior disorders, In Rhodes, W. C., editor: A study of child variance, Ann Arbor, Mich., 1972, The University of Michigan Press.

Schultz, W.: Joy, New York, 1967, Grove Press, Inc.

Skinner, B.: Science and human behavior, New York, 1953, The Macmillan Co.

Skinner, B.: The technology of teaching. In Pitts, C. E., editor: Operant conditioning in the classroom, New York, 1971, Thomas Y. Crowell Co.

Skinner, B.: Beyond freedom and dignity, New York, 1972, Bantam Books, Inc.

Strauss, A., and Kephart, N.: Psychopathology and education of brain injured child, New York, 1955, Grune & Stratton, Inc., vol. 2.

Sye, W.: Social variables and their effect on psychiatric emergency situations among children, Mental Hygiene **55**:437-443, 1971.

Szurek, S.: Psychotic episodes and psychic maldevelopment, American Journal of Orthopsychiatry **26**:519-543, 1956.

Thompson, R.: Foundations of physiological psychology, New York, 1967, Harper & Row, Publishers.

Thorne, F.: Integrative psychology, Brandon, Ver., 1967, Clinical Psychology Publishing Co., Inc.

Thorne, F.: Eclectic psychotherapy. In Corsini, R., editor: Current psychotherapies, Itasca, Ill., 1973, F. E. Peacock Publishers, Inc.

Tracy, M.: Conceptual models of emotional disturbance: some other thoughts. In Rhodes, W. C.: A study of child variance, Ann Arbor, Mich., 1972, University of Michigan Press.

Ullmann, L., and Krasner, L.: Case studies in behavior modification, New York, 1965, Holt, Rinehart & Winston, Inc.

Wender, P.: The role of genetics in the etiology of schizophrenias, American Journal of Orthopsychiatry **39**:447-458, 1969.

Wolpe, J.: Psychotherapy by reciprocal inhibition, Stanford, Calif., 1958, Stanford University Press.

CHAPTER 3

Screening, evaluation procedures, and placement

In discussing the screening and evaluation process, Bower (1960) outlined an ancient Cornish test of insanity that Luther Woodword had described. It went something like this. The subject to be tested was placed in a room containing a water faucet and bucket. The bucket was placed under the faucet, and the water was turned on. As the water began to rise in the bucket, the subject was handed a ladle and instructed to bail the water from the bucket so that the water would not run over. Evaluation of the subject was simple. If he turned off the faucet before he began bailing water, he was considered sane. If he bailed water without turning off the faucet, he was considered insane.

Many individuals might well be considered insane if they had to pass this test of insanity without prior warning. The faucet test was easy to administer, simple to evaluate, inexpensive, and took little professional time to administer. Although these are all marks of a good screening instrument, the faucet test would hardly fit ethical demands for completeness, reliability, or validity. Screening evaluation procedures and placement each represent a logical step in achieving the correct educational program for every child.

SCREENING

Screening is the process of selecting a small number of children who need further evaluation from the total population of a class, school, district, etc. Rather than do a total evaluation process (which might include extensive individual interaction) with all third grade children, the teacher might select or screen out only "high-risk" children who appear to be likely to experience failure and conflict. Screening generally is done within the classroom, using instruments designed for evaluating large numbers of children.

Role of the teacher

The classroom teacher is the primary person in the screening process, generally playing a central role in the total process including screening, identification, placement, and individual programing.

Although some research has questioned the teacher's role and effectiveness in screening children (Goldfarb, 1963; Wickman, 1928), there is a wealth of data that support teachers as effective observers of childhood deviance. Mitchell (1942) reported a positive shift toward agreement of opinions between teachers and mental health specialists. Other studies by Ellis and Miller (1936) and Nelson (1971) suggest that teachers are successful in their evaluation of various behavioral disorders, particularly when behavioral guidelines are provided. Bower (1960) believes that the most critical elements in teacher judgment include self-awareness, insight of self, and personal emotional stability.

Several important factors support teachers as the most logical persons in the identification process.*

1. Teachers are trained in personality development of children.

2. The classroom teaching role provides a variety of normal behaviors on which teachers can base their professional judgment.

3. Teachers interact with children for several hours each day for extended periods of time.

4. Both individual and group activities are monitored by teachers, a fact that enhances teacher judgments when compared to clinical interpretation. An interesting and important consideration of the teacher's role in screening was raised by Woody (1969:44) when he asked, "Is it really necessary for teachers to view behaviors in the same manner as clinicians." From the evidence of research findings and the role assumed by classroom teachers it would appear that both teacher judgment and clinical assessment are effective in the assessment process; however, for screening purposes teacher judgment appears to be most acceptable.

Bower and Lambert (1971:144) list seven broad criteria for selection of a screening instrument for school use.

1. It should be possible to complete the screening procedure with only such information as the teacher could obtain without outside technical or professional assistance.

2. The procedure should be sufficiently simple and straightforward for the average teacher to undertake without long training or daily supervision.

3. The results of the procedure should be *tentative identification* of children with emotional problems—leading the teacher to *refer* to competent specialists

---

*Persons interested in a summary of teacher growth in attitudes toward behavior problems of children should consult Hunter (1957).

those children who could benefit most from thorough diagnosis.

4. As a corollary to 3 above, the procedure should *not* encourage the teacher to diagnose emotional problems, nor to draw conclusions about their causes, nor to label or categorize children; in fact, the procedure should actively discourage the teacher from undertaking any of these highly technical interpretations.

5. The procedure should be one which neither invades the privacy of individuals nor violates good taste.

6. The procedure should be one which does not offer a threat to any child.

7. The procedure should be inexpensive to use.

SELECTED SCREENING INSTRUMENTS
Bower-Lambert scales

Bower and Lambert (1969) have developed a screening instrument that is comprehensive for both the individual child and the range of children served by schools. This scale is designed for both boys and girls from kindergarten through grade 12. It represents a comprehensive model for screening that offers promise for use in the school setting. The procedure covers three domains—the teacher's perception of each child, the child's self-perception, and the perception of each child by his peers. Bower and Lambert's screening device could be labeled a semiprojective technique, which could be further classified as a psychodynamic orientation to screening. Following is a narrative description by Bower and Lambert (1971:142-148) of their pupil behavior rating scales.

Behavior rating of pupils (all grades)

One of the most important and useful kinds of information obtained by the school is the teacher's professional judgment of children's behavior. Teachers see children over a period of time in a variety of circumstances: in stress situations, at work and at play. Their judgment and observation have been sharpened by professional training and by day-to-day experience with the normal behavior of children. Often the teacher's rating can be the single most effective index of a pupil's growth and development.

Few professional persons, no matter how well-trained, can make ratings of others with absolute certainty and complete comfort. Don't spend too much time worrying about whether your rating for a particular child is "right" or "wrong." Make your best judgment of each student, then go on to the next. Remember that it is not your judgment alone that will be used to determine whether or not a pupil is developing emotional difficulties. Your perception of a child's behavior will be combined with the perceptions of the child himself and those of his peers—to make the final judgment about screening a child.

The Class Pictures (peer rating—kindergarten -grade 3)

After you have completed the *Behavior Rating of Pupils*, your next step in screening is to plan for administration of the peer ratings. The peer rating instrument for kindergarten and primary grades, *The Class Pictures*, must be given to each child in your class individually. This may take fifteen to twenty minutes of time for each child. Administration of *The Class Pictures* to the entire class, however, may be spread over a period of time—up to, but not exceeding, one month.

Administer the instrument to children one at a time when the rest of the class is engaged in seat work of some kind or occupied in other activities which do not require constant supervision. Such a schedule will require a minimum of interruption in your regular teaching program.

The Class Pictures are composed of twelve picture cards with a total of twenty scoring items (one or two items on a card). Five of the items are pictures of boys in situations related to emotionally maladjusted behavior; five are pictures of girls in situations related to emotionally maladjusted behavior; five are pictures of boys in situations related to positive or neutral types of behavior; and five are pictures of girls in situations related to positive or neutral types of behavior.

The Class Pictures have been developed as a means of analyzing, in a systematic and measurable way, how children are perceived or "seen" by their peers. The responses of most pupils to the pictures will not surprise you. Some responses, however, may seem unrealistic and inappropriate. *Accept each child's responses without comment unless the child obviously misunderstands directions.* Your role during the administration of *The Class Pictures* is one of test proctor and recorder of responses.

The Class Pictures are used with children who have not yet learned to read or write well. Therefore, the responses of each child will need to be recorded individually by you. You will, of course, have to make special provision for the rest of the class while you are administering *Class Pictures* to individual children. If an additional school person is available, he may work with the class while you administer *Class Pictures*. The actual administration should always be done by you. If you are able to organize the class into working groups, *Class Pictures* may be administered to a few individuals daily during such work periods—but you will decide for yourself how best to accomplish this task.

On the test each child is asked to consider which of his classmates is most like the child in every one of the twenty situations. Some children will pick twenty different names. Others may name one or two peers for several or many different items. Still others may make no response for one or more items. *Do not expect any fixed pattern of responses.*

When the responses for each child in the class are collected, the teacher can tally the number of times a particular child is chosen for each of the twenty pictures. The total number of times a child is chosen for *all* of the pictures indicates how clearly or how vividly he is "seen," or perceived by his peers.

The number of times a pupil is picked for the *negative* pictures indicates the degree to which he or she is *negatively* perceived by his peers. By dividing the number of times a child is picked for the ten negative pictures by the total number of times he is picked for all twenty of the pictures, a percent, indicating the ratio of negative perception by peers, is obtained and used in screening.

The mean or average number of negative selections of emotionally handicapped boys and girls has been found to be significantly different from the mean number of negative selections in the general school population of that grade and sex. Consequently, the percent of negative perception has been found to be a reliable indicator of those children whose behavior, as observed by peers, indicates some degree of emotional difficulty. The higher the percent, the greater the possibility that the child has emotional problems. The percent of negative selections on *The Class Pictures*, when combined with teacher ratings and self-ratings, has been found effective in primary grades for screening children with emotional handicaps.

A Class Play (peer rating—grades 3-7)

A Class Play is a peer rating instrument with greatest applicability in grades 4, 5, and 6, though it has been used with success in grades 3 and 7. It should be administered reasonably soon after you have completed the *Behavior Rating of Pupils*. It should take no more than 35 to 45 minutes.

Section I of the instrument contains descriptions of twenty hypothetical roles in a play, with instructions directing each pupil to choose a classmate who would be most suitable and natural in each of the roles. A second section of the *Play* (Section II) elicits from each pupil an indication of the roles he would prefer, or which he thinks other people would prefer, or which he thinks other people would select for him. This section has thirty different quartets of the twenty roles, with a question aimed at finding out how the child sees himself in relation to each role.

The scoring of *A Class Play* is very much like the scoring of *The Class Pictures*. Each pupil names a classmate for each of the roles in the play. By counting the number of times a pupil is picked for each of the roles in the play, and then counting the number of times each pupil is picked for the *even numbered* (negative) roles, a percentage is obtained indicative of the positive or negative perception of each pupil by his classmates. This score is used in the screening. . . .

Student Survey (peer rating—grades 7-12)

The *Student Survey* is the peer rating instrument for use in the junior and senior high schools. In order for this test to have validity, it is necessary to administer it to a class in which the students have had an opportunity for some social and intellectual interaction, as well as for observation of one another in a variety of classroom situations. Previous work with this test has shown that social studies or English classes are usually best for this purpose.

Some students in the junior and senior high school may be sensitive to the kinds of questions asked on the *Student Survey*. It is important, therefore, that you anticipate the possibility of such sensitivity and take steps to allay any suspicion or resentment. For example, some teachers have found it helpful to have ready an envelope into which all the tests can be placed when the students are finished. This helps to reassure the class that the test results are confidential and reinforces statements made in the instructions that the results will not be discussed with others.

Section I of the *Student Survey* consists of twenty items. Ten are illustrative of maladjusted or emotionally disturbed behavior and ten are illustrative of neutral or positive behavior. For each statement of behavior, the students are asked to list the name of a classmate who is most like the student described in the item.

Section II of the *Student Survey* contains the same twenty behavior statements randomly arranged in thirty groups of four statements each. The student is asked to select one of the four statements in each group as the one which he thinks others in the class might apply to himself. The responses to Section II can be used to compare the peer ratings of a student with his self rating. The value of providing two sections in the Student Survey, a peer rating and a self rating on the same items, is, that after scoring both sections, the teacher is able to measure and analyze how a student sees himself in relation to how he is seen by others. . . .

A Picture Game (self rating—Kindergarten to grade 3)

A Picture Game is designed to give a measure of young children's perception of *self*. It is used along with the *Behavior Rating of Pupils* (teacher rating) and *The Class Pictures* (peer rating) to identify pupils who are vulnerable to, or handicapped by, emotional problems.

A Picture Game consists of 66 pictures, including two sample pictures. Each picture is illustrative of normal home and school relationships and events. With the exception of the two sample cards and the first ten pictures, each picture is emotionally neutral in the portrayal of the relationship or event. The child is asked to sort each picture into one of two categories: "This is a happy picture" or "This is a sad picture." The sorting is done by placing each picture in the "happy" or "sad" side of a two-compartment box, which has a happy face shown on one compartment and a sad face shown on the other. The child categorizes each picture in accordance with his perception of it.

The first ten pictures the child sorts are stereotypes: obviously happy or obviously sad situations. The purpose of including them in the test items is to check on each pupil's understanding of the task. If a child sorts the first ten pictures correctly, you can be fairly sure that he has understood the process well enough for you to use his score in screening. If, on the other hand, he does not sort the first ten pictures correctly, you will need to meet with him individually and ask him to sort the pictures again for you, making certain that he understands the process. Some children *choose* to place pictures differently from others. If you find that such children understand the process but continue, on re-administration, to sort the pictures in an independent fashion, make a note of it on the "Class Record Sheet," and use the child's score in screening. . . .

Thinking about Yourself (self rating—grades 3-7)

The purpose of *Thinking about Yourself* is to elicit from the pupil himself an *intra-self* measure of the relationship between a pupil's perception of his environment and his conception of what it ought to be. What is looked for is the degree of discrepancy between a pupil's self perception of himself as he *is* and as he would like to be.

Many pupils with serious emotional problems cannot bring themselves to disclose their difficulties in writing, or are uncomfortable about disclosing them. Their responses will therefore very much resemble those of other children in the class. These youngsters are most likely to be screened by teachers and peers.

There are other pupils, however, who do not manifest their difficulties to teachers or peers, but who rise to the opportunity to express inner discomfort and *can* communicate their disturbance on a self rating instrument. Since the average discrepancy between self and *ideal* self has been found to discriminate between pupils with emotional problems and those with normal behavior adjustment, *Thinking about Yourself* provides a meaningful and useful screening dimension not available from teacher or peer ratings. . . .

A Self Test (self rating—grades 7-12)

A Self Test is intended to obtain a measure of the difference between the way a pupil sees himself and the way he would like to be—in other words, a measure of the difference between self and ideal self. To the extent that a student is able to disclose the differences or similarities between these two aspects of self, the instrument is useful in screening. However, some pupils with moderate or serious emotional problems cannot bring themselves to disclose the discomfort or dissatisfaction which this instrument invites them to disclose. Their responses, therefore, will very much resemble those of other students in the class. These youngsters are more likely to be identified by teachers and peers in the screening process.

There are other pupils, however, who do not manifest their difficulties to teachers or peers, but who rise to the opportunity to express inner discomfort and *can* communicate their disturbance on a self rating. For these students, the *Self Test* provides the opportunity. Since the average discrepancy between self and *ideal* self has been found to discriminate between pupils with emotional problems and those with normal behavior adjustment, A *Self Test* provides a meaningful screening dimension not available from teacher or peer ratings.

A *Self Test* contains forty statements describing people behaving in a number of different ways. In Section I, the student is asked to indicate how strongly he *would like* to be or *would not like* to be the person described. In Section II, the items are repeated and the student is asked to indicate how strongly he feels he *is* like or *is not* like the person described. The two responses by the student (i.e., whether or not he *wants* to be like and whether or not he *is* like) are then compared in the scoring process, after which the amount of discrepancy between the two "selves" is compared. . . .

The Bower-Lambert scales are an example of a comprehensive screening instrument. Although it may appear to be somewhat cumbersome to teachers, it actually includes rather simple instruments to administer and score. The data from tests are collated and weighted through specific procedures that finally result in a total evaluation for each child.

There are other instruments that show promise for initial screening of children in conflict.

Devereux Elementary School Behavior Rating Scale

Authors: George Spivak and Marshall Swift
Publisher: Devereux Foundation Press
Level: Grades K-6

This checklist consists of eleven areas including classroom disturbance, impatience, inattentive-withdrawn, and need for closeness to the teacher. Forty-seven items are included in the test—forty-four items from the eleven areas and three additional items that cover academic work habits. This behavior checklist is specifically related to classroom achievement.

Walker Problem Behavior Identification Checklist

Author: Hill M. Walker
Publisher: Western Psychological Services
Level: Grades 4-6

This checklist is designed to be used by classroom teachers. It consists of fifty statements describing children's behaviors. The following five factors of behavior are evaluated:
1. Acting-out behaviors such as disruptive, aggressive, or defiant behavior
2. Withdrawal such as avoidance and restricted functioning
3. Distractibility including short attention span and inadequate social skills
4. Disturbed peer relations such as inadequate social skills and a negative self image
5. Immature or otherwise dependent behavior

Devereux Child Behavior Rating Scale

Authors: George Spivack and Jules Spotts
Publisher: Devereux Foundation Press
Level: Ages 8-12 years

This is a rating instrument that can be used by clinicians, child care workers, parents, and others who have had close relationships with a child over a period of time. Seventeen scores are allowed, including such areas as distractibility, emotional detachment, susceptibility to emotional upset, and social aggression. About 10 to 20 minutes are required to administer this scale.

California Test of Personality

Authors: Louis Thorpe, Willis Clark, and Ernest Tiegs
Publisher: California Test Bureau
Level: Grade K-adult

The California Test of Personality covers five levels of personality development by grade. A total of sixteen areas are tested, including self-reliance, feeling of belonging, social skills, and antisocial tendencies. Extensive research is available for the teacher who wishes to use this instrument (Buros, 1965).

Sociometrics

Various forms of sociometrics have been used by teachers for a number of years. For classroom teachers sociometric tests are a simple measure of the attractions and repulsions within a given group of children. Fig.

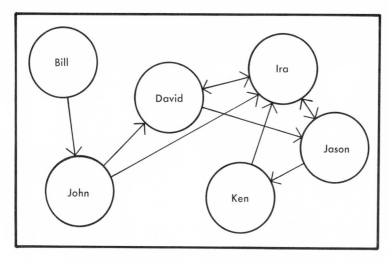

Fig. 3-1. Sociogram of special class of boys.

3-1 shows the results of social questions within a small class of boys.

Several important concerns regarding sociometric tests should be considered before this measure is used for classroom screening (Moreno, 1943).

1. Questions used to stimulate pupil selection should be simple enough to be understood by everyone in the group.

2. Children should be allowed to make choices in private.

3. The limits of choices should be clearly indicated to all children.

4. Children should be permitted an unlimited number of choices or rejections.

5. Each choice should be made with a particular activity in mind.

6. Children should be reacting (as much as possible) to a real situation that will be affected by their decisions.

Sociometric data provide additional information for the classroom teacher. A sociometric test is generally not intended to be used as an isolated screening instrument but rather to obtain supportive information.

In an effort to identify several criteria for identification, Kessler (1966) outlined several variables that are important in identification of children for referral. These include (1) the discrepancy between chronological age and behavior, (2) the frequency of symptom occurrence, (3) the number of separate symptoms that alienate the child from those around him, (4) the view that the child holds toward himself, and (5) the resistance of behaviors to change.

EVALUATION

Once screening has been completed and children in need of further evaluation identified, the first stage of the total evaluation process is completed. Next the educator is ready to evaluate each identified child to determine, so far as possible, specific reasons for deviance to be exhibited. Only those children who are screened out as "high-risk" cases are usually provided with a more complete evaluation. States that have established special funding for emotionally disturbed or behaviorally disordered children generally require specific information before special placement is made. Required information may include observation, psychological or psychiatric interview, individual intelligence tests, achievement tests, medical examination, personality testing, and professional judgment. These evaluations are required to avoid duplication of services and to ensure proper placement for each child. Through the use of evaluative instruments and professional observation the determination of major problem areas is established. When the decision is made to evaluate an individual child, the parents should become involved. This is necessary from ethical, practical, and legal points of view.

Children in conflict can be affected by a variety of other problems. They may be visually impaired, hearing impaired, or physically handicapped; they might also be mentally retarded or suffering from organic problems that might necessitate special placement. The process of sifting through the various physical, mental, perceptual, and emotional processes to determine the major cause of disability is being seriously questioned by teachers, parents, and others interested in the welfare of children. Understandably, educators do not want children whose only problem is a physical handicap, for example, to be placed in a special program designed to serve emotionally disturbed children. In many cases, however, it is extremely difficult to determine which handicap is presenting the major problem for the child. Mental health and adequate interpersonal relationships are not achieved in isolation or are they limited to those who do not have other problems. With the growing emphasis of schools toward the resource room and away from the special class model, many of the categorical breakdowns of the past are being minimized. Resource teachers are trying to help the child without determining the specific "weighting" that should be applied to each problem area. Granted, the child who has a visual limitation, hearing impairment, or other physical limitation is generally more vulnerable to intrapersonal and interpersonal conflicts. The degree of conflict a child experiences can be viewed as the result of two factors: the child's adjustive resources and the degree of stress under which each child lives. Fig. 3-2 shows this conceptualization graphically.

Fig. 3-2 outlines the relative interaction of four children with two factors—adjustive resources and degree of stress. Mary has a high level of coping skills and a low level of problems in her life. She is able to get along well in school. John has a high number of problems and low ability to cope. He presents serious problems in school. John may have physical, social, hearing, and visual

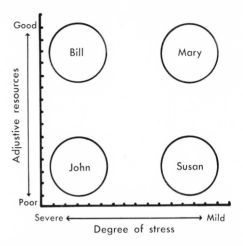

Fig. 3-2. A comparison of adjustive resources and degree of stress with four children.

problems in addition to emotional problems. He needs help to strengthen his ability to cope, and at the same time the number of problems that he must face needs to be reduced if possible. Susan has a low number of problems and has few resources for coping. Her functional level is adequate as long as she continues to be free of stress. Her adjustive resources must be strengthened, since her life will include problems with which she must cope effectively. Bill has a great number of problems but also copes well, which allows him to get along adequately in school. Whereas educators might work with all of these hypothetical cases at some time in school, they generally are most concerned with Susan and John, who have poor adjustive abilities. Secondary handicaps such as vision or hearing problems must be considered in the degree of stress under which a child must function. Although vision and hearing problems should be corrected as much as possible and accommodation of the disability emphasized, the emotional impact often remains. In brief, it is important that emotional problems be dealt with, even if other handicapping conditions are present within the child's behavioral pattern.

Children who are suffering from various physical or mental handicaps may have developed adequate emotional relationships with those around them and achieved an internal self-acceptance. If this is the situation, there is no more need to establish special services for these children than for "normal" children.

Individual evaluation is often done for a variety of reasons including classification or labeling, a means of educational placement, for funding, as a means of establishing the number of handicapped children to be served, and to develop an educational blueprint. Of these and other reasons for evaluation there appears to be only one that is educationally valid and defensible—to establish an educational blueprint for action. Screening and evaluation are reasonably easy operations that can be effectively performed by trained professionals, but what happens after evaluation is closely related to the quality of the diagnostic process and will ultimately determine the success of the program. It seems that professionals have become so enamored by the process of diagnostic evaluation that they have seemingly lost sight of the most important factor in their original plan. Educators might ask themselves several questions. What is the purpose of evaluation? Is it to get rid of children? Is it to satisfy their needs to classify, to label, and to pigeonhole children?

Medical examination

Although evaluation is not a process that proceeds on a predictable course for all children, there are logical steps that seem appropriate to follow as a guide. The first of these is a medical examination. This should not be a routine physical examination with blood pressure, pulse, and respiration serving as the major indicators of normalcy. The teacher should share information with the physician that has led to the recommendation of a medical examination. Information such as hyperactive or hypoactive behavior, sudden bursts of anger, or loss of attention may prove valuable in determining the exact nature of the medical evaluation. A straight pin lodged in the child's leg muscle may be located more readily if the teacher gives the physician information that the child does not

sit still but squirms constantly at the desk. A description of the child's behavior should help the physican to locate and correct the problem if it is one that can be solved through medical intervention.

Teachers and schools have recently received "bad press" because some teachers and/or schools were suggesting that parents take their "hyperactive" child to physicians, who in turn prescribed drug therapy as the solution to the problem. Articles that have appeared in nonprofessional magazines have prompted concern among parents and raise two serious issues for teachers. First, behavior should be described as accurately as possible, but without proposed solutions for the physician. Second, physicians should be recommended only on request, and then the names of at least two physicians should be suggested to the interested parents.

If solutions to the problem are not found in the physical examination, further evaluation is necessary, although additional evaluation generally would be indicated even if possible causation and solutions are arrived at in the initial physical examination. In some cases visual and hearing evaluation might be included in the medical evaluation, whereas at other times this would be a separate consideration. In either case it is important to determine the integrity of these sensory functions.

Psychological evaluation

Since several states require that children given special services for emotional problems be of normal intelligence or above, an individual test of intelligence is often administered. Examples of two commonly used individual intelligence scales include the Wechsler Intelligence Scale for Children (WISC) or Stanford-Binet test. These tests have received sharp criticism in recent years but still remain the major tools for determining the potential intellectual capacity for a given child (Anastasi, 1968). Before any psychological tests are administered the psychologist should spend time in the classroom observing the child. Tests that are given by a person not familiar to the child, in strange surroundings, and without prior observation are highly suspect if interpreted as valid measurement tools (Anastasi, 1968; Ebel, 1972). Although some states still require individual tests of intelligence before special class placement can be made, there appears to be a healthy skepticism developing that will likely diminish "testing for testing's sake."

Although both the WISC and Stanford-Binet test were intended to be used only as intelligence tests, much research has been done to determine their usefulness in other areas such as personality makeup and learning style (Buros, 1965). Various testing professionals have even proposed that brain damage and mental illness can be determined by using individual intelligence tests (Coleman, 1964). Placing much credibility on intelligence tests to evaluate in areas like emotional stability is highly questionable; in fact, Anastasi (1968) suggests that emotional variables are important factors in the adequate measure of intellectual ability.

Once the test administration is completed, the information should be shared with those who are directly responsible for the correct educational placement of each child. This information should include more than test scores, since the testing situation generally yields extremely important data. Proficient test administrators report that the final IQ score is among the least important data gathered during test administration with children in conflict.

Although teachers sometimes believe that the information gained from the intelligence testing is useless, since it represents something they already knew, they should be aware that the psychologist or psychiatrist is really not gathering new information. The alert teacher will soon develop a sense of knowing the approximate intellectual level at which a child is functioning from various school-related tasks. Common findings should lend support to both the teacher and psychologist. The role of the psychologist in testing helps to verify the teacher's suspicions, but more importantly, it looks at the learning style of the child from another perspective, which can contribute valuable insight for educational programing (Anastasi, 1968). When the psychologist is an active participant with teachers and other staff as a helping team, the interaction adds to the overall usefulness of the intelligence testing.

In addition to intelligence testing the psychologist will likely want to do other psychological testing as part of routine evaluation. Personality tests either of the projective or nonprojective type might be used. There are a variety of these tests available from which the most appropriate can be selected. Generally the age of the child and the expertise of the diagnostician are major factors in personality test selection.

Some school districts have negotiated special contractual agreements with mental health centers or professional persons in private practice to evaluate children in conflict. The success of these agreements seems to depend, to a considerable degree, on the process established for assessing behavior of children. Assessment that is done in the isolation of a clinical setting, away from the child's natural world of interaction with other children and adults, is proving to be of limited value for teachers (Ebel, 1972). Under these conditions there tends to be a disruption of interaction and communication between the teacher and clinician. Reports written by clinicians have often been couched in professional jargon, which is of limited value to the teacher in the ongoing educational process. In addition, much of the reporting to teachers concerns static data (the way the child is) rather than process data (the way the child developed). This information is often of limited value, since the teacher generally has good insight concerning the child's present behavior as a result of ongoing classroom interaction. Processing the events that have contributed to the static test information into programing for behavioral improvement appear to be the major necessary components for psychological evaluation.

The total evaluation process can be viewed as beginning with the child and gradually including additional people who, hopefully, possess more encompassing skills. The total evaluation process can be conceptualized as concentric circles, with each additional ring showing movement toward a more encompassing evaluation.

SELECTED EVALUATION TOOLS

Of all the diagnostic tools available, astute observation by teachers, parents, and mental health professionals appears to be most crucial for accurate diagnosis (Akhurst, 1970; Sattler, 1974). Skill in observation does not come easily or naturally; it is generally built on an adequate background and understanding of human growth and development, a basic knowledge of school expectation and the role, effectiveness, and range of formal and informal tests. The teacher who possesses good observational skills can help to avoid unnecessary testing of children. The problems of obtaining accurate assessment with emotional, behavioral, and/or social problems are well documented (Anastasi, 1965, 1968; Davids, 1958; Kleinmuntz, 1967; Lyman, 1971). However, when inappropriate behaviors persist in spite of the best efforts of teachers, additional measures are often indicated. Formalized tests represent one method to verify teacher observations and to provide the teacher with a relatively factual method for gathering new information (Anastasi, 1968; Sattler, 1974).

The formal tests reviewed here are not typically used by teachers of children in conflict. They represent professional measures of emotional stability generally employed by psychologists or others appropriately trained to administer them to children. Their usefulness is determined by the ability of the evaluator to make relevant judgments of educational needs and by teachers' ability to implement educationally sound programs to meet these needs.

Intelligence testing

The study of intelligence testing as it is known today was started with the work of Alfred Binet and Theodore Simon. Binet and his co-workers had been interested in the development of tests to measure intelligence for many years prior to being commissioned

in 1904 by the Minister of Public Instruction to study alternatives to the education of subnormal children who attended schools in Paris. It was to meet this practical demand that Binet, in collaboration with Simon, prepared the first draft of the Binet-Simon scale (Anastasi, 1968). The 1905 scale consisted of thirty items arranged in order of difficulty. A variety of functions were measured, with emphasis being placed on judgment, comprehension, and reasoning.

A major revision of the 1905 test was made in 1908. The number of items was increased, unsatisfactory items were eliminated, and all test items were grouped into age levels. A 1911 revision set the stage for intelligence testing as it is known today. Several revisions of Binet's test were developed in the United States, but the most famous were developed at Stanford University in 1916 under the direction of Terman, called the Stanford-Binet test (Anastasi, 1968).

The most recent major change in either the Stanford-Binet test or WISC came in 1974 with a revision designed to minimize the cultural bias of the WISC. The WISC-R (revised) offers hope that more reliable measures of intelligence, freer from cultural bias, will be made.

Personality tests

Rorschach test. Perhaps the best known of the projective techniques is the Rorschach, developed by the Swiss psychiatrist, Hermann Rorschach (Anastasi, 1968). This test, which was first described in 1921, attempts to predict from the subject's associations to inkblots, how he will react to others in his environment. The Rorschach consists of ten cards, each printed with a bilaterally symmetrical inkblot. Five of the cards are done in shades of grey and black; two have additional touches of bright red; and three combine several of the pastel shades. As the individual is shown each inkblot, he is asked what he sees.

Administering and scoring of the Rorschach test is demanding, generally subjective, and the results are often of questionable value for educational purposes. Not only are the responses considered in scoring but other factors such as popularity of various responses, position in which cards are held, remarks of the examinee, and emotional expressions are considered. Scoring is not only difficult and time consuming but the final results with children are suspect by many professionals (Kleinmuntz, 1967; Ullmann and Krasner, 1965), since some of the normative data were derived from adult groups. Clinical experience with the instrument also lacks an accumulation of information in the qualitative interpretation of protocols for children (Anastasi, 1968). Presently it appears that few children who are placed in classes for the emotionally disturbed or behaviorally disordered are being given Rorschach tests. The reason for this is somewhat unclear but probably relates to the behavioral bent presently held by many mental health professionals: the difficulty of scoring and interpretation and the apparent lack of usefulness for educational programing.

Holtzman Inkblot Technique. An alternative inkblot test that is receiving some attention is the Holtzman Inkblot Technique. This test represents a genuine attempt to meet the technical standards of psychometric instruments. The Holtzman test is patterned after the Rorschach test but is sufficiently different to be called a new test, with little data to suggest any true superiority over the Rorschach test. Age range for the Holtzman test is from 5 years to adult, as compared with preschool to adult age range for the Rorschach test (Anastasi, 1968).

Thematic Apperception Test. Another projective instrument that has been developed is the Thematic Apperception Test (TAT). In contrast to the vague inkblots used in the Rorschach test, the TAT uses more highly structured stimuli and requires more complete and better organized responses. To utilize the advantages of the TAT with children a special Children's Apperception Test (CAT) has been developed. The CAT cards substitute animals for people as stimuli for children and is designed for ages 3 to 10 years. The various animals are shown in typically human situations. The pictures are designed to evoke fantasies that children may hold regarding various problems, such as oral problems of feeding, sibling rivalry, parent relationships, aggression, toilet training, and other experiences of childhood (Anastasi, 1968; Kleinmuntz, 1967).

The Blacky pictures. The Blacky pictures, a series of cartoon drawings, are designed to study psychoanalytical concepts of child development (Blum, 1950-1962). Reliability, validity, and normative data for the Blacky pictures have been challenged as being inadequate (Blum, 1956; Zubin et al., 1965); however, numerous refinements of the original test have been made (Kleinmuntz, 1967). The test consists of twelve cards depicting in cartoon form, a family of dogs. The major character of the test is Blacky, a dog that takes on the role of male or female, depending on the sex of the individual being tested.

Word, sentence, and story completion tests. Various projective techniques have evolved from the more formalized projective tests. These include word association tests such as Jung's list of 100 words, which are presented orally, or the list developed by Kent and Rosanoff. Response to words has been analyzed according to the reaction time of the child, content of responses, nonverbal responses, and frequency of responses (Forer, 1971).

Sentence completion tests, such as the Forer Structured Sentence Completion Test, are used to gain a general diagnostic overview of the child's personality (Forer, 1971). From the individual responses many clinical inferences and behavioral predictions are drawn. Interpretations of fear, hostility, and aggression can be made from sentence completion tests. The Rotter Incomplete Sentence Blank is an example of a sentence completion test (Rotter and Rafferty, 1950). Sentence completion tests are designed to meet a specific population or situation. Typical examples of individual items might include the following:

My dad always . . .
At night I often . . .
On school days I . . .
My sister . . .
School work is . . .

The test begins by the examiner starting a story and the child finishing it. The Madeleine Thomas Stories (M.T.S.) (Wursten, 1960) are an example of this projective technique. Story completion tests are really not tests but they elicit stimuli that encourage children to talk about their inner world freely and with little or no discomfort.

Classroom use of projectives. It is my opinion that educators must avoid the use of projective techniques in the classroom for other than cathartic purposes for children. The teacher can use the techniques as a way of encouraging children to express themselves freely who would otherwise withhold and repress feelings. The perceptive teacher generally is aware of problem behaviors without having the child complete a story or word association test. As exercises of creativity, the techniques described can encourage children to express themselves freely. This expression can often "cleanse" the child of various irrational fears, guilt feelings, and internal conflicts. Being able to express these feelings around a picture or story often precedes confronting the problem on a more realistic level, such as open discussion of inappropriate feelings with the teacher or parent.

The use of formal diagnostic tests with children to ascertain personality development has generally centered around psychodynamically oriented projectives. Behavioral methods include observation and recording of behaviors observable to the teacher. Whereas formalized diagnostic tests serve a useful purpose for clinicians, observation remains the teacher's most often-used tool in behavioral assessment and subsequent educational programing for children in conflict.

Sociological evaluation

Sociological evaluation should generally be undertaken at the same time that other diagnostic information is being gathered. Sociological data include sociometric data such as discussed earlier and social evaluation of the family constellation. Social information is generally gathered by the social worker or school nurse; however, this information could be logically gathered by others in the school, including a teacher who is skilled and interested in social interaction. Social data are extremely important to teachers as they piece together information from a variety of sources and can become the "adhesive" that pulls together various splinter areas of the evaluation process.

CLASSROOM PLACEMENT
Cascade of services

A variety of placement possibilities must be provided to meet the needs of all children in conflict. Deno (1970) proposed what she termed the Cascade System of Special Educational Service. Fig. 3-3 shows how this system would provide service for children with a wide range of educational needs. Four classroom settings by Deno will be discussed: (1) regular class placement with support, (2) the resource room, (3) special class placement, and (4) total care programs. The Cascade System of Special Education Service was part of the policy statement that was approved by the 1973 Council for Exceptional Children (CEC) Delegate Assembly.

Regular classroom placement with support. For children in conflict to be maintained in a regular classroom educators must provide the teacher with support. This support must include more than verbalization and must stop short of removal of the child from the classroom. The specialist assigned to aid the classroom teacher is generally expected to integrate findings from the evaluation and to help the regular classroom teacher develop appropriate educational interventions. The resource teacher can provide this support by working in the classroom whenever possible. The relationship established will often depend on the personalities of the teachers, the needs of the child, and the willingness of each to grow. Often the specialist can best work as an assistant to the teacher. This enables the total classroom coordination to remain with the classroom teacher and provides a nonthreatening atmosphere in which cooperation can flourish.

Working in the classroom marks a dramatic departure from traditional approaches, which often encourage the pulling out of children from the classroom into a more secluded

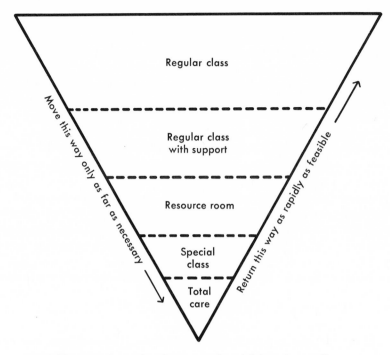

Fig. 3-3. Cascade of services for children in conflict.

atmosphere. Although it takes a great deal of effort and professional confidence to display one's expertise in full view of one's peers, several advantages of this mode of operation seem appropriate to mention. First, the child remains in the regular classroom where the necessity for labeling is decreased and where the trauma that often results from pull-out programs is thus avoided. The child in conflict continues to be part of the class even though there are problems. Second, it discourages the classroom teacher from "giving up" on the child and turning to the "experts" for answers. Third, working within the classroom provides the advantage of the sharing of information between the special teacher and classroom teacher. Both have much to offer in the understanding of and programing for a given child that will likely be lost in a segregated setting. Pull-out programs, by their design, have often encouraged teachers to regress into isolated positions rather than to grow in their understanding and coping ability with children in conflict. Fourth, integrated programing allows children to make use of the modeling process. Children in conflict who are isolated have less appropriate behavior after which they can model

their own behavior. This can result in a potentially unhealthy situation developing (Reinert, 1968). Reality "demands" that "normal" children interact and relate with those who are different from themselves, since the world is filled with diversity of thought and of action. The "normal" adult must be able to cope with this divergence. One way to prepare children for this diversity is to allow them to interact with children who are, in some ways, different. The deleterious effects of homogeneous grouping have been well documented (Coleman, 1966; Dunn, 1968; Meyerowitz, 1967). Part of the teaching process seems to be neglected if educators fail to help every child interact with peers who are different.

Specialists who have capitalized on the opportunity to interact with regular classroom teachers around the needs of children in conflict seldom want to return to the position of isolation that they once knew. But how does the school change direction once a pull-out program has been well established? Obviously many alternatives exist, ranging from simple reassigning all pupils to regular classrooms to gradual mainstreaming through the interaction of specialists with regular classroom teachers. Compulsory reassignment seems to be just as inappropriate as the original assignment to special programs. Establishing an organizational structure that supports continual reappraisal of the educational placement of all children seems to be a feasible goal for most schools.

The resource room. For some children the regular classroom needs to be supplemented with interaction on a one-to-one basis or in small group activity. One approach to meet this need is the use of a resource room, which is a concept that offers several alternatives to the child in conflict so that a child can receive help in the resource room for varying periods of time throughout the school day. For instance, if a crisis develops in the regular classroom that requires the removal of one or more children, the resource room is available as a temporary intervention site. Theoretically, a child could function in the resource room for as little as a few minutes a week to nearly full time during some difficult periods. This is largely theoretical because it rarely functions in that manner. In a sincere effort to serve more children, teachers often schedule specific times for children to come to the resource room. Some scheduling is necessary, but when this scheduling becomes rigid, children often are unable to receive help when it is needed. With rigid scheduling a child cannot have a crisis at times other than from 2 to 2:40 P.M. on either Tuesday or Thursday, for example. The child is out of luck as far as the resource room is concerned if his problems do not occur at appropriate times during the day or week.

A major problem of the resource room concept is the emphasis on expertise and authority of the resource teacher. As long as the resource teacher works in isolation from the regular classroom teacher there is little opportunity for sharing of ideas. Under isolated conditions little personal growth occurs, fears grow, and defensive attitudes often develop. To counteract this somewhat natural division of activity the resource teacher should program as much time as possible in the regular classroom. Time spent in the regular classroom should include working with children seen in the resource room, supporting the teacher in curriculum development, in observation, and in working as a co-worker or professional aide to the classroom teacher.

A second problem area of resource rooms is the role of the resource teacher. Many resource rooms have become no more than glorified study halls, with the resource teacher being the study supervisor. The classroom teacher makes assignments that are brought to the resource room for completion. There seems to be little justification for this relationship—not that study periods and teacher assistance are not important or needed, but the employment of a specialist who is trained to treat emotional problems for a daily study-hall supervisor does not appear to be an economical or effective use of professional personnel. A partial justification for this role might be to develop a relationship with a classroom teacher who is initially reluctant to establish a more meaningful interaction, but this should be only a temporary involvement.

There is no one established role for the resource teacher to assume. Some believe a crisis role is the only acceptable alternative, others believe a remedial role is appropriate, whereas others can accept only emphasis on therapeutic intervention. It seems that strict differentiation of roles for the resource teacher and classroom teacher is necessary to avoid costly duplication. An attempt will be made to draw a simple role definition, knowing that conflicts in the classroom are never so simplistic or easily categorized.

Teachers generally establish their roles according to two major factors: what they are hired to do and the strengths they possess. Being a relative situation, the strengths possessed cannot be discussed in any practical way. In general, resource teachers for children in conflict are hired to act as change agents to help children establish more appropriate ways of interacting with those entering their life space, whereas regular teachers are employed to teach basic educational skills in large group situations.

If educators keep these general job expectations in mind, they will be unlikely to experience serious role conflict. The specialist will generally work with the weaknesses of personality or behavior problems exhibited by the child, whereas the regular classroom teacher will accommodate the deviant behavior as much as possible and at the same time capitalize on things the child can do. A child who is unable to attend to classroom activities and therefore is not learning might be an appropriate example. The resource teacher works specifically on attending behavior each day in the resource room or regular class. By using game activities and positive reinforcement the specialist might try to increase the attending level until the child is attending to the activity at a desirable level.

The regular classroom teacher would also be interested in the attending behavior but would not work directly on the problem. Instead, highly motivating activities, touch control, and other methods aimed at minimizing the opportunity for inattention are employed. This division of effort will help to assure the child a balanced educational program with emphasis on both education and personality development. Another way of explaining this role separation is for specialists to work on the child's weaknesses while the regular teacher capitalizes on the child's strengths. Fig. 3-4 depicts graphically the relative roles of the regular class teacher and resource teacher to the child in conflict.

Three basic interactions are delineated by this diagram. Area A represents the efforts put forth by the regular classroom teacher. Using highly motivating activities, touch control, and other methods of minimizing inattention, the regular teacher tries to accommodate the weakness. Area B represents the efforts of the special teacher to increase attending behavior using game activities along with positive reinforcement. Area C represents the interaction between the regular and special teacher. This might include the specialist's working in the regular classroom and consultation. Much of the effort invested by the special teacher is integrated into the regular class structure, with only a small portion available to isolated activities.

The traveling resource teacher or itinerant teacher is an adaptation of the resource room

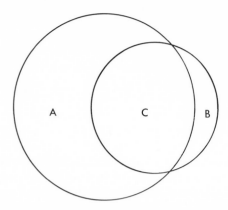

Fig. 3-4. The role of the regular class teacher as opposed to the role of the resource teacher.

that offers services in schools that could not otherwise be provided with services, often because of small enrollments.

Special class placement. During the 1960s special class placement grew rapidly as a placement alternative for children in conflict. Generally the relative importance of special classes has diminished in recent years in favor of more integrated approaches; however, there is still a need for special classes for some seriously disturbed children. Children with serious autistic-like behaviors who have no speech or personal interaction skills are two behavioral types that are difficult to integrate into the most accepting of environments. Integrating these children into routine school activities with normal children seems impossible under the present concept of education. Likewise, severely aggressive children who try to injure themselves or others in a physical way cannot be maintained in less than a special class setting without greatly increased outlays of human resources that are presently unavailable to schools.

The educational goals for special class are considerably different from those described for a resource setting. The special teacher is generally responsible for the total intervention process with additional help from supportive persons such as one or more aids assisting in the classroom so that a ratio of one adult to each three or four children is maintained. The goals for each child are often limited almost totally to social interaction such as developing talking skills and cooperating with others at a minimal level. Once social interaction is established and some minimal cooperative level achieved, partial placement in a resource room should be considered. For some of these children integration in a regular classroom will never be a reality. Some will continue to be maintained in a special class for emotionally disturbed children, whereas a few might require placement in total care facility if they cannot be maintained in the home.

Total care programs. Only the most severe cases of children in conflict should be considered for total care placement, and then only if the child cannot be maintained in the home or in an appropriate home substitute such as foster care. Children tend to become "institutionalized" under total care placement, which complicates future placement in more normal education situations. When total care is indicated, it should be considered to be only temporary, generally not to exceed six months in length. During the child's stay in a total care facility, there should be intervention with the home or home substitute to help establish a suitable environment for the child's return. Parents should understand that total care placement is only temporary and that much of the responsibility for eventual reintegration will rest on the home, with staff support from the total care facility.

Program goals for total care are similar to those for special class, with the added dimension of programing for after-school hours. The child's unacceptable behaviors must be modified to an acceptable level during his stay, and academic skills must be maintained at the highest level possible. Total care programs sometimes represent a capitulation or "giving up" on children with severe problems. Recent litigation in several states is challenging public schools to provide services for all children, regardless of problem severity. The extent to which legal guidelines are followed will undoubtedly depend on several factors: age of the child, the specific type and severity of disability, prognosis for change, relative intactness of the home, and the ability of a given community to re-

spond to individual needs of children (size, location, wealth, and local efforts).

The major goal of screening, evaluation, and placement is one of facilitation—facilitation of the educational process and its attendant intervention techniques. Chapter 4 will introduce the first of several approaches to intervention.

SUMMARY

Screening has a unique role to play in the total educational process. It represents the teacher's first step in recognizing children who need special help to achieve. The teacher's role in the screening process is a vital one, since the teacher is the one who will be responsible for doing the screening. Bower lists several criteria for evaluating a screening instrument. These include the teacher's ability to use the screening instrument without outside professional assistance, a sufficiently simple system that results in tentative identification only, a system that will not encourage premature diagnosis, and a system that neither invades the privacy of the individual nor threatens the parents or the child.

Screening differs basically from educational evaluation in the depth of its activity. Evaluation is the most sophisticated and well-delineated system of the total screening and evaluation process. Sophisticated instruments in both the intelligence and projective areas are available. The teacher generally has a relatively small role to play in the evaluation procedure in schools, a role that could be enlarged to include more observation and input into the evaluation process.

Deno's model of a cascade of services is presented. Several alternatives of classroom placement are outlined, which include regular class placement with support, the resource room, special class placement, and total care programs.

BIBLIOGRAPHY AND SELECTED READINGS

Akhurst, B.: Assessing intellectual ability, New York, 1970, Barnes & Noble, Inc.

Anastasi, A.: Individual differences, New York, 1965, John Wiley & Sons, Inc.

Anastasi, A.: Psychological testing, New York, 1968, The Macmillan Co.

Beilin, H.: Teachers and clinicians' attitudes toward the

behavior problems of children—a reappraisal, Child Development 30:9-25, 1959.

Blum, G.: Reliability of the blacky test: a reply to Charen, Journal of Consulting Psychology 20:406, 1956.

Blum, G.: The Blacky pictures: manual of instructions, New York, 1950-1962, The Psychological Corp.

Bower, E.: Early identification of emotionally handicapped children in school, Springfield, Ill., 1960, Charles C Thomas, Publisher.

Bower, E.: Early identification of emotionally handicapped children in school, Springfield, Ill., 1969, Charles C Thomas, Publisher.

Bower, E., and Lambert, N.: In-school screening of children with emotional handicaps. In Long, N., Morse, W., and Newman, R., editors: Conflict in the classroom, ed. 2, Belmont, Calif., 1971, Wadsworth Publishing Co., Inc.

Buros, O.: The sixth mental measurements yearbook, Highland Park, N. J., 1965, Gryphon Press.

Coleman, J.: Abnormal psychology and modern life, Glenview, Ill., 1964, Scott, Foresman & Co.

Coleman, J.: Equality of educational opportunity, Washington, D. C., 1966, Government Printing Office.

Davids, A.: Intelligence in childhood schizophrenics, other emotionally disturbed children, and their mothers, Journal of Consulting Psychology 22:159-163, 1958.

Deno, E.: Special education as developmental capital, Exceptional Children 37:229-237, 1970.

Dunn, L.: Special education for the mildly retarded—is much of it justifiable? Exceptional Children 35:5-22, 1968.

Ebel, R.: The social consequences of educational testing, In Bracht, G., et al.: Perspectives in educational and psychological measurement, Englewood Cliffs, N. J., 1972, Prentice-Hall, Inc.

Ellis, D., and Miller, L.: Teachers' attitudes and child behavior problems, Journal of Educational Psychology 27:501-511, 1936.

Facts on file: Weekly World News Digest, New York, 1970, Facts on File, Inc.

Fiske, D., and Cox, J.: The consistency of ratings by peers, Journal of Applied Psychology 44:11-17, 1960.

Forer, B.: Word association and sentence completion methods. In Rabin, A., and Haworth, M., editors: Projective techniques with children, New York, 1971, Grune & Stratton, Inc.

Goldfarb, A.: Teachers' ratings in psychiatric case-finding, American Journal of Public Health 53:1919-1927, 1963.

Hollander, E.: Validity of peer nominations in predicting a distant performance criterion, Journal of Applied Psychology 49:434-438, 1965.

Holmen, M., and Doctor, R.: Educational and psychological testing, New York, 1972, Russell Sage Foundation.

Hunter, E.: Changes in teachers' attitudes toward children's behavior over the last thirty years, Mental Hygiene 41:3-11, 1957.

Jacobs, J., and DeGraaf, C.: Expectancy and race:

their influences on intelligence test scores, Exceptional Children 40:108-109, 1973.

Kessler, J.: Psychopathology of childhood, Englewood Cliffs, N. J., 1966, Prentice-Hall, Inc.

Kleinmuntz, B.: Personality measurement, Homewood, Ill., 1967, Dorsey Press.

Lindzey, G., and Borgatta, E.: Sociometric measurement. In Lindzey, G., editor: Handbook of social psychology, Cambridge, Mass., 1954, Addison-Wesley Publishing Co., Inc., vol. 1.

Lyman, H.: Test scores and what they mean, Englewood Cliffs, N. J., 1971, Prentice-Hall, Inc.

Maes, W.: The identification of emotionally disturbed children, Exceptional Children 32:607-613, 1966.

Meyerowitz, J.: Peer groups and special classes, Mental Retardation 5:23-26, 1967.

Mitchell, J.: A study of teachers' and mental hygienists' ratings of certain behavior problems of children, Journal of Education Research 36:292-307, 1942.

Moreno, J.: Sociometry in the classroom, Sociometry 6:425-428, 1943.

Nelson, C. M.: Techniques for screening conduct disturbed children, Exceptional Children 37:501-507, 1971.

Reinert, H.: Decision making in the educationally handicapped and normal child: a comparative study, Ed.D. dissertation, Greeley, Colo., 1968, Colorado State College.

Rotter, J., and Rafferty, J.: Manual for the Rotter incomplete sentence blank, college form, New York, 1950, The Psychological Corp.

Rosenthal, R., and Jacobson, L.: Self-fulfilling prophecies in the classroom: teachers' expectations as unintended determinants of pupils' intellectual competence, In Deutsch, M., et al.: Social class, race and psychological development, New York, 1968, Holt, Rinehart, & Winston, Inc.

Salvia, J., Schultz, E., and Chapin, N.: Reliability of Bower scale for screening of children with emotional handicaps, Exceptional Children 41:117-118, 1974.

Sattler, J.: Assessment of children's intelligence, Philadelphia, 1974, W. B. Saunders Co.

Sharp, E.: The I. Q. cult, New York, 1972, Coward, McCann & Georghegan, Inc.

Ullmann, L., and Krasner, L., editors: Case studies in behavior modification, New York, 1965, Holt, Rinehart & Winston, Inc.

Walker, H.: Walker problem behavior checklist manual, Los Angeles, 1970, Western Psychological Services.

Wickman, E.: Children's behavior and teachers' attitudes, New York, 1928, The Commonwealth Fund.

Woody, R.: Behavioral problem children in the schools, New York, 1969, Appleton-Century-Crofts.

Wursten, H.: Story completions: Madeleine Thomas stories and similar methods. In Rabin, A., and Haworth, M., editors: Projective techniques with children, New York, 1960, Grune & Stratton, Inc.

Zubin, J., Eron, L., and Schumer, F.: An experimental approach to projective techniques, New York, 1965, John Wiley & Sons, Inc.

Classroom application and case studies

CHAPTER 4

Classroom application
of psychodynamic theory

Since children generally have a more limited ability to verbalize than adults, alternate forms of therapy are often necessary to help them assert their feelings in ways that are helpful to the intervention process. Several alternative therapies will be presented for consideration.

MILIEU THERAPY

Milieu therapy is a French term that is used to mean treatment by environment, generally treatment in an institutional or hospital setting. The concept, as described by Redl (1959b) and Lewin (1935), has much to offer school programs that are designed to help children in conflict. Milieu therapy goes hand-in-hand with crisis intervention and life space interviewing. Although most school programs have made concerted efforts to develop a healthy environment for children, these efforts have generally centered around the needs of normal children rather than around children who exhibit deviant behaviors.

Milieu therapy has most often been used in total care programs such as institutions for emotionally disturbed children. It cannot be transplanted to public schools without modification, but it includes useful concepts that

show promise for those who teach children in conflict.

An example of milieu therapy in schools is difficult to outline in a brief description, but it could include the following factors: manipulation of schedules (bus, restroom, classroom, lunchroom, etc.) for the benefit of a child; organization of staff (teachers, bus drivers, aids, school nurse, etc.) to recognize or avoid reinforcement of certain behaviors; and involvement of significant persons in the child's life (parents, teachers, relatives, peers, etc.) to support positive feelings that the child emits. Milieu therapy is similar to behavioral manipulation of the environment but without specific behavioral activities such as counting and recording of behaviors.

Selecting an appropriate setting for each component of a total program is the first step toward developing an appropriate milieu. Special programs should generally be located in schools whose staffs choose to help children in conflict, where the welfare of all children is important, and where administrative support for the concept is evident.

A second consideration concerns the nature of the therapeutic milieu. No milieu that is established is good or bad in itself

(Redl, 1959b); it all depends on the outcome that it helps to promote. The milieu that is established needs careful and continual attention by the total staff so that components of the milieu are not promoted or deleted indiscriminately. Many of the decisions concerning children tend to be made with the group in mind rather than individual children. This practice is defensible to a point; however, the concern for the group can immobilize individualization for children who cannot function in the same mold as normal children are expected to function.

A final consideration involves the degree of deviance that can be tolerated in a school setting. If children are unable to cope with their problems at a very basic level, they may need total environmental support while in school. However, most children will need less than total support. The support level needed and the manner in which it can be effected are concerns for the *total school staff*. Many of the conflicts of children arise in situations and places where the teachers and principal are simply not involved. Parents, aides, custodians, cooks, bus drivers, and other children are often painfully aware of the problems created by and against children in conflict but have little input into the situation. To establish a therapeutic milieu within schools for these children, educators must solicit support from all staff who come into contact with these children as well as parents.

CRISIS INTERVENTION

Crisis intervention is essentially just what the words say, intervention during crises. The crisis teacher is, ideally, an "extra" staff member who is trained to interact with a child during a crisis situation; however, the crisis teacher may be a regular classroom teacher or resource teacher who is freed to work with one child during a crisis. An aide or child can even monitor classroom activities for a short period of time while the teacher attends to an immediate crisis situation.

The crisis teacher concept as described by Morse (1971) offers the flexibility to serve a broad spectrum of problem behaviors in the school setting. Although a wide variety of crisis approaches have been used, they seem to have several common characteristics.

1. An "extra" staff member is employed to act as a "crisis teacher." This person is trained not only in education but in the dynamics of various psychological interventions such as life space interviewing, individual counseling, and group interaction.

2. The school provides a small classroom in which the crisis teacher works with one or more children for brief periods of time.

3. A communication system is developed so that the crisis teacher can be made aware of the impending problems.

4. The most important common component of crisis intervention is capitalization on the crisis situation itself. When a child is embroiled in conflict, some of his defenses are down and in many cases he is open to change. Therefore emphasis is placed on intervention at the time of crisis, not after a cooling-off period.

The crisis teacher concept lends itself to varying degrees of crisis situations and can be used in a variety of educational settings. It has been used in special schools for disturbed children, in special classes for disturbed children, and in regular school programs with behavior problem children. The expertise of the crisis teacher along with the availability of supportive personnel are important factors in determining the variety of children served. Since no one person is capable of solving all problems that are brought to the attention of the crisis teacher, other professionals must support the crisis teacher if correct solutions are to evolve.

The role of the teacher in crisis intervention is total involvement. The child might be seen at a mental health center or in private therapy in addition to crisis intervention, but this is not mandatory. The crisis teacher not only is available to children but is available to other teachers on the staff. This consultation is vital; the crisis teacher can receive tremendous help from regular classroom teachers and, in turn, can be supportive to problems that arise in the classroom.

Pitfalls that have developed from abuses to

the crisis teacher concept include (1) using the crisis teacher to complete mundane tasks between crisis situations such as grading papers, filling out reports, etc.; (2) having poorly qualified persons fill the role of the crisis teacher, leading to poor results; and (3) scheduling children into the crisis room, which often diminishes flexibility to the extent that crisis situations cannot be handled effectively when they arise.

LIFE SPACE INTERVIEW

Life space interview, an approach generally credited to Redl (1959a), is essentially a cathartic technique that lends itself to use during a crisis or potential crisis situation.

Redl lists two major components to life space interviewing as follows: (1) emotional first aid and (2) clinical exploitation of life events. An example of these two interventions is described by the following brief encounter.

Your class is ready for lunch. As the children reach the lunchroom, it is discovered that another class has "slipped" in front of your class. A brief period of delay follows at which time pushing and verbal attacks ensue. One of the cooks finally challenges Dennis, one of the instigators of the conflict. At this point Dennis comes "unglued" and runs for the classroom with occasional pauses to deliver very specific verbal barrages.

According to the goals established for life space interviewing, one of two behaviors would be appropriate. First, you could return to the classroom with Dennis to reconstruct the events of the crisis in such a way as to get Dennis back to lunch as quickly and painlessly as possible. This would be called *emotional first aid on the spot*. Second, you could spend your lunch hour with Dennis to begin piecing together the events that precipitated the problem and to relate these to other similar events in which Dennis typically becomes involved. The goal here is not to "dig up old bones" but rather to help Dennis gain some insights into how problems begin, develop, and finally end in conflict. Redl calls this technique *clinical exploitation of life events*.

Emotional first aid

Redl (1971) lists five subcategories of emotional first aid that offer specific alternatives for the classroom teacher.

1. Drain-off of frustration acidity. Frustration often arises when children must discontinue something they like to move on to another less pleasing activity. Disappointment leads to an explosive situation for the child who has experienced so much defeat and who often has a low threshold for frustration. The life space interviewer might be able to take some of the "sting" out of this frustration by explaining why a change in schedule is necessary or warning of possible changes in time to arrest a crisis from developing.

2. Support for the management of panic, fury, and guilt. Children who have too much hate, guilt, anxiety, or anger are particularly vulnerable to their feelings. Often the child not only has these feelings but, in addition, is unable to cope effectively with them, even when these feelings occur at times they should. An adult who is available during times of stress to be supportive, particularly after the episode is completed, seems extremely important for helping the child to sort through the events and to put problems into their proper perspective.

3. Communication maintenance in moments of relationship decay. Positive relationships are difficult to maintain when the teacher is forced to intervene in a problem behavior. In the process of stopping inappropriate behavior the communication link between the child and teacher is easily broken. The teacher must therefore hang on to any thread of communication so that the child does not slip into a totally autistic state of daydreams or self pity. The child must be free to choose alternative behaviors and still be able to "save face."

4. Regulation of behavioral and social traffic. Rules help to establish guidelines for behavior that offer much needed support for children in conflict. Whereas rules are not a goal in themselves, their consistent application by patient and benign adults will help these children through critical situations where their behavior must come under better "ego control." The adult must not moralize or be dictatorial in the process of pointing out the rules or in helping children live within their intent. Some children need an authority figure in sight to support appropriate rule-following behavior, at least until better inner controls can be developed.

5. *Umpire services.* The role of an adult who can be fair with all sides is vital to children in conflict. Many situations are too dangerous to be left to chance alone. When children begin to develop and, more importantly, to rely on a sense of fairness with other children, it is vital that an adult sometimes act as umpire. This umpire role is important for both intrachild and interchild conflicts. Interchild services might include acting as an impartial referee during a wrestling match. Helping a child to tell the truth rather than lie is one example of solving an intrachild conflict.

Clinical exploitation of life events

Emotional first aid is a first line of defense against runaway emotions and deviant behaviors. No specific guidelines are suggested for the use of either emotional first aid or clinical exploitation of life events. Redl (1971) suggests that a correct approach cannot be predicted in advance; it can only be arrived at through involvement with the child. Two factors are critical in determining whether to go deeply into clinical exploitation of life events: (1) the time available at the moment of need and (2) the receptivity of the situation to therapy. When time is available and the situation correct, Redl offers five techniques to exploit the crisis.

1. *Reality rub-in* (making the child aware of what really happened). Many children appear to be "perceptually impaired" in their ability to see problems that they have stimulated. Redl calls this "socially nearsighted" behavior. Other children get caught in a "system of near to delusional misinterpretation of life" (Redl, 1971). Unlike socially nearsighted behavior in which children fail to read the social meaning of their behavior, these children tend to gloss over obvious

situations that should be interpreted correctly. In both cases reality rub-in is an effective tool to point out inappropriate behavior. Doing so immediately is vital, since any period of delay will only allow the child to rationalize and further gloss over the real problem.

2. *Symptom estrangement* (help the child to "let go" of inappropriate behaviors). In symptom estrangement the task of the person doing the life space interviewing is to help children in conflict to let go of the symptoms that are ruling their behavior. It is important that other staff who interact with the children also support this letting go of pathological behavior. Children have learned that pathology does get results even if the behavior is seen as deviant. Educators must tell and show children how they can let go of their symptoms and still reach the goals that pathological behavior has been able to provide.

3. *Massaging numb value areas* (awaken appropriate values that are dormant). Redl suggests that many children simply have had sensitive areas of their personality numbed by the pathology and resulting conflicts, both internal and external. The life space interviewer can slowly chip away at this numbed area and reawaken the potential for acceptable behavior that exists in most children. This process is generally not a dramatic change but rather is a painfully slow process both for the child and for teachers.

4. *New-tool salesmanship* (promoting new behaviors as alternatives). A major problem of children in conflict is their inability to approach problems with any flexibility (Bower and Lambert, 1971). When faced with a crisis, the child reverts to a common behavior pattern that appears not to vary with experience. Redl suggests that the life space interviewer can offer new alternatives for children in conflict. Giving a child a new socially acceptable behavior to replace an old unacceptable behavior seems to be necessary to avoid trading one inappropriate behavior for another inappropriate behavior.

5. *Manipulation of the boundaries of the self* (desensitize the child to deviant behav-

ior). The manipulation that Redl is speaking of concerns the child who is always getting "sucked in" by peers who enjoy seeing the child do the wrong thing and get into trouble. By increasing the number of interviews with the child and providing needed support, he can often be desensitized to the contagion around him and be able to redirect his behavior.

The following example describes how this contagion develops. A group of boys screw out a light bulb until it is about to fall. Then one of the "deviant" kids is told to jump up and touch the light bulb. When the bulb falls to the floor, everyone points the finger at the "culprit" who is subsequently punished for breaking the bulb. This type of setting up a deviant child is common in schools. Punishing those who prey on children in conflict will only make the problem worse; deviant children must be desensitized so as not to be "sucked in" by those around them.

• • •

For the teacher who is doing life space interviewing a major portion of time and energy will be spent on emotional first aid rather than clinical exploitation. In fact, teachers who are effective in administering emotional first aid will decrease the time spent solving more serious problems.

Teachers who have worked in a life space interviewing role have been quick to point out some of the problem areas. First, a competent person must be selected to do the major share of life space interviewing, particularly if it is used as a supportive technique in a specialized administrative structure such as crisis intervention. Although many teachers in a typical school probably can and should develop competence as life space interviewers, this is not an easy or quick task for already overburdened teachers. Selecting a resource teacher trained in life space interviewing techniques seems to be a likely alternative. In this way other teachers can share in the expertise exhibited by the trained person while their own personal skills are being developed. Since correct application of life space interviewing

skills is relative to the problems presented, it is important that good judgment is used in determining when and at what levels to become involved. The interviewer must also be aware that children may learn to manipulate the teacher so as to receive individual attention through life space interviewing.

A second problem area is communication. How does the classroom teacher communicate in an effective manner with those doing life space interviewing? Those who have worked in clinically oriented systems are aware of the vast amounts of time spent in communication with other staff. Teachers have generally operated in an autonomous environment that easily leads to noninvolvement and isolation. Team teaching situations offer hope that this isolation may dissipate into a cooperative effort with effective communication.

A third problem for the teacher using life space interviewing is timing. What does the teacher do with thirty other children while spending time with one child? If a teacher is not convinced that life space interviewing can work effectively, that teacher will not have the "administrative courage" to facilitate time for one child when he needs it—not after school or tomorrow at 10:30 A.M. but at the time of need. This problem can be solved by commitment to the concept and a resulting determination to solve the administration problems. Some have supervised other teachers' classes by combining classes on a temporary basis to free one staff member to help one child. Other programs have used aides, parents, the principal, and more mature children in a temporary role so that life space interviewing could be implemented by the teacher. Using a staff member who is trained to interview children (a crisis teacher) and who is free of other school duties is an ideal solution but by no means the only solution to the time problem.

A fourth problem centers around the role of teachers who function as life space interviewers. Although the teacher's role cannot be one of junior psychiatrist, psychologist, or social worker, some allied skills are necessary. The teacher using this technique must have an understanding of individual and group personality dynamics, be able to work effectively on a one-to-one basis, and be able to initiate productive educational tasks in short periods of time.

THERAPIES WITH SUPPORTIVE MEDIA

Several supportive therapies have been developed that offer assistance to classroom teachers who must deal with serious behavioral problems. These techniques have developed largely in clinical practice where they continue to be used; however, their strengths are not limited to that setting. Teachers have discovered that many are usable in the classroom. These include play therapy, which is the most sophisticated of the supportive therapies, art therapy, music therapy, occupational therapy, and therapeutic play.

Play therapy

Play therapy makes use of the child's natural world of play for therapeutic purposes. As a form of psychotherapy, play therapy seeks to unfold the child's inner world, to help the child gain insight into his own behavior, to be able to live within limits, and to grow in his ability to solve problems (Axline, 1947). Psychotherapists have suggested that the basic principles of play therapy are applicable to the classroom, especially classrooms that are serving children in various stages of conflict (Nelson, 1966). There are definite limits placed on using play therapy in an educational setting; however, the teacher can utilize some of the therapeutic principles that have shown promise in more structured play therapy sessions. The intent of this discussion is to explain how the classroom teacher can use the *philosophy* of play therapy. There is no intent to suggest the establishment of a clinical play therapy situation within a school classroom; however, a therapeutic attitude is a possibility. The principles of play therapy, as outlined by Axline (1947), are summarized here.

1. Permissiveness is allowing the child to be free to express his feelings completely. In an educational setting the expression of feelings necessarily must have some limits; however, allowing the child the freedom to create his own painting, to write ideas, and to develop creative talents in music, drama, and free play are all important. Self-expression, while important for the child, does not solve problems the child may have. It only allows the behaviors to come to the surface where the teacher can deal with them in a productive manner.

2. Establishing a warm, friendly relationship is generally accepted by teachers in theory but difficult to implement (Fig. 4-1). Children in conflict have often lost their trust in adults, which makes teaching even more difficult. It is a more arduous task to build a warm, friendly relationship in a classroom than in a one-to-one-therapy situation, but it can be done if the children are viewed and treated as individuals rather than an amorphous group. Individual children must be encouraged to interact with the teacher and other children if security and trust are to be developed.

3. Limits are established only as needed to anchor the therapy to the world of reality. In the classroom these limitations must be more numerous and stringent than in individ-

Fig. 4-1. The teacher can develop a warm, friendly relationship in several ways. Sitting on the floor with a child for a brief period of time is one technique.

ual therapy, but limits are never established just for the sake of having limits. The child should only have enough structure so that he does not injure himself or others and so that property is protected from willful destruction. Limitations are not set out as a list of rules to be followed but are introduced as needed to maintain a productive environment for learning while still maintaining respect for every individual in the classroom. Limitations do not place demands on the child but allow growth within some reasonable structure. Reasonable limits allow the timid child a "safe place" in which to explore and grow and provide needed bounds for the more volatile child.

4. The therapist should be aware of expressed feelings and reflect these feelings back to the child. This guideline has been misinterpreted more often than any of the guidelines of play therapy. Reflecting the child's feelings does not make a mockery of the child or is it "selling out" to the whims of the child. The ability to recognize feelings and to reflect them back to the child is difficult. For most teachers it is easier to tell, to explain, and to solve the problem for the child rather than to allow the child the time and freedom to solve his own problems. Although some have suggested that teaching and therapy are antithetical, this principle shows that this should not be the case; good teaching and good therapy are parallel activities rather than oppositional.

5. Complete acceptance of the child seems to be the most difficult to operationalize of all the guidelines presented. Accepting children completely does not imply that teachers also must accept their behavior. It is relatively easy to accept a child who has limitations that are visibly apparent such as a broken leg or a severe vision problem. If the handicap is not readily visible, however, teachers may view the child as lazy, uninterested, and rebellious. A teacher's persistence in comparing one child to another in school activities betrays a willingness to treat each child as an individual. In a clinical setting complete acceptance is more easily effected, since there is no other child readily available for comparison and no implied criticism that can be transmitted to the child as a result of this comparison.

6. A respect for the child's ability to solve his own problems must be maintained. This principle is indirectly related to all of the other principles and the structure that regulates behavior during therapy sessions. If the teacher can have the respect for the child's ability to make decisions, even though the decisions will likely be different from those the teacher would make, the child will be helped to gain insight into the decision-making processes. The teacher must make some logical determination as to the level of decision making at which the child is presently functioning. For example, a first grade child should not be expected to make decisions that will have serious implication for his future existence unless the child is certain to make correct decisions. Whether the child practices words for reading now or 2 hours later today is not too big a decision for a first grader to make. Whether the child practices reading words or not is too big a decision to make, since the punishment that might conceivably result from failure in learning to read would be too big a price for the child to pay. If the teacher will allow the child to make small decisions, where the price of failure is equal to the child's ability to handle failure, growth in problem solving should result.

7. The teacher should allow the child to lead the way in both conversation and action. This principle has been successfully demonstrated by the discovery method often used in teaching mathematical concepts, reading skills, and spelling rules. However, when inappropriate behavior is the issue, it is tempting for the teacher to tell, to direct, and to manipulate—temptations that must be avoided if this principle is to be implemented.

8. Therapists tend to think in terms of time, but therapy often does not follow a time schedule. Behaviors that have taken years in formation generally respond slowly to significant change. Teachers understand the process of change in cognitive skills extremely well but often are unrealistic when

affective behaviors are under consideration. This principle of play therapy emphasizes the importance of time in changing affective behaviors.

When teachers are able to incorporate the therapeutic principles of play therapy into their teaching style, the atmosphere for learning often is improved for all children.

Art therapy

Art therapy, as used in this text, means a therapeutic process that provides children with the opportunity to interact with the various visual arts as the vehicle of therapeutic intervention (Fig. 4-2). Finger painting, working with clay, and free-hand drawing would be examples applicable to children in conflict.

A

B

Fig. 4-2. A, This child's picture takes on a new meaning if you look at **B. B,** Picture of the child's teacher in **A.** The child views his teacher as an extremely important person in his life and is concerned with how his teacher feels about him. Through art media he expresses these feelings.

The various art media can provide additional channels of communication. Just as play therapy encourages children to express themselves through play activities, art therapy encourages communication through the various art forms. Children can show when they are sad, happy, and afraid; and they can share their dreams, ambitions, and innermost thoughts. Art can also show deep psychological conflicts such as aggression, compulsive behaviors, sublimation, substitution, and various unconscious feelings (Kramer, 1971; Naumberg, 1958). This communication does not preempt the need for other forms of information—it only supports and enhances these forms in most cases. In a situation where a child is not speaking, as might be the case in autism, the art therapy can become even more critical as a communication link.

Although teachers can often determine that children are experiencing conflicts from viewing children at work with various art forms, this realization only supports the teacher's original concern, since the troubled child will generally give many indications of conflict. The classroom teacher generally should not use art as a diagnostic tool; rather it should be a catalyst for the child to try, to express, and to identify in new and creative ways those feelings that cannot surface in other ways. Care must be exercised so that just enough structure is provided so that children are not rigidly controlled or allowed to be carried along by art that is too stimulating. For the teacher who is aware of the students' emotional needs and problems, art therapy adds one more dimension of understanding and expression.

Art therapy should be seen as supplementary to other therapeutic interventions, not as an isolated panacea. Art should help children to share their inner feelings with the teacher in an acceptable and nonthreatening manner. It also gives children an outlet for the release of inner tensions, which ultimately can have beneficial effects on future learning experiences that will demand a child's complete attention.

The art therapist should become an ally of the child's creativity. Kramer (1971) says that the therapist should lend both technical assistance and emotional support. By requiring that materials be used to produce works of art, the therapist counteracts any tendencies toward "dissipation into fantasy or play." Kramer is not suggesting that the end product is the goal of art therapy but neither is therapy per se. The emphasis is on therapy through the art media. Whereas art therapy is strongly allied to psychotherapy, it does not follow that its use cannot serve other therapeutic models such as a behavioral approach, for example, as long as the basic premise of freedom to create is not endangered.

Music therapy

Music therapy is in many ways a parallel to play therapy that can be used to bring out feelings that would otherwise fail to surface. Music has become a way of life in the United States. Everywhere people go they hear music—in church, in bars, at football games, and in the supermarket. Music has various effects on people; it can relax them and put them in a mood for sleep, or it can stir them to action. Football marches played on a crisp autumn afternoon have one effect on an individual's feelings, whereas soft dinner music puts the individual in quite a different mood. Music can promote many similar reactions from children.

Soft background music in the classroom will often have a quieting effect on active children and aid in the concentration of children, since it helps to shut out noise that might otherwise be distracting. Teachers have, at times, used music in the classroom only as a reward for appropriate behavior. Since many schools are equipped with classroom speaker systems, there seems to be the possibilities of background music for those who would care to implement its use in the classroom. Since there has been little research on the effect of background music on children in conflict in regular classroom settings, teachers will need to develop much of their understanding and techniques through trial and error.

Music can have a therapeutic value in addition to its use as background stimuli.

These could include singing or playing songs on a piano or other instrument, which gives the child a feeling of success. Playing certain instruments (drums, piano, clappers) allows the child an acceptable outlet for physical aggression, it can provide a healthy reward activity for less desired tasks, and it provides a medium of self-expression, for example, dancing to the music, acting out the beat, and so on.

In music therapy the emphasis should not be on the aspects of music or should it encourage behavior that perpetuates existing problems. For example, the overly active child may become even more out of control with certain stimulating music, or the withdrawing child may become more isolated with music that is self-stimulation. Careful monitoring of the therapeutic situation is needed to ensure productive outcomes.

Occupational therapy

Occupational therapy is the use of manual activities such as carpentry or building, leather work, and plastic work to treat emotional problems. Occupational therapy has long been accepted as a productive method of treating disturbed children and adults. However, its use has been abused in schools that have relied too heavily on its use as a tool of pacification. Keeping a child busy and "out of the teacher's hair" has it merits, but it cannot be the goal for any child who is to grow emotionally. Although occupational therapy has typically been a part of institutional therapy, it is often a part of school programs under the guise of arts or crafts. The use of activities that allow children to express themselves, to create, and to be productive with their hands can have many beneficial outcomes for both children and teachers. Many of the same benefits outlined for art and music therapy are also applicable here.

Occupational therapy, as a part of total intervention procedures, seems appropriate for schools. Concentration on an activity that is enjoyable is therapeutic for everyone. In the elementary school these activities generally should be limited to no more than 5 hours a week with most children. Young adults might reasonably spend more time in occupational therapy, since their activities could be related to work activities that might shortly be a part of their lives.

Therapeutic play

One of the most promising interventions that can be implemented in the school is therapeutic play—the structuring of play activities so that maximum therapeutic benefits can be achieved. Although most teachers try to individualize educational activities, they often encourage play for individual children that is unsuited to their developmental level; for example, teachers want all children to participate in games during recess. The problem is that all children are not ready for this rather sophisticated level of interaction. With children in conflict it is not unusual to have individuals who cannot yet play effectively alone. They may need to develop satisfactory skills of individual play and parallel play with one other child before proceeding to play with other children. The necessary growth may take weeks or months in some cases, but the time for growth must be taken. The troubled child may initiate interaction with another child by attacking his sand castle or kicking the child's football into the street—both encounters that appear to be of negative value. This stage of relationship development should be tolerated by the teacher only until it can be guided into more cooperative activities.

When a child is able to play alone, it is time to encourage individual skill development. Activities that encourage running, jumping, and climbing are generally appropriate. As muscle coordination develops, the child can be taught individual skill activities such as swimming, table or lawn tennis, bowling, fly casting, wrestling, handball, gymnastics, and camping (Fig. 4-3). These individual skills, along with many other appropriate to various age groups and geographical location, seem to be helpful to prepare the child for interpersonal interactions that are to follow.

Group activities that require sharing, cooperation, and rule following generally should be delayed until some individual skills have been mastered. If this is not done,

Fig. 4-3. Learning to bowl, even with a little help, can have therapeutic benefits for children.

group activities are likely to deteriorate into chaotic disputes over rules, who pushed whom first, and eventual refusals to participate.

The teacher should maintain sufficient structure to ensure continued growth through play. Recesses should not be aimless happenings but planned periods of growth. Conflicts that develop during play activities can often have a deleterious effect on an entire school day, whereas success experiences can promote additional success. Conflicts that arise during play can often be resolved in ways that are not possible in any other setting. A fight that erupts on the playground might be conveniently ignored so that a valuable lesson in "starting fights" is learned by one child. This lesson cannot be learned in the classroom for several obvious reasons.

Many other interventions that have therapeutic value that can be used include puppetry, big brother and big sister programs,

community recreational programs, scouting, dance therapy, and drama therapy. It appears that many of these activities are supplementary to or could become a part of therapies already mentioned, with the teacher providing the imagination necessary for implementation.

THE MENTAL HEALTH CENTER APPROACH

During the late 1950s and early 1960s when formal educational programs for emotionally disturbed children were being initiated in the schools, the typical emphasis was the mental health center approach or a cooperative approach, in which schools "handled" the academics and the mental health personnel "handled" the therapy. Although some schools were in direct communication with mental health centers regarding the concerns of both groups, many were carrying out their roles in nearly complete isolation.

In terms of pull-out programs (intervention away from regular classroom), the psychodynamic approach has been a classical example. Therapy was done, almost exclusively, away from the school by various mental health professionals, including the psychiatrist at the mental health clinic or in private practice, the psychologist, the social worker, or various combinations of these mental health professionals who interact with the child and/or parents. Gradually this relationship shifted to a significant degree until many school programs were no longer working with mental health centers except on an "on call" or referral basis.

This mental health center approach has several advantages for schools that should be noted.

1. Professionals who are trained in working with children and adults are available for support and consultation to the teacher.

2. The child and/or parents and other family members might be seen at the local mental health center. Communication of this fact to the school is enhanced through a close working relationship.

3. Services need not be duplicated; that is, schools do not need mental health services, and mental health programs generally do not need educational programs.

Some weaknesses of the mental health approach have included the following:

1. The child is often out of the mainstream of life for treatment; it represents the ultimate in pull-out programs.

2. The system is wasteful of human resources, both the children and professionals. This intervention simply cannot accommodate the numbers of children who need help in the public schools.

3. Individual therapy only helps the child. No one else, such as the teacher, has the possibility of growth. The therapist is the expert, and little communication is possible with any other helping professional.

4. The process often has led to a defensiveness rather than a team effort.

5. Little in the way of verification of success has been demonstrated. Research data are painfully scarce, and when they are available the interpretation is risky, since the setting of school and therapy are often physically apart.

6. Too much emphasis is placed on the past status of the child at the expense of programing for the present and future.

In reviewing the strengths and weaknesses of the mental health approach, there appear to be few problems that could not be overcome, at least to some degree, through a commitment to cooperative programing. A major concern of cooperative mental health efforts must include the pull-out nature of such programs—a weakness that pervades all of the areas of concern.

To demonstrate the effectiveness of the various psychodynamic tools with children in conflict, I have chosen to present a series of vignettes. These brief case outlines and research studies were selected to (1) show specific psychodynamic techniques and (2) evaluate their use. Most techniques are a combination of two or more psychodynamic constructs, although one may appear to be the dominant tool.

Vignette 1: Music therapy
  Reported by Nordoff and Robbins (1971)
  The child in this case was a 9-year-old girl, Y, who was diagnosed as a schizoid personal-

ity. Her behavior prior to labeling had been described as bizarre and hallucinatory. She would attack both physically and verbally when she became angry. The occurrence of this behavior was limited to her neighborhood. In school she was described as withdrawn, preferring to be alone both in the classroom and on the playground. She had no friends among her peers and felt that adults, including her parents and her teacher, were mean and hated her. Y was referred to the music therapist because of her apparent music aptitude. The goals of music therapy were to develop an adequate relationship with an adult, change her attitude toward adults, provide an intellectual challenge, afford group recognition, and provide an acceptable emotional outlet.

Y took piano lessons twice a week for 5 years with the exception of 2 weeks' vacation each summer. During the first few months, lessons were devoted to learning fundamentals of piano and developing an acceptable relationship with her therapist. During this time she consistently tried to manipulate the therapist into rejecting her. The therapist resisted the temptations successfully by describing the behavior without condemnation. Gradually a warm and friendly relationship was developed with the therapist, she became less shy in school, and began to play with other children. During her second year this progress continued, as did growth in musical ability. In her third year outbursts of anger began to develop, which were caused, according to her physician, from her mother's illness, irritability, and lack of consistent discipline. A rebellious teenage sister also contributed to the unsettled nature of the home. This situation continued into the fourth year. At one point Y told her therapist she had picked up a butcher knife and was going to kill her mean old mother but she did not. The therapist said, "No, and you never will. If you start to do anything like that, you will always stop yourself." She then resumed the music lesson. Y played wildly, inaccurately, and loudly for a time after the incident. When she finished her lesson, she left without saying a word, only to return and say to her therapist, "I love you—you are good to me." The therapist reported the incident to Y's psychiatrist so that these feelings could be dealt with in psychotherapy sessions.

Y developed good musical skills, played in

school recitals, and according to her parents, often played the piano for relaxation.

Vignette 2: Life space interview
Reported by Newman (1963)

Six severely disturbed preadolescent boys who had spent their previous 5 years at the Child Research Branch of the National Institutes of Health were integrated into an educational program away from the institute. Newman discusses the role of the life space interviewer or crisis interviewer in these cases. The problems that these boys exhibited centered around their poor self-image, that is, uncontrolled behavior, withdrawal, violence, grandiose delusions, and acting-out behaviors. Crisis situations often grew out of otherwise bland situations: A nail that bent in woodworking, a potter's wheel that failed to turn at the right speed, an arithmetic problem that failed to come out right, reading *was* for *saw*, or the cancellation of a promised trip all brought down the wrath of the boys on the teacher.

Over a period of time the life space interviewer was able to deal with these on-the-spot crises effectively. In addition, the life space interviewer was able to disarm potential crisis situations by the following interventions:

1. Warn the boys of changes in routine in advance, for example, "You will have your tutoring session after science today."
2. Help prepare the child for the grade he is going to receive, for example, "What grade do you think you will receive?"
3. Help the child organize himself to do his homework assignment, for example, "What part of your homework do you need for tomorrow?"
4. Practice test taking with the boys to help them master the technique of test taking.

In brief this report suggested that life space interviewers can work effectively in helping troubled youngsters over the "rough spots" in their everyday life, to avoid problems when possible, and to overcome them when avoidance fails.

Vignette 3: Play therapy with puppets
Reported by Kessler (1966)

Ralph was in therapy from the age of 5 years suffering from several chronic problems, including enuresis, phobias, destructive and aggressive behavior, and separation anxiety.

After 3 years of therapy he became interested in puppets, and for the following 10 months he was engrossed in making and playing with puppets during therapy sessions. Through the puppets he was able to show the conflict between his wishes and his conscience. Two characters dominated therapy situations: Good Bob (Ralph) and Bad Bill (the therapist). Good Bob had everything going for him; he was a model child, bright and wealthy. Bad Bill, on the other hand, was in constant need of money, brains, friends, and advice. Bill was unhappy and always getting into fights.

Bob was able to reform Bill by showing him how he had trained a room full of wild animals. He said he had trained them through patience, love, and rewards. As therapy continued, Bob began to indulge himself by eating sweets all the time, going to bed when he wished, and spending money at will. The therapist began questioning his position of Good Bob, since he was not living by the rules, etc. Bob's behavioral deterioration stopped; however, he continued to be very successful in everything he did.

Bob preferred to relate only to boys, whereas the therapist related to girls like his sister and mother. The therapist could not get Bob to relate to girls or to discuss topics of sex. He would always pretend to know everything there was to know about babies, pregnancy, and so on, but when pressed by the therapist, he would forget the details of information he claimed to have. As the puppets (Bob and Bill) grew older, they went through the stages of being interested in girls, of conflicts with big brothers, and of induction into the armed services. When the therapist suggested they were leaving the world of girls for a world of men, Ralph suggested they return to the age of 10 years. The therapist interpreted this as a desire to regress to a more comfortable state and avoid marrying and making babies.

In this vignette the therapist used puppetry at the child's request to ease the way to change. After Ralph was able to solve his problems through play he was ready to relate these solutions to real life.

Vignette 4: Art therapy, milieu therapy, and psychotherapy
Reported by Kramer (1971)

Martin was admitted to Wiltwyck School at the age of 10½ years. He was an only child and was admitted on the request of his mother. Wiltwyck School is a residential school for emotionally disturbed boys from the slums of New York City. The home can serve 100 boys aged 8 to 12 years who have normal intelligence with emotional disturbance that does not require the safety of a hospital setting.

Martin's behavior prior to coming to Wiltwyck was highly erratic. He was often truant from school, and he had been involved in a number of minor delinquent acts and conflicts with his mother. Martin's father was a seemingly dependent man who was unable to control the family situation effectively. His mother was the major breadwinner and also responsible for monitoring Martin's behavior, which she did by beating him severely after his provocations. Martin's first encounter in art therapy was extremely revealing of his internal thought processes. He came to the art room and drew an island scene surrounded by a dark green sea. When he finished, he picked up several aprons and put them around his neck, ran into the yard, and twirled around in a whirling dance. Then he threw the aprons aside and ran from the area. Later he came back and apologized for his behavior.

The therapists interpreted this behavior as: (1) the painting represented isolation and a preoccupation with far away places, (2) his dance indicated an exhibitionism, and (3) his return and apology represented a desire to maintain a relationship. Martin became one of the most intolerable boys at the school. He was unable to get along at all with men and only occasionally with women. He showed his only real interest in art, and it was in art therapy that the staff was able to tolerate him part of the time.

Martin's art had a distinctly angry tone in its message. He also produced works that showed his intense emotion and strong sexual stimulation. After 6 months in school Martin was placed in psychotherapy as a supplement to art therapy and milieu therapy. With this team effort he gradually began to grow in his ability to let go of his pathological behaviors.

His therapist reported a major breakthrough, which occurred in an art session with prior stimulation during psychotherapy. Martin had been walking in the woods with his therapist when he spoke of one of the many bird nests in the trees. This led to a discussion about the feelings of a bird that would be robbed of its freedom. Martin said he would give the bird partial freedom by tying a kite string to the bird's leg. Slowly he came to verbalize that the kite string idea was similar to his mother's relationship with him. The following day he came to the art room and painted an intricate picture of an apple with an apple tree inside and branches, leaves, and smaller apples. In the center of the tree was a bird's nest with a mother bird feeding her baby. He had worked for 7 hours one day and finished it the following day. When it was completed, he presented it to his counselor, Mr. Frank. This was the first gesture of friendship he had made to any male since he came to the school.

Kramer believed that Martin survived because of art and eventually used art as a form of recognition.

Vignette 5: Life space interview
Behavior

David is generally a quiet 10-year-old boy who exhibits a violent temper when he becomes frustrated or angry. During these temper tantrums he hits, kicks, bites, and verbally abuses those around him. His vocabulary abounds with sexual terms, particularly when he is angry. He has few friends but relates extremely well to animals.

Family background

David belongs to a middle to lower middle class white family. He has one younger brother. David's mother abandoned both boys when David was 6 years of age. Since that time, he has lived with his father and a series of baby sitters. The mother left the family to become a stripper in a local club. Subsequently she married a black man and adopted a black son.

Psychological information

David is of average intellectual functioning. No personality or psychiatric evaluation is available, and it was decided that none was needed at this time. David appears to be intact, and his frustration and anger appear to develop only as a result of family situations.

Medical information

Physical evaluation shows no abnormalities that should interfere with educational or social functioning.

Educational information

David is academically retarded in all but arithmetic. He lies continually in school situations, particularly if he does not have his work completed as requested. He exhibits an exaggerated masculinity but has a very soft heart. When things are going well at home, David will work hard in school, but at the slightest problem he comes unglued and his educational growth stops or regresses.

Placement recommendations

It was recommended that David be placed in a special class for a short period of time. The use of life space interview was suggested to allow David to talk out his frustration and anger. It was also suggested that a female teacher try to build relationships with David so as to rebuild his trust in women. Finally it was suggested that attempts be made to build relationships between David and other children.

Evaluation

The major portion of life space interview time was spent in clinical exploitation of life events with David. When a conflict occurred and David had a temper tantrum, his teacher tried to "rub in" what really happened without asking David to accept this or reject it. In these cases his teachers pointed out David's inappropriate behavior and tried to help David let go of his inappropriate behaviors of kicking, biting, and verbal abuse. The main concern in working with David was to reawaken appropriate values that David had in his personality but that were covered up by his external callousness. Finally David was taught new ways to handle his frustrations such as talking out his anxieties, exercise, and various physical games in which he could vent his frustrations more appropriately. David showed continuous progress. He had some regressions because his teachers would not allow him to manipulate them into a life space interview session through inappropriate behavior. As these situations were recognized and ignored, gradual improvement was made.

The major change in his life came when his father remarried, and a stable home environment was created. David was able to return to the regular classroom within 6 months after being placed in a special class, and within 1 year all support services except those administered by the regular classroom teacher were dropped. David continued to have sporadic regressions at which time he exhibited temper tantrums but to a much lesser degree than previously experienced. The classroom teacher used emotional first aid techniques to get David back into classroom activities after these brief episodes.

Vignette 6: Play therapy
Behavior

Julia is 7½ years old. Her behavior has been typified as well behaved, in fact, too well behaved. She seldom talks when she is with more than one person. She is extremely nervous. She sucks her thumb and pulls her hair when she becomes tense. She is a bed wetter and occasionally has bladder control problems during the school day.

Family background

Julia comes from a middle class white family. She has two brothers in the family, both of whom are older. She lives with her mother, father, and two brothers, and since the first grade in school, her grandmother has lived upstairs in the same house. The family had continual problems for several years. The grandmother has probably stabilized the family somewhat. It is reported that the father would go around the house naked when Julia was small and even come to the dinner table without any clothes on. This upset the mother a great deal. Since the grandmother's arrival, the family has been in therapy at the local mental health center.

Psychological information

Julia had no serious problems, according to the parents, until she started school. The nervousness and enuretic behavior, thumb-sucking, and hair pulling all started at this stage of her life. The individual test of intelligence that was administered to Julia indicated that she is functioning slightly above average.

Medical information

Physical evaluation shows no abnormalities that should interfere with educational or social functioning.

Educational information

Julia is functioning above her grade level expectancy in arithmetic, but in all other academic subject areas she is much below expected level of functioning. She seems to try hard and want to learn but appears to be so tied up emotionally that she cannot concentrate on the subject at hand. She memorizes words easily but forgets them almost immediately. The words in reading that she knows one day will likely not be remembered the next day. When she is trying to learn, she is constantly twisting her hair and swinging her feet nervously.

Placement recommendations

Julia was placed in a regular classroom program with help from the remedial reading teacher and resource teacher. The remedial reading teacher was working on skill development utilizing a multisensory approach. The resource teacher was concentrating on the emotions that surrounded Julia's educational functioning. This included a "watered-down" play therapy situation through the use of puppets, dolls, and other toys. Julia was encouraged to play out the roles that seemed to trouble her in her life. Through this technique it was learned that Julia had a great deal of concern around learning to read. Through the use of puppets she told the teacher that everyone in her family wanted her to read. She felt that her whole world evolved around reading. She read in her home room classroom, in the remedial room, and then when she went home her mother would read with her. Later her older brothers would read to her. When her father returned home in the evening, he would read with her, and in the evening her grandmother would come downstairs and read with her. It was decided that everyone should reconsider their position regarding reading, with only the remedial reading teacher working in the reading area. The parents were instructed to back off from their forceful approach to Julia's reading problem and allow her to be a little girl at home.

Evaluation

Placement in the regular class with help from the remedial reading teacher and resource room teacher proved to be ineffective until it was found that the child was simply being inundated with the reading process. When pressures were relieved, the parents started to reinforce Julia just for being a little girl and interact with her on a social level rather than an academic one and Julia gradually began to show progress. After 1 year in the special resource room Julia was placed full time in the regular classroom with only support from the remedial reading specialist. She continued to do well in arithmetic and at last report was doing average work in reading. She is not working up to expected level in reading according to her indicated ability; however, the changes that have occurred indicate that much progress has been made. Julia now verbalizes her feelings in the company of others and has stopped her enuretic behavior and thumb-sucking. She still indicates an occasional tic such as hair pulling when she is under some strain to perform.

Vignette 7: Crisis intervention
Behavior

Tom, 9 years of age, is a very angry boy. It has been common for him to hurt other children by pushing, hitting, kicking, and biting them. He has also had a history of cutting up baby kittens, killing birds, and even killing trees with a sharp object by stabbing them to death.

Family background

Tom is from an above-average income family. The family has been intact, although the mother has some emotional problems. Tom was adopted through a private agency. He has two brothers and one sister, all adopted, also through a private agency. Tom's mother appears to be uncertain in her acceptance of the children. On the one hand she loves and wants the children badly; however, at times she locks them out of the house until dinner in the evening. Tom has had more than his share of toys, clothes, and other material goods; however, he lacks appropriate adult attention.

Psychological information

Tom's early records show no psychological problems that can be identified. On entering school his behavior problems prompted the parents, on recommendation from the teacher, to seek psychiatric help for Tom. As a result of the psychiatric interview, it is reported that Tom had weak ego strengths and an underdeveloped super-ego. His intellectual functioning was considered to be above average according to the score achieved on the individual test of intelligence. The parents report psychological problems with Tom in the home but nothing that they cannot manage.

Medical information

Physical evaluation shows no abnormalities that should interfere with educational or social functioning.

Educational information

Tom is academically retarded in all skill areas. He is extremely capable in verbal skills but is unable to transform these verbal ideas into written communication. He is an extremely nervous child in school, often biting his fingernails until his fingers bleed. He appears to be seeking constant attention from others.

Placement recommendations

Tom was placed in a regular classroom with support from a crisis intervention teacher. On signal (a buzzer) the crisis teacher would come to the classroom and take Tom for brief periods of time. Tom was to be taken from the classroom only in situations where his behavior was so inappropriate that it could not be tolerated in the regular classroom situation. The classroom teacher was to be the judge of this behavior. The crisis teacher tried various approaches with Tom when he was taken from the classroom. These included (1) ignoring Tom and allowing him to complete whatever work he was supposed to be doing at the time of the crisis, (2) helping Tom with assignments that were being completed at the time the crisis arose, (3) visiting with Tom about his problem and encouraging him to get back to the task that he was working on when the crisis arose, and (4) using life space interview techniques.

Evaluation

Much success was gained through crisis intervention with Tom. Initial problems included Tom's trying to manipulate the classroom teacher so that he could be with the crisis teacher whenever he chose. When it was thought that Tom was manipulating his way out of the classroom and into the crisis situation, he was not allowed to leave the classroom. Developing a more structured crisis intervention system in which Tom could carry on with the same work he had left from the regular classroom also helped solve this problem. As soon as Tom discovered that he could not escape the reality of the classroom by creating a crisis, he began to grow emotionally. Tom's need for support during crisis situations was intense for about 6 months, followed by a period of approximately 1 year when occasional support during crisis was needed. After 1½ years Tom was able to function within the regular classroom situation without unusual intervention other than that normally provided by the classroom teacher.

SUMMARY

Five major psychodynamic techniques are presented in this chapter. These include

milieu therapy, crisis intervention, life space interview, therapies with supportive media, and the mental health approach. Although these therapies are not generally appropriate in all educational situations, the concepts that they outline are useful for a wide array of educational interventions. A series of vignettes outline how each of these interventions can be applied to children in conflict.

BIBLIOGRAPHY AND SELECTED READINGS

Axline, V.: Play therapy, Boston, 1947, Houghton Mifflin Co.

Baumgartner, B., and Shultz, J.: Reaching children through art, Johnstown, Pa., 1969, Mafex Associates, Inc.

Bower, E., and Lambert, N.: In-school screening of children with emotional handicaps. In Long, N., Morse, W., and Newman, R., editors: Conflict in the classroom, Belmont, Calif., 1971, Wadsworth Publishing Co., Inc.

Dmitriev, V., and Hawkins, J.: Susie never used to say a word, Teaching Exceptional Children 6:68-76, 1973.

Gaston, E.: Music in therapy, New York, 1968, The Macmillan Co.

Glasser, W.: Schools without failure, New York, 1969, Harper & Row, Publishers.

Grump, P., and Sutton-Smith, B.: Therapeutic play techniques. In Long, N., Morse, W., and Newman, R., editors: Conflict in the classroom, Belmont, Calif., 1971, Wadsworth Publishing Co., Inc.

Kessler, J.: Psychopathology of childhood, Englewood Cliffs, N.J., 1966, Prentice-Hall, Inc.

Kramer, E.: Art as therapy with children, New York, 1971, Schocken Books, Inc.

Lewin, K.: A dynamic theory of personality, New York, 1935, McGraw-Hill Book Co.

Morse, W.: The crisis or helping teacher. In Long, N., Morse, W., and Newman, R., editors: Conflict in the classroom, Belmont, Calif., 1971, Wadsworth Publishing Co., Inc.

Naumberg, M.: Art therapy: its scope and function. In Hammer, E., et al., editors: The clinical application of projective drawings, Springfield, Ill., 1958, Charles C Thomas, Publisher.

Naumburg, M.: Psychoneurotic art: its function in psychotherapy, New York, 1958, Grune & Stratton, Inc.

Nelson, R.: Elementary school counseling with unstructured play media, Personnel and Guidance Journal 45:24-27, 1966.

Newman, K.: The school centered life-space interview as illustrated by extreme threat of school issues, American Journal of Orthopsychiatry 33:730-733, 1963.

Nordoff, P., and Robbins, C.: Therapy in music for handicapped children, New York, 1971, St. Martin's Press, Inc.

Powers, H.: Dietary measures to improve behavior and achievement, Academic Therapy 9:203-214, 1973-74.

Redl, F.: The concept of a therapeutic milieu, American Journal of Orthopsychiatry 29:721-734, 1959a.

Redl, F.: The concept of the life space interview, American Journal of Orthopsychiatry 29:1-18, 1959b.

Redl, F.: The concept of the life space interview. In Long, N., Morse, W., and Newman, R., editors: Conflict in the classroom, Belmont, Calif., 1971, Wadsworth Publishing Co., Inc.

Robbins, C., and Nordoff, P.: Clinical experiences with autistic children. In Gaston, E., editor: Music in therapy, New York, 1968, The Macmillan Co.

Skinner, B.: Beyond freedom and dignity, New York, 1972, Bantam Books, Inc.

Stainback, S., Stainback, W., and Hallahan, D.: Effect of background music on learning, Exceptional Children 40:109-110, 1973.

Waterland, L.: Actions instead of words: play therapy for the young child, Elementary School Guidance and Counseling 4:180-187, 1970.

CHAPTER 5

Classroom application of behavioral theory

Behavioral theory offers the classroom teacher a practical alternative to psychodynamic theory, which was presented in Chapter 4. Whereas many commonalities exist within behavior modification, there are several distinctive theoretical differences that offer the practitioner a variety of methodological approaches. Three of these systems will be discussed, including operant conditioning, contingency management, and behavior modeling.

OPERANT CONDITIONING

Behaviorists delineate two basic systems of conditioning. One is classical (Pavlovian) or respondent conditioning, the other is operant conditioning (Ullmann and Krasner, 1965). In general, respondent conditioning is associated with the involuntary muscular movements such as response to touching a hot stove or response to a mild shock. Respondent behavior is not used in typical learning situations, although its use has been demonstrated with severely disturbed children (Lovaas et al., 1965).

From the time children are born they make an enormous number of random responses to their environment. Children literally "operate" on their environment through motoric and verbal responses. Operant behaviors are conscious responses to the child's environment, which are maintained through reinforcement. As such, operant behaviors are clearly a major concern of teachers who attempt to modify children's behaviors. Whether operant behaviors are modified depends on what happens immediately after each operant behavior. If a child completes a good piece of work and is complimented by the teacher, this is likely to affect that child's work in the future. Whether the teacher's compliment will increase the strength of the operant (good work) or not depends on whether the teacher's praise is a positive reinforcer or punishment to the child.

Operant conditioning, in simplest terms, means reinforcing desired behaviors in ways that will cause the child to repeat the desired behavior. Another way of saying it is "catch the child doing what you want and reinforce his behavior." Operant conditioning can be used in a simplistic setting with no formal counting or reinforcement schemes, or it can be part of an extremely sophisticated system in which each behavior is counted, charted, and reinforced appropriately. Whether a teacher uses a simplistic or a highly sophisticated system often depends on the nature of the behavior being modified. The child who exhibits an occasional moodiness on Monday mornings probably needs no formal intervention, whereas another child who has a major temper tantrum each Monday is an entirely different problem.

Children in conflict who are identified as needing special intervention should be among those whose behavior should be monitored closely to effect desired behavior changes. Operant conditioning should begin as soon as a determination is made that serious problems exist. Hopefully, the child will be observed and inappropriate behaviors counted while he is still in the mainstream (regular class) or as close to the mainstream as possible.

Data collection

Three steps can be delineated in implementing operant conditioning systems. The first is data collection. Data collected before intervention begins are called *baseline data*. They help the teacher in several ways. First, baseline data help the teacher to determine if a problem actually exists. On one occasion I was invited to a classroom to observe a child in conflict who was exhibiting "nervous habits" including nose-picking behavior. Over a period of 2 weeks in which the teacher observed and counted the behavior it was found that nose picking occurred an average of once every 10 hours, and then for an average duration of 10 seconds. After counting and charting this behavior the teacher decided that it was not the frequency of the deviant behavior but her dislike for the behavior that caused serious concern. The decision was made not to intervene formally to change the child's behavior, since it was occurring at such a low level of frequency and duration.

On another occasion I discovered, through counting talk-out behaviors (talking without permission in the classroom) that the rate of inappropriate talk-outs for one classroom was over seventy an hour, with one child contributing over forty of the total number. The

boy who was dominating the classroom was a favorite of the teacher and was never suspected as being a behavior problem, only an "outgoing" child.

These two examples emphasize the importance of gathering baseline data to determine the exact nature of the behavior being considered for modification. To obtain accurate information, behaviors should ordinarily be counted and charted for a period of 1 or 2 weeks. During this time nothing new in the way of intervention should occur. The goal is to establish which behaviors are being exhibited and how often they occur. The teacher can gain information concerning the specifics of behavior counting by reading one of the many fine texts on the subject. Buckley and Walker (1970) and MacMillan (1973) are examples of easily read texts on the process involved in behavior modification, whereas Ullmann and Krasner (1965) represents a more detailed and in-depth study of the process.

Second, baseline information can also help the teacher to identify environmental stimuli that are supporting or maintaining the inappropriate behavior and that environmental stimuli would likely produce the desired behavioral change. This step is rather involved and takes considerable thought and skill on the part of the teacher. To determine the reinforcing stimulus (stimulus that follows behavior) or eliciting stimulus (stimulus that precedes behavior) the teacher must observe closely what happens immediately after the deviant behavior and also recall what environmental stimuli preceded it. A simple chart can be used to collect data on both reinforcing and eliciting stimuli.

Table 6 outlines a series of behavioral events that were either preceded or followed by stimuli. Deviant behaviors often occur in rapid succession, although the events could occur as separate behavioral entities. If a chart similar to this is kept, the problem areas soon become apparent. Table 6 shows that the teacher was involved twice in eliciting inappropriate behavior and four times in reinforcing deviance. At other times peers provided eliciting and/or reinforcing stimuli.

Table 6. Acting out behaviors (David, age 12 years)

Eliciting stimuli	Behavior	Reinforcing stimuli
Teacher asks question	David shouts out	Teacher says "Be quiet"
	David mumbles under his breath	Peers laugh
Tim walks past	David hits Tim on the arm	Tim cries
Teacher scolds David	David talks back	Peers all watch David
Tim snickers at David	David swears	Teacher sends David to the principal
	David refuses to leave	Teacher starts toward David
	David runs from classroom	Teacher follows

Third, baseline data provide teachers with a standard against which future progress can be measured. Without this standard it becomes increasingly difficult to measure success or failure. Teachers' memories tend to be inadequate when specific behaviors are compared; especially when several weeks or months have elapsed.

Arranging consequences

Once the baseline data have been gathered, the teacher must decide whether or not to proceed with an intervention process. If a decision is made to modify specific behaviors, the teacher then determines which of the stimuli are maintaining the deviant behaviors. If either the reinforcing stimuli or eliciting stimuli can be removed behavior will often change. In the earlier example (Table 6) if the teacher could avoid reinforcing David's inappropriate behavior, a noticeable change in the behavior should become evident. However, some cases will require additional intervention for change to occur. The teacher may need to reinforce appropriate alternative behaviors, for example. The successful arrangement of consequences requires specific attention to behaviors and how they are affected by reinforcement—a requirement that makes this a difficult stage of operant conditioning. Arranging consequences requires the teacher to decide (1) which reinforcers to use (types), (2) how much reinforcement is necessary (rate), and (3) the schedule of reinforcement to employ.

Any or all of these variables can contribute to the failure of intervention approaches.

Phasing out reinforcers

The third step in operant conditioning is the phasing out of reinforcers so that the child continues to exhibit appropriate behaviors with a "normal" level of social reinforcement. The phasing-out process has not been given as much attention in behavior modification texts as other issues, but it appears to be an important teacher concern. Reinforcers should gradually be reduced in both type and rate to a level acceptable to those with whom the children interact. The goal is to have the individual feel good about his behavior and achieve internal satisfaction. Children vary in their individual needs for reinforcement; however, this range does have its limits beyond which most teachers and parents will not continue (at least for long periods of time) to reinforce behaviors.

Reinforcement tips for teachers

Several reinforcement ideas have survived the trial and error of classrooms and have proved useful for teachers (Fig. 5-1). These include the following:

1. The most potentially powerful consequence in the classroom is the teacher (Anderson et al., 1972). Teacher attention can be in the form of verbal praise, physical contact, attention, allowing special privileges, etc. Whether teachers are the most powerful reinforcer in children's lives depends on the

Fig. 5-1. The faces of the child and teacher both suggest that the reinforcement is having a positive effect.

age, sex, environmental relationships, and a host of other variables. At any rate the teacher is "potentially" a high-level reinforcer for children.

2. Behavior modification can be used in a variety of educational settings, but it has no educational content of its own (Gearheart, 1973). Although behavior modification has only been a "technique" for teaching, its use has become so widespread that persons outside education have sometimes misinterpreted the technique as having educational content.

3. Operant conditioning is just as applicable to "normal behaviors" as to "deviant behaviors" and "regular class" as to "special class" (MacMillan, 1973). Children can be helped to change deviant behaviors through the use of operant techniques, but appropriate behaviors can also be increased through this technique.

4. Whereas "do-it-yourself" methods, which are readily available to teachers, can help to foster professional knowledge, they cannot ensure adequate training (Woody, 1969).

5. Behavior modification techniques are actually a refinement of traditional teaching techniques that have been practiced by effective classroom teachers. Many of the commonsense ideas teachers have been using are theoretically sound when they are compared to "proven" behavior modification techniques.

6. The process of extinction will generally bring an increase in deviant behavior (Ullmann and Krasner, 1965). Teachers have noticed this phenomenon to occur in the case of positive and negative reinforcement as well as during extinction processes. It almost seems that some children are afraid to grow in educational and social skills for fear that it will not last or that the expectation for growth will continue.

7. Three crucial elements of classroom behavioral control include (a) sensible rules, (b) appropriate praise, and (c) planned ignoring of deviant behavior (Madsen et al., 1968).

Operant conditioning provides teachers with the theoretical construct to change behaviors. Two systems will be discussed that add form to this theory: One is called contingency management or contracting, and the other is called behavior modeling.

CONTINGENCY MANAGEMENT

Contingency management is a close ally of operant conditioning that relies on basically the same concepts of other forms of behavior modification, that is, reinforcing appropriate behaviors by using positive reinforcement with punishment used sparingly, if at all. The basic difference between contingency management and other behavior modification systems is the degree of structure. Contingency management is essentially a contractual agreement between the teacher and the child. The contract can vary, depending on the needs of the child and the school setting. Generally more severe conflicts require more severe structure, whereas less severe problems require fewer external controls.

In contingency management LPBs (Low Probability Behaviors) are rewarded with HPBs (High Probability Behaviors). LPBs generally include such things as grading papers, doing homework, and studying for tests; HPBs generally include such things as eating, free time, coffee, and watching television.

An excellent outline of contingency management is available to teachers through the Instructional Materials Center Special Education, University of Southern California, Los Angeles. This package presents the basics of contingency management by means of cassette tapes, filmstrips, and a written manual. In their contingency management package Langstaff and Volkmor outline the basis of contingency management as (1) of any two alternative behaviors, one is preferable to the other and (2) if the preferred behavior is given only after the less preferred behavior has been performed, the less preferred behavior will occur more frequently in the future. Thus the preferred behavior becomes "contingent" on the performance of the less preferred behavior.

Contingency management has four basic components, which include (1) contracting for a specific amount of work, (2) making a contract that is fair, (3) rewarding behaviors that approximate desired goals, and (4) rewarding performance only after the behavior occurs.

1. Contracting must be for a specific amount of work. The child must know what is expected, even to such an extent that each contract is put in writing and signed by all parties concerned. If a child has lost faith in adults, it may take more than words to assure the child of good intentions. A contract can often provide the vehicle to reassure the child.

2. The contract must be fair to both sides involved, not just to the teacher or just to the child. This implies that both sides have agreed to its content.

3. Behaviors that approximate the desired outcome should be rewarded. This is the principle of shaping that allows the child (and the teacher) to have partial successes on the way to terminal goal attainment.

4. Behaviors are rewarded after they occur rather than in advance. This principle appears to be an unnecessary statement except that teachers often are tempted to reward before the fact or before the contract is completed.

Homme (1970) has written a helpful outline to contingency contracting in the classroom in which he presents ideas useful to the teacher. This easily read and applied text is written in a self-instructional format with pretests, intermediate tests, and posttests to guide each step of the instruction.

Contingency management is becoming a popular system of behavior management to use with children in conflict. It is simple, straightforward, and includes input from the child at every step, from deciding on a contract to reinforcement for work completed. The basic assumptions that underlie operant conditioning also apply to contingency management, making it supportive to this powerful modification tool.

Contingency management has also been found effective for teachers to modify their own behavior. Tasks such as grading papers can often be made more palatable by using contingency management. The teacher can grade ten papers then reward this appropriate behavior with something pleasant, for example, having a cup of coffee before grading more papers.

BEHAVIOR MODELING

Bandura (1965, 1969, 1971) outlines a social learning theory that he calls behavior modeling, which is based on the concept that many behaviors are learned most effectively through modeling or imitation. Although trial-and-error learning is an effective learning tool, it is extremely time consuming, and in many cases dangerous to the learner. No thinking parents would allow their children to learn to cross a busy street through trial-and-error learning for fear the punishment would be too great if they were to make an error. Parents take them by the hand and show them how to cross the street. Parents try to present a good model by their own behavior and also through verbalizing their knowledge and concerns.

Such behaviors as batting a baseball, swimming, and driving a car are other behaviors that are best learned through the modeling process rather than breaking these complex behaviors into individual components to be reinforced independently. Bandura (1965) delineates what he considers to be the difference in teaching procedure between operant methods and modeling methods. He sees modeling techniques as most viable for learning a new language. The teacher says a word in the foreign language, and the students in the class attempt to imitate the teacher's pronunciation. Once the individual words or language are mastered, operant techniques would be used to increase and improve on the already learned behavior.

It should be pointed out that operant conditioning and behavior modeling are extremely supportive to one another. When a child swings a baseball bat correctly or develops a swimming skill, the coach or parent might reinforce this behavior with appropriate words of encouragement or a pat on the back. In this way reinforcement, as used in operant conditioning, is much in evidence in reinforcing the modeled behavior. Bandura found that there are several variables that either enhance or detract from the effectiveness of the model the child is observing. Some of these variables include the sex of the model, the age of the model, and whether the model is live or on film. In short, the prestige of the model as seen by the student will either encourage or discourage new learning. An example of this might be a high school football star who is demonstrating passing and catching techniques to a group of third grade boys. In this case the learned behavior would probably be much more effective than if the same demonstration were conducted by one of the local high school cheerleaders to a group of third grade boys, even though the techniques might be similarly demonstrated. The high school football player model would likely be held in a higher prestige value, and therefore modeling would be more easily effected.

Some children model behavior more readily than others. It seems that whereas some children learn much deviant behavior as a result of modeling or seeing deviant behavior performed, other children seem to avoid learning of this type. Withdrawing children often regress into a self-stimulating world and do not appear to be affected by those around

them who are very active. Other more outgoing children appear to model much of their behavior from others in the environment. The teacher can determine which children will learn through modeling by observing and determining which children respond to the contagion of behaviors around them.

Children in conflict who react readily to the behaviors of those around them should be placed in a location in the classroom or in a special classroom where they might imitate appropriate behavior rather than inappropriate behavior. Educators do not have the same concern for children who do not model their behavior after others, since they are less vulnerable to either appropriate or inappropriate behavior.

In a study of the decision-making patterns of normal and educationally handicapped (emotionally disturbed and perceptually impaired) children, Reinert (1968) found that many children capitulate to the value judgments of their peers. Whereas it was found that normal children and educationally handicapped children tend to conform to judgments to a similar degree, their conformity took an interesting form. The educationally handicapped children, as individuals, tended to conform either to a small degree or to a great extent. This study seems to indicate that some disturbed children tend to conform a great deal (are followers who might benefit from appropriate models), whereas others conform little (are leaders themselves who are unlikely to follow).

The practice of putting all children with similar behaviors into isolated classes with others who have similar behaviors would seem to be highly questionable if one subscribes to the concept that many behaviors are learned through modeling of peer behaviors.

The role of the teacher in modeling needs careful attention, since adults also serve as models. Teachers who are hyperactive themselves, who scurry around the classroom, yell at children, and otherwise present a frantic disorganized and uncoordinated model to children can hardly expect children to be calm, soft spoken, and quiet in their classroom. The modification of the teacher's own behavior is likely to have a dramatic effect in calming the classroom if the children can observe this type of model. Many young men teachers have observed that the young boys in their classroom often model their behaviors in such ways as copying the belts that they wear, imitating their walk, combing their hair in similar fashion, and trying to imitate speech patterns. Little girls often model their teachers, particularly if they are female, in related ways.

Bandura (1965) has done many studies to demonstrate the social implications and value of the modeling process. He suggests that no trial learning occurs once a child is under the control of discriminative stimuli. In other words, a child can learn from others once he has learned to view others as sources of information.

Behavior modeling is more effective in learning new behaviors when no reliable eliciting stimuli are available to the teacher (Bandura, 1965). For example, how would you teach a child to say "I'm sorry" without using a behavioral model? Would a child ever say "I'm sorry" without ever having heard someone say the words before? Bandura doubts this would happen and therefore believes in the modeling process, a process that avoids the painful slowness of the operant conditioning model.

Although the concept of behavior modeling has been researched extremely well (Bandura, 1969), its use with children in conflict must be considered a part of other modification systems. Modeling becomes a component of change rather than an isolated change in its own right.

Educational concerns of using behavior modification

Many claims and counterclaims have been made regarding the use of behavior modification in the classroom. Following guidelines should help the classroom teacher to bring some of these concerns into perspective.

1. Behavior modification is not a panacea for all children. It is one technique that offers promise if used with discretion.

2. Behavior modification will not overcome poor teaching. Whereas reinforcement will never replace a well-planned lesson, it can certainly enhance the lesson if used appropriately.

3. It is incomprehensible to believe that a teacher could function without using some behavior modification techniques. Social reinforcement is as real as life.

4. Behavior modification was not invented yesterday. Teachers have used behavior modification techniques for many years, even though the labels of behavior modification were not applied. Many behavioral techniques were not scientifically grounded by research, but they were still being used. For example, the Romans are said to have put an eel into wine glasses as an aversive stimulus for those who had a drinking problem. Teachers have successfully used negative reinforcement, positive reinforcement, and counterconditioning long before theorists developed the supportive research for these techniques.

5. Society is based to a great extent on principles of behavior modification. Individuals receive pay for working, supposedly in some relationship to their contribution to society. If individuals drive too fast, they are punished; if they have an accident-free year, they are sometimes rewarded with a deduction on their automobile insurance premium —a form of negative reinforcement.

6. Proper use of behavior management techniques will help to avoid the conflict between those who support the use of token reinforcers and those who favor only internal controls (an individual's feeling good as a result of his behavior). Children who can function without token reinforcers should be encouraged to do so. (Teachers would never think of putting all the children back into reading readiness material simply because one child in the classroom needed to be at that level.) Neither should teachers use token reinforcers, like candy, for all children when only one child needs this type of reinforcement to function. The goal should always be to achieve as much inner control and motivation as possible for each child.

7. Reinforcement cannot overcome a lack

of structure and common sense in teaching children. At times teachers must learn to close doors, to vary schedules, and to separate personalities rather than to use behavioral manipulation to solve these problems.

8. Behavior management is not a subversive activity. Teachers have always been interested in changing the behaviors of children whom they are paid to teach. Whether behavior is changed through the discovery method or through conscious manipulation on the part of the teacher does not really matter; to be effective the one who teaches must have a plan for change. As a change agent, the teacher has certain rights and obligations to students that remain intact regardless of the system advocated in helping to bring about desirable behavior changes. Behaviorists believe that their system is more open and honest than systems that encourage change through discovery or through gaining insight.

9. An often-heard complaint of behavior management is that it is unfair to reinforce one child while ignoring another. If this is happening, it certainly is unfair, since all children need some reinforcement. Even university students on occasion will "let it slip out" that they have achieved all A's during a given quarter. Parents often remind their children of the high marks they had in school. It seems that everyone needs reinforcement, although they generally want this reinforcement to be appropriate to their level of maturity and to the situation.

10. One principle of behavior management appears to be beyond reproach—making systematic observations of what is going on. This is what the push for accountability is all about. No matter what system is used to teach children, teachers need to be accountable to students, to parents, and to whomever else they serve.

Most teachers indicate that behavior management is a powerful tool for behavior change. Still they are often reluctant to implement it in their classrooms. Teachers apparently view behavior modification techniques with some fear because of its tremendous potential for changing behavior.

Most teachers feel a deep obligation to children and are fearful of the ethical implications that manipulation raises. As long as teachers are aware of this powerful tool and desire to help rather than hurt children, there appears to be no real danger of misusing it in the classroom.

The following vignettes should be helpful in showing how various forms of modification have been applied to children.

Vignette 1: Behavioral theory
  Reported by Patterson (1965)
  Karl, a 7-year-old boy, exhibited an unusual fear of school (anxiety separation from leaving his parents), a condition often called school phobia. Karl began to exhibit a fear of leaving home during nursery school. He often needed to go into his house to check on his mother. If she planned to go to the store, he would demand that he also go along. All attempts to keep Karl in school or to avoid his fears of separation were fruitless.

Karl was tested and found to have normal intellectual functioning but was low in reading readiness and rather immature in social interaction skills. Treatment was undertaken in a clinical setting, with reinforcement (M & Ms) given for time spent in the playroom without looking at his mother. During discussion sessions (held after treatment) the mother was encouraged to praise Karl for remaining in the playroom without her. The mother was also instructed to praise Karl for not "checking" on her at home for periods of over 30 minutes.

Through the continued process of reinforcement of mother separation, Karl gradually allowed his parents to stay in the reception area rather than sit outside the playroom door. Gradually in sessions 11 through 23 he attended school, accompanied by the special teacher. Three months after the individual sessions were terminated Karl remained in school. Teachers reported a general improvement in school adjustment with no evidence of the return of fearfulness. The process took approximately twenty bags of M & Ms and 10 hours of staff time.

Vignette 2: Contingency management
  Reported by Dee (1972)
  Dee reports the use of contingency management with a crisis class of children experiencing emotional problems. The children involved

in the study were placed in the special class as a result of fighting behaviors, hostility to authority, school truancy, and disruptive behavior. Special class goals included modification of existing behaviors so as to allow each child to return to regular class.

The day was divided into work periods and play periods to provide the disturbed children with consistent boundaries. During work periods each child worked from an assignment book individualized to meet his needs. When the work was completed, the child brought the work to the teacher for any help and correcting. The work had to be within the contractual limits established prior to completion (e.g., three mistakes or less) of the task. If the contract was completed, check marks were awarded, as agreed on in the original contract. When the specified number of check marks was reached, each child could take his free time, which he monitored with a timing clock.

Free time was spent in a variety of activities, including games, eating, art activities, or any other high probability activities available at the time. The success of individual contracts was based, to a large extent, on the ability of the staff to identify reinforcers of positive value. If a child did not play well, he had to return to academic activities or go to a quiet area for a specified period of time, for example, a 5-minute period where no reinforcement or work was completed (Fig. 5-2).

Fig. 5-2. A quiet time-out area where a child cannot receive reinforcement is often helpful for children whose emotions are out of control for brief periods of time.

Classroom example: Fred

Fred was in the special class for 8 weeks, working under a contractual program with the special teacher before he was ready to return to his regular class. He was a belligerent child with average or better intelligence who was considered to be a potential dropout. His functional academic level in the classroom was extremely low. When Fred entered the special class, he was offered several alternative contracts for which he could earn free time, candy, and teacher attention. He worked well initially, but eventually tested the situation to see if there were "holes" in the system. After the honeymoon period he became belligerent and was placed in the quiet area, where he became even more obnoxious. Some of his hard-earned points were then taken away.

This case is extremely "believable" for classroom teachers who must adjust programs for individual children in ways that do not disrupt the good things that are happening in the classroom.

Vignette 3: Behavior modeling

Reported by Bandura, Ross, and Ross (1963)

This vignette describes a classical study in modeling theory. The study was designed to research the modeling effects of aggressive behavior presented on film. Subjects for the study included ninety-two children (forty-six boys and forty-six girls) enrolled in the Stanford University Nursery School. They ranged in age from 35 to 69 months, with a mean age of 52 months.

One group of children observed real-life aggressive models, a second group observed the same two real-life models performing their aggressive acts by way of a motion picture, and the third group viewed a film of a cartoon character exhibiting aggressive behavior. After exposure to these aggressive models each group was subjected to mild frustration (not allowing them to play with some special toys).

The results of the study indicated that children exposed to filmed aggression (both human and cartoon) exhibited nearly twice as much aggression as did children in the control group who were not exposed to aggressive films. Children who viewed aggression of real-life models showed less tendency toward aggression than either of the groups that viewed filmed aggression and more than children in the control group.

This study is open to many interpretations, but several important findings appear to be important for teachers and parents: (1) both normal and deviant children model aggressive behavior when frustrated; (2) both boys and girls model aggressive behavior when frustrated; and (3) the sex of the model influences the aggressive behaviors of children.

Vignette 4: Behavior modification of selectively mute child
Reported by Dmitriev and Hawkins (1973)
Prior to coming to the Olympic Center Susie, age 9 years 4 months, had been in a regular kindergarten for 2 years. She was referred to the center because of muscular twitching and refusal to talk to anyone outside her immediate family (she talked primarily to her 10-year-old sister).

During her first 2 years at the center Susie showed periodic gains but always regressed into periods of twitching and digging at her arms, causing considerable bleeding. Speech was absent in school during this period of time. Susie was placed full time in the center for a while, but still speech was absent, although other social gains were reported.

Through the consultation of Valentine Dmitriev it was determined that the various behavior modification plans that were tried and discarded had failed because the staff was actually reinforcing Susie for *not speaking*.

Treatment centered around giving cues for speaking, that is, "say chair," "say work," or "say lunch." After 2 years of silence Susie began speaking. The breakthrough came on the fifth day of intervention, when seven of ten cues met with verbal response. This number increased rapidly, until verbal responses reached 421 words on the twenty-second day. Susie returned to public school 6 months after the procedures for implementing speech were undertaken. The authors report that Susie entered junior high school in 1973 and was doing well in school and community activities.

It should be emphasized that Susie was different from other mute children in that she was selectively mute. Her rapid progress under treatment obviously was a result of this fact. A totally mute child undoubtedly would react differently to treatment.

Vignette 5 describes the basic program used at the University of Northern Colorado Laboratory School during my teaching tenure. It could be described as a contingency management program with support services from a psychiatrist from the local mental health clinic, the school psychologist, the director of special education, a visiting teacher, and graduate students attending the university.

Vignette 5: Contingency management in a special class
Reported by University of Northern Colorado Laboratory School
John came to the classroom reluctantly one early spring morning (being carried by two husky males). John was 9 years old at the time and had been in school for an average of about 30 days a year through his first 4 years of school. He was a member of a large migrant family who spent part of their winter in Texas and part of it in Colorado, depending on the work that the father could do.

From John's cumulative folder it was learned that John disliked authority, was hyperactive, and was unable to keep at a task for any appreciable length of time. Our first contingency with John was to have him remain "in the vicinity" of his desk for 5 minutes and thereby earn a 5-minute break to do as he chose. We were sure that John did not know what vicinity meant and that was all well and good. We could interpret the word *vicinity* as we saw fit and thereby allowed John the freedom to cope with the situation without imposing rigid standards that he perhaps could not meet. For the first 5 minutes John laid on his chair, sat under his desk, sprawled over the top of his desk, and looked out the window. He was told that he had done a good job of staying at the vicinity of his desk, and he had earned 5 minutes of free time to play outside or in the classroom as he chose. John immediately went out to the playground and found a multihandicapped youngster playing in a wagon. He quickly separated the wagon from the handicapped child and began riding around the school yard. This activity pointed out that the red wagon had a high reinforcing value for John. We made appropriate arrangements with the classroom teacher whose wagon John had commandeered so that John could use the wagon for his reinforcement whenever he was on the playground. John must get permission to use the wagon from the teacher, which she would readily give on his asking, but he must not dump a child from the wagon. In addition, no other children in our classroom were to use the wagon. This was to be John's sole possession when he had earned his reinforcement. The wagon proved to be a highly reinforcing agent for John since he continued to stay in the vicinity of his chair for 5 minutes and thus earned 5 minutes of free time. We allowed this to continue for 2 days, until John began to show signs of tiring of this activity. During this first 2 days, which we call the honeymoon period, John tried to manipulate the reinforcement process by overstaying his 5 minutes with the wagon, even though he had a kitchen timer that warned him when his time was up. When he returned to the classroom, we said nothing but had him continue earning more reinforcement. When he got ready to return to the playground for another 5-minute break, we told him that he had overstayed his break time on the previous period and therefore he must lose the amount of time he overstayed plus an additional 1 minute from his next 5 minutes. This left him only 1 minute on the playground. We specifically waited until John had earned more free time before breaking the news that he had overstayed his last free time break so that he would not become discouraged. Please note that we did not ask John if he had reset the timer or why he was late returning but simply stated the fact that he had overstayed his time. In this way we tried to avoid the conflict that might arise if we asked questions as to why he did not return.

After the 2 days of earning reinforcement by staying in the vicinity of his chair, we indicated to John that he would need to sit in his chair to earn his free time. John seemed to be pleased to make this advancement toward the behavior that he was seeing modeled by other children in the classroom. The second phase of modeling John's behavior lasted only 1½ days before John gave signals that indicated he was ready to do more than sit in his chair. These signals included taking a pencil and paper from his desk and doing some scribbling on the paper, forming a few crude letter symbols, and drawing some pictures. At this point we introduced John to the letters of the alphabet using the Sullivan reading program. John continued to earn 5 minutes of free time for every five pages of the reading material that he was able to complete correctly. John learned

quickly, since he did have good ability and was older. We had few conflicts with John, and he liked school. He even rode his bicycle 4 miles from his home to school when he missed the bus.

A contingency management program helped John to become responsible for his behavior. The reinforcements that were earned were the type that are acceptable to most teachers in the public school so that John was able to make the transition to regular class without a difficult phasing out of reinforcers. In our program we avoided such reinforcers as candy, gum, and toys, which would not be readily accepted by teachers in future placements. We also found that the social reinforcers that we were using were much more easily phased into a reinforcement system that could be carried out in the regular classroom. Since several graduate students interacted with the children, we were forced to have specific guidelines for interaction so that consistency would be maintained.

The following guidelines were established for all staff:

1. Try to be positive at all times—even when correcting a child's behavior.

2. Prepare all work for the day before school begins. Prepare more work than generally needed so as not to be caught short.

3. Keep lessons short and to the point. Cut through the redtape of learning.

4. Individualize work so that each child can work on his own as much as possible. Each child should have an individual "in" and "out" folder so that he can pick up his work without interrupting others.

5. Check work as soon as possible. Generally work should be checked immediately so that children receive immediate reinforcement.

6. Children should come to the teacher to have work corrected. The teacher is seated at a table near the entrance to the classroom.

7. Verbalize as little as possible. Show by actions rather than words. Do not argue with children.

8. Be alert to everything positive a child does. Ignore inappropriate behaviors as much as possible.

9. Try to give each child something positive to look forward to the next day.

10. Maintain positive relationships with parents.

11. Always pair reinforcement with a smile or verbal praise.

Reinforcement for the children was not expensive, since we relied mostly on social reinforcers. When token reinforcers were used, they were generally supplied by the children. We allowed children to bring their bicycles to ride during free time, models to build, and games to play. The children played chess, checkers, cards, and dominoes. One of the most novel reinforcers that we observed was an old cowboy hat, which one boy brought from home. His mother did not allow him to to wear it around the house so he took special delight in having it in school. During his reinforcement period he would sit in the reinforcement area of the classroom with his cowboy hat on his head and a big grin on his face.

SUMMARY

Three systems of behavior modification were discussed, Operant conditioning, contingency management, and behavior modeling. All three of these systems represent efforts to explain and formalize the learning process in schools. Although all are highly related, each has components distinctive to its individual process. Operant conditioning relates closely to the other systems. Contingency management varies from operant conditioning in that it is a contractual arrangement rather than just a process of reinforcement. In the contingency management process the child is totally involved. The child, hopefully, recognizes his deviant behavior and knows exactly what is being done to help him change the behavior. Behavior modeling is also a process of behavior change, but one slightly different from contingency management. In the modeling process the child behaves because of an exemplary model that he chooses to follow. Sophisticated behaviors are believed to be more easily taught by use of the modeling concept.

The advantages and disadvantages of behavior modification are also discussed. The use of behavior modification has increased rapidly in the public schools during the past decade. The proposal is made that professionals should take a healthy reassessment of its use so that needed changes can be made. The major concerns delineated include the use of hard-sell approaches to behavior modification in the classroom, the feeling that behavior modification will overcome poor teaching, the ethical implications of behavior modification, and the need for behavior modification techniques to be included in the repertoire of all teachers.

Chapter 5 concludes with a series of behavioral vignettes that give examples of the practical application of behavioral modification.

BIBLIOGRAPHY AND SELECTED READINGS

Altman, R., and Meyer, E.: Some observations on competency based instruction, Exceptional Children **40:** 267-271, 1974.

Anderson, D., Hodson, G., Jones, W., Todd, F., and Walters, B.: Behavior modification techniques for teachers of the developmentally young, Greeley, Colo., 1972, Rocky Mountain Special Education Instructional Materials Center.

Bandura, A: Behavioral modifications through modeling procedures. In Krasner, L., and Ullmann, L., editors: Research in behavior modification, New York, 1965, Holt, Rinehart & Winston, Inc.

Bandura, A: Principles of behavior modification, New York, 1969, Holt, Rinehart & Winston, Inc.

Bandura, A: Social learning theory, Morristown, N.J., 1971, General Learning Corp.

Bandura, A., Ross, D., and Ross, S.: Imitation of film-mediated aggressive models, Journal of Abnormal and Social Psychology **66:**3-11, 1963.

Buckley, N., and Walker, H.: Modifying classroom behavior, Champaign, Ill., 1970, Research Press Co.

Dee, V.: Contingency management in a crisis class, Exceptional Children **38:**631-634, 1972.

Dmitriev, V., and Hawkins, J.: Susie never used to say a word, Teaching Exceptional Children **6:**68-76, 1973.

Fargo, G., Behrns, C., and Nolen, R.: Behavior modification in the classroom, Belmont, Calif., 1970, Wadsworth Publishing Co., Inc.

Forness, S., and MacMillan, D.: Origins of behavior modification with exceptional children, Exceptional Children **37:**93-100, 1970.

Gearheart, B.: Learning disabilities: educational strategies, St. Louis, 1973, The C. V. Mosby Co.

Homme, L.: How to use contingency contracting in the classroom, Champaign, Ill., 1970, Research Press Co.

Lovaas, O., Schaeffer, B., and Simmons, J.: Building social behavior in autistic children by use of electric shock, Journal of Experimental Research in Personality, **1:**99-109, 1965.

Lovitt, T.: Behavior modification: the current scene, Exceptional Children **37:**85-91, 1970.

MacMillan, D.: Behavior modification in education, New York, 1973, The Macmillan Co.

Madsen, C., Becker, W., and Thomas, D.: Rules, praise and ignoring: elements of elementary school control, Journal of Applied Behavior Analysis 1:139-150, 1968.

Patterson, G.: A learning theory approach to the treatment of the school phobic child. In Ullmann, L., and Krasner, L., editors: Case studies in behavior modification, New York, 1965, Holt, Rinehart & Winston, Inc.

Reinert, H.: Decision making in the educationally handicapped and normal child: a comparative study, Ed.D. dissertation, Greeley, Colo., 1968, Colorado State College.

Ullmann, L., and Krasner, L., editors: Case studies in behavior modification, New York, 1965, Holt, Rinehart & Winston, Inc.

Woody, R.: Behavioral problem children in the schools, New York, 1969, Appleton-Century-Crofts.

CHAPTER 6

Classroom application of biophysical, sociological/ecological, and counter theories

Each of the theoretical approaches of biophysical, sociological/ecological, and counter theories has a relationship to the education of children in conflict, but none can currently be considered as important as the psychodynamic or behavioral theories of Chapters 4 and 5. Each approach will be discussed separately within this chapter to point out the teacher's role within each system.

CLASSROOM APPLICATION OF BIOPHYSICAL THEORY

The biophysical system is an area where the teacher's role is supportive to medical intervention. Although teachers are not physicians, they need to become aware of the progress being made in the biophysical area and to work as supportive team members with medical personnel whenever feasible. A knowledge of and interest in the work being carried on by the biophysical disciplines could help promote an understanding and cooperative spirit that will benefit children.

Although physicians have always been interested in the educational development of children, their involvement seems to have grown dramatically in recent years. Although only a few schools utilize the services of a pediatrician on even a part-time basis, the increase of consulting psychiatrists, pediatricians, and full-time nurses is encouraging. This growing medical involvement is generally viewed as a positive step toward solving the medical aspects of problems that often manifest themselves in school. It should neither be viewed as a new panacea for children's behavior problems nor should it threaten the role of the teacher. Even if it is found (although there is no imminent danger of this happening) that *all* deviance is biophysically related, teaching will still be required for individual children to achieve their fullest potential within these limits.

Medical intervention generally centers around three areas.

1. Physical examination or medical evaluation is generally specified to determine the role of physiological problems in deviant behavior. Most school programs rely heavily on the family physician or pediatrician to provide this information prior to placement in any special programs. Although the medical evaluation generally does not provide immediate intervention, it does outline the strategy for intervention if a medical basis of the problem behavior is discovered.

2. Manipulation of physiological functions are sometimes indicated to "cure" the child. Examples include surgery to correct physical defects, which in turn have an impact on emotional health; dietary controls, which have a direct effect on behavior, for example, phenylketonuria, diabetes, and weight problems; and prosthetic devices such as glasses and hearing aids. In cases where the "cure" is effective, the child can often function in somewhat of a "normal" fashion.

3. Treatment of the symptoms of biophysical defects often becomes the most common medical intervention. Procedures aimed at remediating behavioral problems through artificial means have become common in today's medical practice. The use of tranquilizers and energizing drugs are two recent examples of treatment of symptoms through artificial means.

Role of the teacher

Teachers obviously cannot prescribe drug treatment, put children on diets, or perform surgery. They can and should alert medical persons to problems that might be helped through medical intervention. Referral therefore is one of the teacher's major roles. Generally the school has specific guidelines for the referral process that the teacher should know and follow. Suggestions to the referral agency should be made either in writing or by telephone so that the physician is alerted to the specific educational concerns. The school nurse, if available, should play a major role in this process. Once the medical evaluation is completed and the intervention decided on, the teacher has a continuing role in communicating the educational results of such intervention. This role need not be formal or time consuming in most cases; an occasional telephone call or note to the physician is often all that is needed to maintain adequate communication.

CLASSROOM APPLICATION OF SOCIOLOGICAL/ECOLOGICAL THEORY

Sociological/ecological application is combined because it is difficult, in practice, to separate their components. Both offer a wholeness or holistic approach to working with children, although the ecological view is somewhat more encompassing; both have cautioned educators against looking only within the child for the cause of deviance; and finally, these theories have taught educators that children in conflict cannot be treated in isolation.

Project Re-Ed

One of the most widely publicized and duplicated sociological/ecological systems is Project Re-Ed, which stands for "a project for the re-education of emotionally disturbed children" (Hobbs, 1966). The program described here represents a compilation of interpretations (Hobbs, 1966; Lee, 1971; Lewis, 1967; Weinstein, 1969). Although no major variance of description is made by the writers who describe the Re-Ed process, there appears to be a healthy variance in program implementation. The intention is to discuss briefly the Re-Ed process from a theoretical viewpoint and then to describe its implementation in one school setting.

The Re-Ed approach holds to the principle that the conflict is within the child, but this conflict is maintained through inappropriate interface (interaction) with the environment. Lewis describes this conflict as a discordance between the role prescriptions of the primary socializing systems with whom the child interacts and the child's role performance. This discordance may develop for one of three reasons: (1) the child may not have the ability to perform the role prescription; (2) the child may not be aware of this role prescription; and (3) the child may find the consequences of competing role prescriptions more attractive than those of expected roles. Fig. 6-1 depicts the ecological system as interpreted by the Re-Ed approach.

As indicated by Fig. 6-1, there is a close relationship among various components of the child's primary socializing systems. Traditional psychotherapy, including the exploration of inner personal dynamics, transference, and intrapersonal conflicts are avoided in the Re-Ed process. Since inappropriate behaviors are seen as bad habits that have

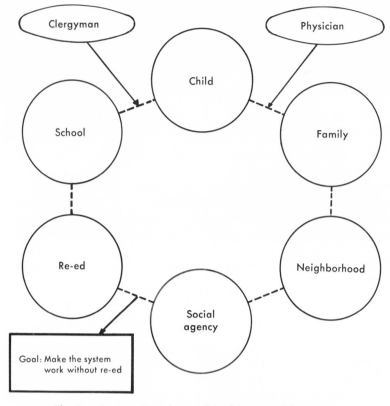

Fig. 6-1. Project Re-Ed. (Modified from Hobbs, 1966.)

been learned by the child in conflict, major emphasis is placed on establishing improved relationships between the child, family, and home community (Hobbs, 1966).

The Re-Ed approach is generally labeled a pull-out program by those who favor keeping children in the mainstream of education. Those who espouse the Re-Ed approach believe that a temporary pulling out from the regular school situation, which is contributing to the disturbance, is a positive factor. The environmental setting established by the Re-Ed process is a residential 24-hour care unit that focuses its attention on the educative process. To maintain some orientation to reality the children are returned home each weekend to be with their families.

The center of the intervention system is the teacher counselor. Teachers selected for this role are generally those with teaching experience and a year of special training for emotionally disturbed children. The teacher counselor is assisted in program development by consultants from social work and mental health and by a liaison teacher. These consultants do not interact directly with the child but relate with the teacher counselor concerning the child's specific needs.

The philosophy of the Re-Ed approach is well stated by thirteen processes of reeducation, as described by Hobbs (1966).

1. Life is to be lived now. This process points out a basic difference between Re-Ed and traditional approaches, which often look to solutions to problems in terms of a therapy hour. The Re-Ed approach does not put the child in a "holding pattern" for another intervention to effect change. Re-Ed is the change agent; each hour is important to the child and the reeducation process.

2. Time is an ally. This process supports the concept that time heals. When a child is taken from his home, the family is often at a low point in its ability to cope with the child. Things must get better. Re-Ed tries to capitalize on this belief without sentencing

Fig. 6-2. Trust is an important element in teaching, whether it be in the classroom or swimming pool.

the child to a 2-year stay before he can "get well." The goal is to use time for the advantage of the child, with 6 months considered a justifiable period of stay.

3. Trust is essential (Fig. 6-2). Children in conflict have often lost all trust for adults. They have been "let down" too often; they have been coerced in various ways by adults and often resent the intrusion into their lives. To teach, to change, and to reeducate the child, trust must first be reestablished. Hobbs suggests that teaching this skill to adults is impossible; this would underscore the importance of the selection of teacher counselors rather than training.

4. Competence makes the difference. Much of an individual's perception of others is based on what they can do. In teaching children it is necessary to begin with the acceptance of their limitations and lack of competence; however, as teachers we must not be satisfied with this situation. Children must feel that they are good at some things. The most common characteristic of children who are labeled disturbed is a lack of school achievement; therefore in the Re-Ed approach, school is important. It is part of the change process, not to be put off. In addition to the gaining of competence in school subjects, individual skills are stressed. These often include learning to swim, skate, to cook

on a Dakota Hole, to paddle a canoe, to be assertive, and a myriad of other social skills that give the child a feeling of personal satisfaction and group stature.

5. Symptoms can and should be controlled. This process points out a specific variance of the Re-Ed process from traditional interventions. In psychotherapy, for example, symptoms are often not treated, with emphasis being placed on the underlying conflict. Re-Ed theory encourages the study and control of symptoms whenever possible. Symptoms can either endear children to those around them, or they can alienate children. It is important that symptoms that alienate children be changed or replaced by more acceptable ones. Explanations of inappropriate behavior that assume minimum pathology are preferred to those that assume in-depth explanations.

6. Cognitive control can be taught. Emotionally disturbed children can learn to monitor their own behavior if taught to do so. Emphasis is on today and tomorrow, on immediate and short-term goals. This is done by teacher counselors interacting with the child around life events that are underway. Much talking is done to develop personal insights into social occurrences. Each night a group session or council ring is held to talk over what went right and what went wrong

during the day and to encourage appropriate changes for the following day. The youngsters are encouraged to verbalize their problems so that eventually self-control might be brought under the child's own verbal control. It is hoped that verbal interaction will carry over into the home, with a strengthening effect for that relationship.

7. Feelings should be nurtured. In contrast to those who would "turn feelings off," the Re-Ed approach encourages the healthy expression of feelings. Feelings that have been blunted by experiences with adults or other children are not easily restored to their full resiliency. The child might first wish to establish relationships with an animal before entering into a more complex human relationship. This approach also emphasizes the release of feelings in productive ways such as throwing clay on a potter's wheel, drawing, painting, or writing the script for a puppet show.

8. The group is important to children. A sense of belonging, comradeship, and responsibility are all factors that can be encouraged through group processes. Groups are kept small, usually around eight persons. Various sharing activities, including the council ring or pow-wow, are made possible through the group interaction.

9. Ceremony and ritual give order, stability, and confidence. In an effort to bring order to otherwise chaotic lives, the Re-Ed philosophy encourages rituals such as regular meetings, a nightly backrub, or other small but important occurrences. The healthy family traditionally has developed rituals that are important to and held "sacred" by family members. Celebrations around family successes, parties, and family outings can never be replaced by rituals developed in a residential setting, but a certain closeness can be developed.

10. The body is the armature of the self. A wholesome physical self-image seems to be associated with a wholesome psychological self-image. To enhance the psychological self, the Re-Ed approach encourages physical activities such as swimming, canoeing, climbing, tumbling, and walking a monkey bridge.

11. Communities are important. Families of disturbed children often have failed to develop adequate community ties. The child can be encouraged to be aware of community activities and to participate in them. Field trips to the police and fire stations, health department, and community recreation facility might be helpful in pointing out the useful community relationships. A boy might be encouraged to become actively involved in Boys' Club or Young America Football to help develop a positive association with community agencies.

12. A child should know joy. Joy is promoted by the teacher counselor who knows each child and what he enjoys. Re-Ed schools believe that joy is more than reinforcement given for some minute behavior. The child should have something to look forward to each day that will promote joy and a desire to anticipate coming events.

13. Middle class values should be taught. Children who are considered "normal" by their peers can deviate considerably in their relationships to others and still be seen as normal. Children whose behavior has been inappropriate are often labeled as deviant and have a more difficult time expressing themselves in acceptable ways. Children in conflict must learn good manners, cleanliness, and acceptable language to be accepted by middle class teachers. Often their behavior must be superior to that expected of more normal peers.

The Re-Ed process offers one way to deal with children in conflict as an indivisible unit, that is, child, school, home, and neighborhood. Its goals are concerned with reality and self-fulfillment rather than illness. Teacher counselors are employed as change agents, and specialists are used only in a consultant role. In addition, the Re-Ed process capitalizes on the abundant energy of young teachers; thus allowing professional expertise, which is in short supply, to be spread to the needed population of children.

Vignette 1: Sociological/ecological theory
  Reported by Project Re-Ed, State of Tennesee
  Jimmy, age 6 years 3 months, was enrolled

in the first grade of an elementary school in Tennessee. Jimmy was originally recognized as a serious behavior problem. He had been seen at a mental health services clinic earlier because his mother thought he was mentally retarded or organically damaged. His behavior included a preoccupation with knives and hatchets, a serious lag in educational achievement, and inability to control his anger. According to a problem behavior checklist, the teacher indicated twenty-four separate behaviors that were severe problems in the classroom.

Jimmy was evaluated for the Re-Ed school at the age of 7 years. On the Stanford-Binet test he was found to have normal intellectual ability but was thought to have perceptual and emotional problems. On the WISC Jimmy's scores were: verbal scale IQ 89; performance scale, IQ 89; and full scale, IQ 88. Subtest scores were as follows:

	Scaled score
Verbal	
Information	7
Comprehension	11
Arithmetic	8
Similarities	8
Vocabulary	7
Performance	
Picture completion	11
Picture arrangement	12
Block design	10
Object assembly	6
Coding	3

The scatter noted on the subtest scores indicated the possibility of learning disabilities, whereas the mannerisms and explosive reactions to the testing situation prompted the examiner to believe that Jimmy was experiencing emotional difficulties.

Other tests were administered after intake. These included the Metropolitan test, in which he scored at the 67th percentile; the ITPA and Frostig tests, which indicated acceptable functioning, although some scatter; the Wepman Auditory Discrimination Test, which was normal; the Beltone Audiometric Analysis, which was normal; and the Keystone Visual Survey Test, which placed him in the unsatisfactory range, with correction possible.

In all academic areas Jimmy was considered to be functioning below normal, although some scatter was noted. A comprehensive educational program was developed to remediate areas of educational concern.

Jimmy's early childhood was a stormy one. His mother and father experienced continual marital problems, which ended when his father was killed in an automobile accident. Jimmy was the oldest of three children; the youngest child is his half-brother and the second child is his sister. The mother generally believes that Jimmy is having some difficulties but not less than others believe he is having.

In Project Re-Ed a behavior modification program was used with Jimmy, including positive social reinforcement, a token economy and point systems. He became a member of the Tomahawks, a group of twelve younger boys from 6 to 8 years of age. Camping experience, a structured environment, and group rituals were among the many activities in which Jimmy was involved.

A Family Service Agency case worker was assigned to the family to help improve any home situations needing attention. Communication with the home indicated steady and continual growth.

Jimmy was 7 years 2 months old when he entered the Re-Ed program. He was terminated at 7 years 9 months. At termination his academic achievement was average and his social relationships were adequate. The growth demonstrated during his brief stay can best be indicated by a statement in the case report. "Jimmy was a little bitty baby when he came to Re-Ed. He was a second grade boy when he left" (State of Tennessee, p. 77).

CLASSROOM APPLICATION OF COUNTER THEORY

Counter theory appears to have a growing acceptance among those who teach children in conflict. The educational approach of countertheorists has no common bond that holds them together against more established practice; however, they do have points of contention on which they tend to agree. Tracy (1972) lists four assumptions made by traditional educational institutions that are opposed by countertheorists.

1. Countertheorists oppose the idea that education possesses a quantifiable set of knowledge that should be passed on to generations of children.

2. The role of the teacher as holding a reservoir of knowledge that is to be syphoned to each student is rejected.

3. The question of literacy, which is a value system generally expected in American society, is seen as a political tool for spreading information to the populace.

4. The institutional character and destruction of the individual personality that results from schools is a further concern.

Some writers would abolish the formalized educational system as it is known, whereas others would only seek to modify its structure severely (Reimer, 1972; Tracy, 1972). Countertheorists have been proposing changes to the educational system for years. In general, they are dissatisfied with the "system" of education that has evolved (Cleaver, 1968; Farber, 1970; Glasser, 1969; Goodman, 1964). They are also generally dissatisfied with the medical model of deviance (Szasz, 1961, 1970). Bron (1972:464) aptly stated the position of countertheorists: "There are no organizations, schools, publications, or authors which can lay exclusive claim to the title and thereby define the parameters to be explored. Each person is left to apply the label to whatever overlapping and divergent views strike some chord of recognition, some feeling of 'ah, here seems a thread of counter psychology.' "

Counter theory is needed. It adds a new dimension to educational thought. Although controversy often accompanies a new theoretical approach, there seems to be new growth by all professionals as a result of the theory.

In this chapter the contributions of three countertheorists, A. S. Neill, William Glasser, and Elliot Shapiro, will be discussed. These theorists were selected for several basic reasons. Glasser represents a "humanistic-behavioral approach," which emphasizes individual responsibility as a necessary component of mental health. Neill presents a contrast to Glasser's reality-oriented approach; whereas Glasser encourages the mainstreaming concept without labeling, Neill's approach separates the child from his peers in a "freedom oriented residential approach." Shapiro's work is described by Hentoff (1966). As a principal, working in Harlem, Shapiro blended hard work, a caring

attitude, and community involvement for productive educational programing.

A. S. Neill

The concept of education that Neill espouses in *Summerhill* might be described as a "free school." In a Summerhill school there are few demands placed on the students, with most issues being decided by each student having a single vote. Education in its traditional sense is a secondary issue at Summerhill with emphasis placed on students becoming healthy persons. In his forward to Neill's test, Erich Fromm lists ten principles that guide the work carried on at Summerhill.

1. There is a firm faith in the "goodness of the child."

2. The aim of education is to find happiness.

3. Education is both intellectual and emotional.

4. Education must be geared to the capacities of the individual child.

5. Extensive disciplining of the child should be avoided.

6. Freedom is important, but it is a mutual arrangement.

7. The child must be told the truth by his teachers.

8. Primary ties with parents must eventually be severed.

9. Guilt feelings impede growth toward independence.

10. No religious training is fostered at Summerhill.

Summerhill was started in 1921 in a village about 100 miles from London. Boys and girls may attend the residential school, which operates during the usual school term. Pupils generally do not come to the school before 5 years or after 15 years of age; however, they may remain past 16 years of age if they choose. Children come to the school from a variety of countries and for various reasons. Growing and developing into happy adults is Neill's wish for those children who come to Summerhill—happiness being the ability to find interest (Neill, 1960). The children who attend the school are often from middle to upper class families because of the high costs involved in maintaining a private facility.

Summerhill continues to be one of the most controversial of educational programs. It has been labeled a fraud, an atheistic institution, a holy place, a myth, a religion, permissive, a contradiction to reality, and the Dr. Spock of the next generation (Hart, 1970). When Neill's book on Summerhill is read and the arguments that surround the school are heard, it becomes obvious that many critics are drawing opinions about Summerhill that were never intended by Neill. Many question Neill's theory and his understanding, but few have questioned his sincerity and love for the children he served (Hart, 1970).

It appears that Neill's work is as he says it is—not theory, but the results of practice. As such, it often lacks the completeness and perhaps the logic of well-formed theory. It is a theory that is designed to refute the critics in addition to helping the children. One must also consider the man, A. S. Neill, who is the "soul" of Summerhill. Nearly everyone who has visited the school comes away with a belief in Neill the man, even though his system may not be accepted (Hart, 1970).

Among the factors that must be evaluated are the goals of the institution, the type of children served, and the setting of the school. When these three points are considered, Summerhill begins to take on a tarnished view as a public school model. The goals of Summerhill are admittedly different from those of the public school. The basis of Summerhill is isolation—isolation not for 6 months or a year, but for several years. The public school, on the other hand, is trying to maintain children as much as possible in the mainstream of education and life activities. Goals such as finding happiness and freedom appear to be unusual because of the words used rather than the ideas conveyed. Freedom in Summerhill does not mean license to do as one pleases but only the freedom to grow in a natural way without impeding the growth of others. To Neill, happiness is the aim of life. The goals of the typical

school include both intellectual and social learning. Although happiness and freedom are generally encouraged, they are not the *goals* of education.

The children served are also different. Neill's children have generally been "normal" children from homes that seek an alternative school for their children. Public school programs must deal with these children and many more severe cases of conflict. The school setting is probably the most contrasting element between Summerhill and the typical school system. Children live at Summerhill by their choice or that of their parents; people choose Summerhill. In the public schools choices are limited for the consumer by the nature of the school system—a system that is large, complex, and often cumbersome. Although many of the principles of Summerhill are attractive for children in conflict, the typical school does not offer an appropriate environment for implementing Neill's total theoretical approach. This does not mean that his theoretical construct cannot become a part of a teaching style of a given teacher, but carrying out a total Summerhill approach in a public school setting would appear to be an inappropriate consideration in view of the educational goals of the school as they now exist.

William Glasser

William Glasser was trained as a dynamically oriented psychiatrist. During his training he became convinced that traditional therapy, which stressed transference, exploration of the past, the unconscious, and interpretation of behavior was not meeting the needs of those under treatment. In his book, *Reality Therapy*, Glasser did not attempt to soften the Freudian concept but adopted a theoretical position that in many ways is in opposition to Freudian theory.

Glasser (1965) is opposed to labeling, and the system he proposes is geared to the mainstream of education. His opposition to labeling is based on the premise that deviance is an indication that the person is not meeting his essential needs. The degree of severity is determined by the extent that needs are not being met. Glasser is unable to explain why patients exhibit such a wide variety of inappropriate behaviors. In an effort to fulfill their needs these patients deny the reality of the world they live in. Glasser puts it this way:

> In their unsuccessful efforts to fulfill their needs, no matter what behavior they choose, all patients have a common characteristic: they all deny the reality of the world around them. Some break the law, denying the rules of society; some claim their neighbors are plotting against them, denying the improbability of such behavior. Some are afraid of crowded places, close quarters, airplanes, or elevators, yet they freely admit the irrationality of their fears. Millions drink to blot out the inadequacy they feel but that need not exist if they could learn to be different; and far too many people choose suicide rather than face the reality that they could solve their problems by more responsible behavior. Whether it is a partial denial or the total blotting out of all reality of the chronic backward patient in a state hospital, the denial of some or all of reality is common to all who exhibit deviant behavior. Therapy will be successful when they are able to give up denying the world and recognize that reality not only exists but that they must fulfill their needs within its framework. [1965:6]

Glasser defines reality therapy as "a therapy that leads all patients toward reality, toward grappling successfully with the tangible and intangible aspects of the real world, might accurately be called a therapy toward reality, or simply reality therapy" (1965:6).

The basic needs that are mentioned so often in reality therapy include the need to love and be loved and the need to feel worthwhile to ourselves and to others. These two basic needs are closely related, but they can and do stand alone. Human beings must not only love but be loved. Children must not only achieve for the satisfaction of those who care for them, but they must feel worthwhile themselves. Glasser says that to be worthwhile human beings must maintain a satisfactory standard of behavior by learning to correct themselves when they are wrong and to approve or reward themselves when they exhibit correct behavior.

The ability of individuals to fulfill their needs in a way that will not deprive others of the ability to fulfill their needs is called responsibility or acting responsibly. The responsible child then is the healthy child, whereas the irresponsible child is emotionally disabled (Glasser, 1965).

The task for teachers is to teach children to become more responsible. This is not an easy task; it takes extreme courage and unheralded dedication to stand firm in the process of teaching children in conflict. Holding firm in the face of a child's anger has given many teachers sore shins and numerous broken noses. Giving in to irresponsible behavior has caused much more serious and lasting damage for the child, even though the teacher might escape personal attack.

Glasser does not propose that teachers should become psychiatrists or usurp the professional relationship of the psychiatrist with the child. He suggests that teachers work more in a role of preventive therapy in the classroom. The difference is one of intensity; the psychiatrist works on a more intense level with children who are acting out their irresponsibility in ways totally unacceptable to the school situation.

Whether the therapeutic intervention is attempted by the psychiatrist, the teacher, or the parent, there are three basic steps to intervention. First, the therapist must achieve some level of involvement with the child; second, the therapist must reject the inappropriate behavior; and third, the therapist must teach the child more appropriate ways to fulfill his needs. The teacher has a real advantage in this scheme of intervention because involvement is not only the cornerstone of therapeutic intervention but of good teaching as well.

Reality therapy is concerned with behavior as well as with attitudes. It aligns itself with the behavioral approaches and with psychodynamic theory. As such, reality therapy does not rely on exacting behavioral techniques such as counting, charting, and direct reinforcement of appropriate behaviors, nor does it utilize strict psychological interpretation of life events and labeling as in dynamic orientation. It is concerned with psychic surface, with behavior that occurs now, and with the reality of these current behaviors. Although Glasser carefully avoids labeling himself, his behaviors seem to categorize him as a countertheorist.

Elliott Shapiro

Elliott Shapiro is a tough-minded realist, who has fought long and hard for children in his school. The book from which much information about him was gained is *Our Children Are Dying*, written by Nat Hentoff (1966).

Shapiro worked as the principal of Public School 119, a black school in Harlem. He supports the common claim of those who have experienced inner-city slum schools— that failure is due to poor schools rather than inferiority of children. His attack is from a position different from that taken by several other theorists, many of whom have never experienced what they attempt to change. Shapiro has not only been actively involved in the teaching-learning process with slum children but he also has developed a program to effectively change the children served. He has turned his frustrations and anger into productive programing for the culturally different child.

Children who are different, who cannot conform to the rituals established by the school such as appropriate behavior, have variously been labeled personality disordered, delinquent, troubled children, and culturally deprived. The labels have often been nothing more than salves to the educator's conscience and tools for further delay.

In reading about the work of Shapiro in a school that is 96% black, the balance being Puerto Rican and Chinese, the educator must be impressed with two factors. The first factor is his ability to attract and hold teachers who choose to work with children from a slum area. It is obvious, from the dialogue, that teachers are important in this school. Innovation is encouraged by the principal. The teachers tend to respond with a sincerity and warmth that give the children a message of caring and of hope. The second factor is Shapiro's willingness to enter a controversy if it will help the children he serves. Personnel at the school are encouraged to take a stand alongside parents when "issues which count" are being decided. Shapiro has been involved in getting better housing for parents, heating for apartments, and supplemental welfare payments for needy children. An example of Shapiro's willingness to "confront the system" was the "incident of the rat," which occurred after publication of an advertisement on the school page of the *World Telegram* on May 22, 1961. The advertisement outlined, in eleven separate items, the problems faced by children who must attend school in a building constructed in 1899. The advertisement was paid for by teaching, clerical, and administrative staff of Public School 119. Item number one indicated that the school was infested with rats and roaches on every floor. Response came quickly in the form of news media and television cameras. Mayor Robert Wagner visited the school shortly after the advertisement appeared, and this is when the rat incident occurred. While touring the building, the group entered the auditorium. Suddenly a teacher and group of children pointed to a corner and yelled, "Rat!" Shapiro seized a broom and chased the rat back into his hole before the mayor could actually see the rodent. Higher administrators yelled "Foul" and said that the incident was rigged, but repairs were eventually made. Incidently, exterminators worked during the following Memorial Day weekend and killed forty rats in the school.

This is not the first time a staff member has put his "job on the line" for what he believed, but it does represent doing something for children. Teachers have often been accused of getting involved only when trivial matters were at stake or only when salaries were being discussed. Shapiro and his staff have been extremely successful at getting meaningful parent involvement and developing trust among parents.

It is interesting to note that success in an inner-city school is often based on the teacher's willingness and ability to become meaningfully involved with children, parents, and the school community. Teachers who have worked in both inner-city schools and rural schools often draw similar comparisons regarding their expected roles in community involvement. Teachers are expected to live, shop, and seek social interaction within the community. They are often distrusted if they "escape" to a neighboring city to live or to entertain themselves, even on weekends. The people who live in these communities are often defensive about their life-style. Any teacher behavior that suggests nonacceptance of the community is seriously questioned by those who live there.

Shapiro has made a real contribution to children in need. His work has not been marked as a fly-by-night operation. He was born in Brooklyn in 1911, taught in the children and adolescent wards of Bellevue Hospital, and developed a day school for disturbed children. His work shows one way to help children in conflict through understanding, enthusiasm, conviction, and a tough-minded realism (Hentoff, 1966).

Vignette 2: Reality therapy with an entire sixth grade class

Description of class

Children from this sixth grade class included twenty-nine boys and six girls. They are from the lowest section academically of all the sixth grade students, numbering approximately 120. They live in a middle to lower middle class environment, and their parents have occupations including skilled labor, blue collar work, nonskilled labor, and some unemployed. The boys were generally showing acting-out aggressive behavior, whereas the girls tended to be very withdrawing in their behavior.

Educational information

The grade point average for this class was about 2 years below expected grade achievement. The parents were generally supportive of school activities but tended toward punishment as a way of solving educational problems that their children encountered. There was a noticeable lack of interest in educational activities by the students. Homework was seldom if ever completed, and classroom assignments generally were ignored.

Psychological information

Group intelligence testing indicated that the class was in the normal range of intelligence. A few of the children had been identified as

having emotional problems, and some borderline retarded children were included in the class. In addition, two mildly crippled children and one visually impaired child were members of the class. There were extensive psychological workups available to the classroom teacher for the exceptional children.

Implementation of reality therapy

It was decided to implement reality therapy techniques for two basic purposes: (1) to hold students in the classroom responsible for their own behavior and (2) to establish group meetings each day to get individual children's feelings out into the open where they could be dealt with.

Evaluation of reality therapy

Through continued efforts of the classroom teacher to hold each pupil responsible for his or her own behavior, students gradually developed more self-responsibility. The aggressiveness, fighting behavior, and tattling behavior decreased remarkably. This was a slow process with many regressions. The group meetings generally deteriorated into gripe sessions about other teachers and about other kids on the playground. After the first 3 weeks it was decided to suspend the group meetings of a therapeutic type, except when classroom situations indicated a need. Other class meetings were held around academic areas with discussion topics being announced and each child doing a small amount of research to prepare for the discussion. Using this method, the class meetings improved significantly. Problems around behavior, social interaction, and feelings were handled in class meetings, but these occurred only sporadically throughout the school year. The students learned many discussion skills, were able to give and take, to take turns, to listen, and to evaluate ideas through the process of group meetings. In addition, class meetings proved to be highly supportive for those who need to let their feelings out in a group situation. Some of the children never felt comfortable in the class meetings and continued to withdraw from interaction with more than one person.

As a result of this experience, the classroom teacher believed that class meetings, designed for therapeutic value, were unnecessary on a daily basis but should be used only as needed to support individuals within the class. Other days could better be utilized in educational types of meetings as described by Glasser (1969).

Vignette 3: Diet control and behavior
Reported by Powers (1973-1974)
The relationship of blood glucose (CHO foods) and brain metabolism are studied in this research report. A total of 260 children with behavioral and learning problems are reported in the study, and several cases are discussed briefly on an individual basis. The workup for each child was strictly a medical one; with assessment of "soft" neurological signs, routine laboratory studies (blood count, urinalysis, glucose tolerance test), and additional medical studies as needed.

Studies centered around the glucose curves (milligrams of blood glucose present over a period of time) of each child. Generally it was found that children's blood glucose levels (1) were too high for too long a period, (2) were too high followed by too great a drop, and (3) remained at a "flat" level.

Treatment centered around (1) the limitation of carbohydrates and the exclusion of sugar, stimulant beverages, and cola drinks, (2) the administration of digestive enzymes to promote the use of protein as a source of glucose, (3) the supplement of concentrated vitamins B and C, (4) vitamin and mineral additives, and (5) hormonal supplements when needed.

Powers' studies suggest that the regulation of carbohydrates and blood glucose levels has a considerable impact on the behavioral and learning problems of children and that all problems do not emanate from environmental stress or inadequate teaching.

SUMMARY

The teacher's role in the biophysical system is a limited one. It evolves around supporting the physician as a professional observer and co-worker for behavior change in the child. Obviously, the teacher does not prescribe medication or give medication to the child. The teacher can report the effects of medication on the child's behavior in the classroom.

Biophysical intervention centers around three important areas, including medical evaluation, manipulation of physiological functions, and treatment of symptoms.

The Re-Ed process is discussed as one possible sociological/ecological system of intervention. Although the Re-Ed approach has generally been labeled a pull-out program, many variations of the program have been implemented in public school classes. The basic premise of this approach is aptly stated by a process of thirteen reeducation principles, which include life is to be lived now, time is an ally, trust is essential, competence makes the difference, symptoms can and should be controlled, cognitive control can be taught, feelings should be nurtured, the group is important, a child should know joy, and middle class values should be taught.

In this chapter three countertheorists were presented. The first was the Summerhill residential school concept of A. S. Neill. Ten principles are outlined that guide the work carried on in Summerhill, including a firm faith of the goodness of the child, the aim of education is to find happiness, education is both intellectual and emotional, education must be geared to the capacities of the individual child, extensive disciplining of the child should be avoided, freedom is important but it is a mutual arrangement, the child must be told the truth by teachers, primary ties with parents must eventually be severed, guilt feelings impede growth toward independence, and no religious training is fostered. The Summerhill concept represents one of the most controversial of educational programs. It has been called a fraud, a myth, and a contradiction to reality.

The second countertheorist is William Glasser, who defines reality therapy as therapy that leads all patients toward reality, toward grappling successfully with the tangible and the intangible aspects of the real world. It might accurately be called therapy toward reality or simply reality therapy. Whereas much of Glasser's theory appears to be behavioral, his theory also encompasses a humanistic bent, which relates more closely to psychodynamic theory.

The third countertheorist studied is Elliott Shapiro. Shapiro's theory of working in an inner-city minority school leans toward a sociological or an ecological emphasis. Shapiro tends to blame the failure of children on poor schools rather than inferiority of the children who attend them. He believes that teachers should not only be active in the teaching-learning process but also should interact intensively with children outside the school, in their homes, and in their communities. Success of the school can probably be attributed to Shapiro's ability to attract and hold outstanding teachers, allowing them the freedom and security to be innovative, and his ability to be intimately involved with the community without being inundated by it.

A series of three vignettes are presented that suggest practical applications for the theoretical constructs presented.

BIBLIOGRAPHY AND SELECTED READINGS

Bron, A.: Some strands within counter psychology. In Rhodes, W. C. A study of child variance, Ann Arbor, Mich., 1972, The University of Michigan Press.

Cleaver, E.: Soul on ice, New York, 1968, McGraw-Hill Book Co.

Farber, J.: The student as nigger, ed. 2, New York, 1970, Pocket Books.

Glasser, W.: Reality therapy, New York, 1965, Harper & Row, Publishers.

Glasser, W.: Schools without failure, New York, 1969, Harper & Row, Publishers.

Goodman, P.: Compulsory miseducation: community of scholars, New York, 1964, Vintage Books, Inc., Division of Random House, Inc.

Hart, H., editor: Summerhill: for and against, New York, 1970, Hart Publishing Co., Inc.

Hentoff, N.: Our children are dying, New York, 1966, The Viking Press, Inc.

Hobbs, N.: Helping disturbed children: psychological and ecological strategies, American Psychologist **21:** 1105-1115, 1966.

Lee, B.: Curriculum design: the re-education approach. In Long, N., Morse, W., and Newman, R., editors: Conflict in the classroom, Belmont, Calif., 1971, Wadsworth Publishing Co., Inc.

Lewis, W.: Project Re-ed: educational intervention in discordant child rearing systems. In Cowen, E., Gardner, E., and Zax, M., editors: Emergent approaches to mental health problems, New York, 1967, Appleton-Century-Crofts.

Neill, A.: Summerhill, New York, 1960, Hart Publishing Co., Inc.

Powers, H.: Dietary measures to improve behavior and achievement, Academic Therapy **9:**203-214, Winter, 1973-1974.

Reimer, E.: Unusual ideas in education. In Rhodes, W. C.: A study of child variance, Ann Arbor, Mich., 1972, The University of Michigan Press.

State of Tennessee: One child: a case study, Department of Mental Health (grant from National Institute of Mental Health).

Szasz, T.: The myth of mental illness: foundations of a theory of personal conduct, New York, 1961, Harper & Row, Publishers.

Tracy, M.: Conceptual models of emotional disturbance: some other thoughts. In Rhodes, W. C.: A study of child variance, Ann Arbor, Mich., 1972, The University of Michigan Press.

Weinstein, L.: Project Re-ed: schools for emotionally disturbed children—effectiveness as viewed by referring agencies, parents and teachers, Exceptional Children **35:**703-711, 1969.

CHAPTER 7

A synthesis of theoretical positions and classroom application: case studies

This chapter will show how various theoretical constructs can be molded together into a workable educational program for children. Although the various component theories have been studied individually, it has been consistently pointed out that in the reality of the public school the clear-cut models generally do not exist. The child with only one problem is an exception rather than the rule; the child with a variety of problems is the rule. To cope with the numerous problems presented by children in conflict and to prepare to interact with a variety of professionals and staff the teacher must be able to orchestrate many points of view. The teacher must be able to separate the real problems from the superficial, to select the right technique for each problem, and to have the patience and determination to follow through despite the temptation to give up.

The various theoretical constructs are generally easier to reconcile in practice than in theory, probably because the practitioner has no better alternative than to bring harmony through their use. A theoretical construct (Fig. 7-1) will be used to indicate how this reconciliation can be made.

Several rather significant relationships can be illustrated by this diagram.

1. The child is the center of the theoretical construct, not only being acted on by those around him, but in turn interacting on the environment.

2. Biophysical factors form the base on which the child develops. When biophysical factors are intact, the child has a solid foundation on which to develop. Conversely, if the biophysical foundation is impaired through prenatal or postnatal injury, genetic accident, or a chemical imbalance, the child has a shaky base on which to grow.

3. The legs of the triangle include the behavioral and psychodynamic factors that help the child to develop into a wholesome individual. Behavioral factors include learned behaviors, both appropriate and inappropriate, that shape a child's future. As the child grows, his psychological development has an effect on his personality. The resolution of childhood conflicts and child-rearing practices helps to determine the child's eventual mental health.

4. The two concentric circles totally surround the child and all other theoretical con-

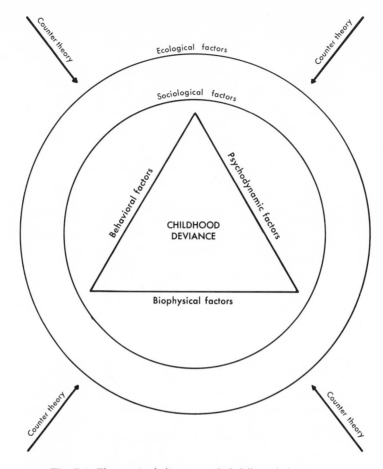

Fig. 7-1. Theoretical diagram of childhood deviance.

structs. Social and ecological theory bring a wholeness to the otherwise fractured interpretation of personality development.

If a teacher looks at one theoretical approach as having all of the answers for children in conflict, it is similar to looking at only part of the diagram; one side of the triangle hardly presents the total picture of personality.

To demonstrate how a child might be studied from several viewpoints a series of case studies will be presented and analyzed to show their various theoretical components.

The case studies that follow all represent real cases involving children who have been identified as having various behavioral or emotional conflicts. They come from a variety of settings and represent a cross section of problems in school. Specific cases were selected for their interest, genuineness, and

usefulness for discussion. Names, places, and any other factors that might lead to specific identification of children have been changed to preserve anonymity of all concerned.

CASE 1 (Tony P.)
Personal data

Tony is a 14-year-old boy whose small stature (4 feet 9 inches; 82 pounds) and young features give him the appearance of an 8- or 9-year old instead of a teen-ager. He is Chicano and speaks fluent Spanish (mainly in the home), although he has no Spanish accent when speaking English. He is a very attractive boy physically.

Tony has two older brothers, Alberto, 16 years, and Roberto, 15 years, and one younger brother Richard, 9 years. Tony has two younger sisters, Maria, 6 years, and Belin, 1½ years. All the children except the baby are attending the public school and are doing extremely well. Tony is the middle child and is the only one who did not adjust well to school.

Tony lives with his mother and stepfather (whom she married in 1971) in project housing. His stepfather works at night as an assembly-line man in a mattress factory. He is a rather passive man (34 years old) who speaks little English. Tony's mother is a lively woman (30 years old) who did most of the talking during the interview. One of the first things she said was that Tony had a normal childbirth, although she went into some detail in saying that she was running from Tony's natural father when she was pregnant with Tony and had a terrible fall. She states that Tony slept "day and night" after birth until he was about 1 year old. She stated that when she wanted him awake, she had to keep him awake and even this did not work. Since he seldom cried, she never sought a medical examination or advice concerning his sleeping problem. Mrs. P. stressed that Tony's natural father is an alcoholic. She said that Tony was very close to his natural father and may have been hurt by their divorce in 1970.

There seems to be a symbiotic relationship between Tony and his mother for several reasons. Tony was sick as a child and required much more of his mother's time than did the other children. She was constantly needing to meet his needs, and for unknown reasons she has continued to relate to him as more important than the other children. She seems guilty and defensive about her marriage to her present husband to the extent that she may be feeling that Tony's needs should come before hers. If she projects this feeling to Tony, the relationship of his behavior to the home situation becomes clear. His acting out began at the same time she remarried. He exhibited temper tantrums regularly to assert his need to be of first importance to his mother. This problem is further compounded by the fact that Mrs. P. must spend time away from the home helping to support the family.

Behavior

Tony has had a history of deviant behavior both during and outside school. School problems include erratic school performance, tantrums, and emotional outbursts. Tony's activities outside school were largely responsible for his being labeled as deviant and in need of special help.

Tony was somewhat successful at stealing;

however, this activity led to serious problems with police. He was charged with a total of nine burglaries, although the police believe he was involved in approximately 125 such actions. He is presently serving a 2-year probation term.

Psychological data

Wechsler Intelligence Scale for Children

Full scale	IQ 73
Verbal scale	IQ 74
Performance scale	IQ 78

On the triad of subtests most specifically related to verbal comprehension, Tony attained a prorated IQ of 69. On the triads related to attention-concentration and perceptual-analytical factors Tony attained prorated scores of 62 and 80, respectively. From this information one could judge Tony's performance to be in the low normal range.

Bender-Gestalt test. There is evidence of perceptual difficulty. Tony exhibited three rotations of 180 degrees as well as some more minor difficulties in angulation and closure of figures. Sometimes during this test he switched his pencil and seemed confused as to which hand he should write with. There are indications that he may have a generalized difficulty in laterality and problems crossing the midline.

Rorschach test. There is some indication of pathological thinking and also evidence of confused thinking processes. There was, for example, a fusion of responses on two cards so that the same part of the blot was two different objects at the same time as far as Tony was concerned. It is difficult to tell whether this relates to primarily emotional or primarily perceptual difficulties.

Educational information

Tony's functional level in school-related tasks was extremely low. He is working at first grade level tasks in both reading and arithmetic.

Chronological age 14-0
Peabody Individual Achievement Test

	Grade equivalent
Reading recognition	1.4
Reading comprehension	Preschool
Spelling	1.4
General information	4.0
Wide Range Achievement Test	
Mathematics	3.6
No other WRAT scores available	

Teacher evaluation: Functioning much below grade level

Medical evaluation

All areas of the medical evaluation were within the normal range, including physical examination, visual acuity, and auditory acuity. His electroencephalogram was in the borderline range, although this should not be indicative in itself of an organic pathology.

Summary statement

In summary, Tony can be considered a moderately disturbed youngster who, under conditions of stress, is capable of functioning in a psychotic-like fashion. It would not seem appropriate to label him as a childhood schizophrenic. There is evidence of a moderate perceptual difficulty, and there is some substantiation for organic difficulty in a borderline abnormal electroencephalographic record. It would appear that the emotional difficulties, in conjunction with an underlying perceptual deficit, can well account for periods of erratic and sometimes explosive behavior.

Intervention strategies

From all that can be learned from this case it is apparent that the school and community made minimal efforts at solving Tony's problems. He received some individual help in school, but nothing of great duration or intensity. The lone exception to this was a 6-month placement in a nearby residential treatment center for emotionally disturbed children. He apparently "adjusted well" to this situation but little change occurred.

Shortly after Tony's return to the community and school he was caught burglarizing a home in the neighborhood (fingerprint identification). He went to trial in the Fall of 1974 and was found guilty. His probation officer is attempting to have him placed in a closed treatment center for adolescents.

Theoretical interpretation

In this section I will attempt to raise specific questions and in some cases make recommendations regarding the case under discussion. These recommendations are made after reviewing the data and visiting with concerned persons surrounding the case.

Each case in this chapter will be viewed in essentially the same way: (1) by viewing the case from each theoretical position, that is, psychodynamic, behavioral, biophysical, sociological/ecological, and counter theory and (2) suggesting alternative courses of action

if appropriate. I will not attempt to raise *all* of the possible questions that could be considered, but only practical ones that might be realistically pursued.

Psychodynamic position. Several questions regarding Tony's personality development could be explored.

1. Has Tony's only success been in stealing?
2. What is the specific nature of Tony's apparent pathological relationship with his mother?
3. What is the mother's emotional maturity in regard to her family and her husband?
4. What recommendations could the psychologist make to the school regarding Tony's abnormal Rorschach test?
5. What is the family relationship?

Behavioral position
1. What problem behaviors actually exist (baseline information)?
2. What is reinforcing the stealing behavior?
3. What is reinforcing Tony's avoidance of learning tasks?
4. What is reinforcing Tony's tantrum behaviors?

Biophysical position
1. Are other factors such as biochemical imbalance or diet a consideration that should be evaluated?
2. Could perceptual problems have significant impact on Tony's performance of educational tasks?
3. Would drug therapy affect his extreme tantrum behaviors?
4. Is Tony receiving adequate rest and a proper diet?

Sociological/ecological position
1. Is Tony's tantrum behavior a legitimate effort on his part to gain his mother's attention?
2. What is the dynamic interaction that exists within the family constellation?
3. What is the present family posture in terms of supervision outside of school?

Counter theory position. It is difficult to consider individual concerns that might be raised in this case, since countertheorists do not follow any predictable pattern (other than divergence).

Questions that could be asked might include the following considerations:

1. The need for Tony to learn the educational skills required by the school
2. The relative problems of Tony as op-

posed to those of a "sick" environment which (a) allows children to go unsupervised, encourages family problems through job scarcity, and forces both parents to work to supply necessary material goods, (b) requires success in superficial and unimportant school activities, and (c) discriminates against minority groups, which often adds to school frustration

Alternative courses of action

When everything is considered, it seems that Tony's case evolves around two important issues: (1) the social and cultural interaction, which is generally inappropriate, and (2) educational programing, which appears to be far less than might be expected. These two problems are mutually supportive in that they often lead to a circular stimulation that grows to encompass more of Tony's life. Although other theoretical concerns should not be ignored, the social/ecological, the behavioral, and to a lesser degree the psychological area should be emphasized. The following procedures would appear to be helpful.

1. A complete family social evaluation should be undertaken to determine the interaction of Tony and his family. This evaluation should lead to a determination of goals and activities within the family that could promote (a) attention and reinforcement for appropriate behaviors, (b) realistic monitoring of after-school activities, and (c) additional activities as determined in the evaluation.

2. If at all possible, Tony should be maintained in his home with support to the family or in a structured group home rather than a state institution.

3. Family support as needed should be made available to ensure Tony's success in the home environment.

4. A structured behavior management program appears to be a viable alternative for Tony during school time. Tony should be allowed to earn free time or tokens, which could be turned in for small objects. The ability to earn small items and receive attention for this could have a positive effect on his stealing activities.

5. Educational tasks need to be geared to Tony's chronological age level of interest while remaining concrete enough to allow success. Work-oriented emphasis would seem to be appropriate.

6. Relationships between the home and school need to be nurtured through the efforts of the teacher or a specialist.

7. In addition to the behavior management program developed at school the parents might be trained to recognize and reinforce appropriate behaviors as they occur within the family.

8. Crisis intervention in the form of life space interview techniques should supplement the natural consequences of the reinforcement system.

9. Family therapy sessions designed to modify and work through family problems might serve a useful purpose. Much of this effort would depend on the outcome of the family evaluation discussed in number 1.

CASE 2 (Kenny)
Personal data and behavior

Kenny is now 12 years old. He is the third child of a family of four children with two brothers, aged 16 and 18 years and a sister aged 8. Both parents are well educated. The father with a Ph.D. works in a specialized scientific field, and the mother with a master's degree is a full-time homemaker. Family life appears to be stable although not a typical life-style. Kenny is a handsome child who appears to be loved and well cared for. He can be sweet and loving with an endearing quality that is irresistible. He is aware of his charm and often uses it for his own desires.

At the age of 4 years Kenny attended a special school where he exhibited hyperkinetic behavior, expressed wishes to burn the school, and verbalized his desire to attack teachers. His psychiatrist recommended patience, firmness, supervised large muscle play, and constant presence of an authority figure to help control his impulses.

Kenny has been a student in an open-space concept school for almost 6 years and has not been labeled as emotionally disturbed but, rather, was integrated into the regular class activities with all modifications of work or therapy done in the class setting. This is not to say that anyone is unaware that he is different. His bizarre behavior is unlikely to go unnoticed by teachers, classmates, neighbors, or even casual visitors to the school.

Kenny has had and continues to have a problem in relations with his peers. Because of behavior patterns that are rarely acceptable by social standards, many parents do not consider Kenny a good playmate for their children. Those who do accept him as a friend find it difficult to understand his uncontrolled outbursts. Adults often find these same outbursts, foul language, inappropriate gestures, refusal to cooperate, and lack of responsible behavior intolerable.

Psychological data

Extensive testing has been done with Kenny. The following test scores are representative.

Chronological age 6-3
Wechsler Intelligence Scale for Children
Verbal scores   5-5   20%   Slow learner
               (mental age)
Peabody Picture   5-10   41%   Average
   Vocabulary   (mental age)
   Test
Bender-Gestalt Test
   Koppitz scoring: Maturation level is prekindergarten; many psychological indicators of brain dysfunction

Personality assessment

Children's Apperception Test: Emotionally disturbed
Wechsler Intelligence Scale for Children
   Verbal scale   IQ 87

Educational information

Chronological age 10-5
Peabody Individual Achievement Test

	Raw score	Grade equivalent
Mathematics	15	1.1
Reading recognition	27	2.6
Reading comprehension	No basal	
Spelling	27	2.5
General information	23	3.4

Illinois Test of Psycholinguistic Abilities

	Raw score	Age equivalent
Auditory reception	38	9-2
Visual reception	27	8-10
Visual memory	8	3-10
Auditory association	35	10-1
Auditory memory	30	8-8
Visual association	24	7-2
Visual closure	25	7-6
Motor expression	32	10-4

Auditory channel appears stronger than visual; visual sequential memory is very impaired and area needing most help
Peabody Picture Vocabulary Test
   Chronological age 12
   Raw score 89   IQ 106
   Percentile 73   Mental age 12-9

Detroit Tests of Learning Aptitude
   Chronological age 12-5

	Raw score	Age equivalent
Verbal absurdities	28	13-0
Verbal opposites	42	10-6

Informal Reading Inventory
   I.R.I. word recognition list—grade equivalent
     Independent level 4-1
     Instructional level 4-5
   Informal reading passages—Betts series based
     Independent level 3-5
     Instructional level 4-1

Kenny has developed good word skills and makes use of them in decoding words in a list. Good comprehension is lacking in silent reading. In directed oral reading, comprehension is adequate at the fourth grade level. Reading level is subject to variation according to emotional attitude at the time of testing.

Medical evaluation

Kenny was born after a full-term pregnancy and was normal weight. His mother reported no medical problems other than some bronchial problems during pregnancy. Kenny did not walk until 2½ or 3 years of age. He did not talk until 3 years of age. At 2 years of age he had surgery for muscle imbalance in his right eye. At 4 years of age he had an operation on his left eye. He began receiving psychotherapy in the city of his former residence at the age of 4 years.

An electroencephalogram done in June, 1969, was within normal limits. Hyperactivity and distractibility were not modified by methylphenidate (Ritalin) in 1969. He has not received such medication since.

At the present time (1974) Kenny appears physically healthy and of normal size and strength for his age.

Intervention strategies

The efforts of the school to keep Kenny in the mainstream of educational reality are commendable. The teacher reports that Kenny has made some academic gains but still lacks friends among children of his own age. His relationships with adults are still erratic, although there is some improvement. A regular classroom placement has been chosen for Kenny because he tends to mirror the behavior of those around him. Providing appropriate behavior models was believed to be helpful in this regard.

Kenny is being seen by a psychiatrist in private practice who has been helpful and supportive to teachers and parents. He has basically been advocating the use of a behavioral approach, although some play therapy, leathercraft, music therapy, and puppetry have been used. With so many different adults interacting with Kenny it is difficult for everyone to be consistent with their expectations and reward systems. There are some indications that Kenny is capitalizing on this by manipulation of the situation whenever possible.

Theoretical interpretation

Psychodynamic position. Several questions arise from statements that teachers have made and behaviors Kenny has exhibited:
1. Several resent behaviors, that is, bringing soiled diapers to school daily for several weeks and "finding" matches in great numbers, which could be explored with Kenny.
2. Now that Kenny is 12 years old could he talk through his problems with the psychiatrist in addition to the behavior modification techniques being applied?

Behavioral position
1. Kenny's teacher reports that he responds well with consistent treatment. Could a management system be employed that would ensure consistency?
2. Emphasis on punishment should generally be avoided. Kenny apparently allows punishment to take away his guilt for inappropriate behavior; that is, he often washes his mouth out with soap (voluntarily) when he says a nasty word.
3. Behavioral emphasis toward building peer relationships could be encouraged more strongly.
4. What is reinforcing Kenny's lack of responsiveness to his peers?

Biophysical position. The electroencephalogram report for Kenny stated that everything measured within the normal range. No physical disabilities were noted, and no suspicions of medical problems are present. Although his behavior sometimes indicates an internal drive that could be biophysically oriented, no objective measures that have been used support this notion.

Sociological/ecological position. The school has apparently done a good job in the social area. Labels have been generally avoided, and intervention efforts have been developed. The teachers and family know he needs help and are getting help for him. Little has been said regarding the relationship of the parents to Kenny, except that the father holds a Ph.D. and mother a master's degree. It might be helpful to explore the interaction that is ongoing between Kenny and his parents as well as his brothers and sisters. Having parents who are well educated has certain advantages and certain disadvantages and cannot be judged on external appearances alone.

Counter theory position. A case could be made for allowing Kenny to work more independently within the school as long as he would pay a price for inappropriate behavioral choices. He comes from a well-educated family and has a different life-style from that of most children. A school environment that would allow the freedom to choose, to decide, and to do with only the natural consequences of success and failure might provide Kenny with the treatment he seems to want and perhaps need.

Alternative courses of action

The behavioral approach seems to offer the best hope for Kenny at present. When the demands are simple and inappropriate behavior is met with the expected response, Kenny seems to get the security he needs. He likes token rewards but is becoming better able to exhibit appropriate behavior for merely the reward of a pat on the shoulder or a sincere word of praise. He also responds well to the reward of added responsibility that improves his self-concept, for example, being allowed to assist with media equipment for other areas, to help younger children with simple drill work, or to perform on the drums for younger children, although he cannot yet handle this with his own age level. His teacher believes that he would make progress if he had one accepting, primary relationship with someone with whom he could identify. Although several people have partially filled this role, his teacher believes he has not yet developed adequate primary relationships.

It appears that the school and home are providing a good program for Kenny. One notable exception exists. Coordination of effort seems to be a problem that threatens to disrupt progress. This coordination could probably be developed through brief meetings (maybe once a week for a few minutes) of all those interacting with Kenny or through the efforts of one adult, for example, the classroom teacher or resource teacher coordinating the work with Kenny.

CASE 3 (Bobby)
Personal data and behavior

Bobby is 9 years 4 months of age; he appears well kept but slightly heavy for his age and height. He seems to be in constant motion —shifting his feet, cracking his knuckles, and moving his eyes. In times of stress his eyelids drop half-shut, and he seems to peer from under them.

Bobby's mother works to support Bobby and herself. She has been divorced for 2 years and dates frequently. She is concerned about Bobby but is confused about ways to handle him. She is willing to come to conferences and to supply Bobby with the support she can offer.

Bobby is unable to contain his impulses in neighborhood activities. He has no apparent respect for property boundaries or landscaping niceties. He is destructive with his own toys and others' toys. He uses obscene language, and neighborhood parents do not allow him to play with their children or to come in their homes. During leisure time Bobby often loiters in the nearby shopping center or watches television.

Bobby demonstrates aggressive behavior in all school activities. He uses verbal and physical aggression in the classroom, teasing, ridiculing, hitting, and tripping his peers. His acting-out behaviors disrupt playground activities and cause him continually to be involved in fights. He has no close friends but seems to attract others into breaking the rules with him, after which he loudly blames them for his troubles.

Psychological data

Chronological age 9-4
Wechsler Intelligence Scale for Children
Full scale	IQ 91
Verbal scale	IQ 83
Performance scale	IQ 98

The drawing he made of himself was only 1½ inches high with no facial features except the ears, only one hand, and no other distinctive body parts included.

Educational information

Chronological age 9-4
Illinois Test of Psycholinguistic Abilities
Language age	8-10

Peabody Individual Achievement Test
	Grade equivalent
Reading recognition	1.8
Reading comprehension	2.0
Spelling	2.4
Arithmetic	3.1
General information	3.7

Medical evaluation

Bobby is within the normal range in both auditory and visual acuity. He is physically healthy and normal, as documented by an apparent comprehensive medical examination.

Intervention strategies

Bobby has been maintained in the regular classroom with the help of professional staff consisting of a resource room teacher who works with him for 30 minutes, 4 days a week, and counseling at a local mental health center. He is also being seen in the corrective reading program within the school. In addition, Bobby has been on 10 mg. Ritalin, morning and noon.

Bobby has made little, if any, progress in developing satisfactory emotional stability; however, a limited gain in academic progress has been noted. His social relationships are bitter and frustrating to him, and his aggressive behavior continues.

Theoretical interpretation

Psychodynamic position. This case certainly raises some serious questions regarding Bobby's level of personality development and his self-image. Both the drawing of himself and teacher observations support this contention.

Since Bobby has been receiving therapy at the local mental health center without apparent success, it seems that a change in strategy would be indicated. It appears important for the therapist and teacher to decide on future therapy in terms of the following questions.

1. Should therapy continue?
2. Should the therapy become part of daily school activities or be isolated from school?
3. What is the relationship between Bobby and his mother?
4. Could some male adult relationships be developed for Bobby?

5. Would further psychological evaluation be of any benefit?

Behavioral position. The record indicates that the behavior modification techniques employed with Bobby were of little sophistication, since his teacher, in her first year, was at a loss as to the correct teaching procedures. Several questions might help bring out important behavioral concerns.

1. What is maintaining Bobby's aggressive and antisocial acts?
2. What is the exact nature of Bobby's problems (number of times deviant acts are exhibited, etc.)?
3. What contingencies would Bobby work for?
4. Could behavior modification techniques be used to build a better self-image for Bobby?
5. Could behavior counting and charting help to identify areas of success and failure?

Biophysical position. The medical information makes no mention of any medical problems; however, medication is being prescribed with no evidence of success. It seems that this practice should be explored carefully by those competent to evaluate such procedures. Unless some defensible rationale and/or success with medication can be shown, it should be discontinued in favor of other intervention techniques.

Sociological/ecological position. A study should be made to determine Bobby's relationship to his mother, other adults, and children in his school environment. The personal records yield little information regarding social history. Bobby's problems appear to include more than school conflicts. A comprehensive evaluation of these relationships would be helpful in planning a coordinated effort between home and school in helping Bobby to solve his problems. Three comments made in the cumulative record indicate that many of the problems could be related, that is, (1) the child's father has moved out of state and has no contact with Bobby; (2) Bobby's mother dates frequently; and (3) the father does not support the family, so that Bobby's mother must work outside the home. These comments could prove to be useful leads in gaining the information necessary to develop a program for Bobby.

Counter theory position. Several questions might be asked by those who look at this case from nontraditional viewpoints.

1. Is Bobby really the problem or are his reactions correct in view of the situation? Bobby has had little opportunity to develop a male image and has been deserted by his father, and his mother has had a series of male companions. What does this do for his self-image?
2. Is Bobby simply fulfilling the expectations of a system that labels him as deviant both overtly and covertly?
3. What is the probability of success for Bobby as long as he is forced to live in an environment that is hostile to the goals he is asked to achieve?

Alternative courses of action

Since almost every child is adequate in some areas, whether art, music rhythms, identifying dinosaurs, assembling things, telling time, or whatever it is, this is an area for beginning remediation. Bobby's scores on the Peabody Individual Achievement Test indicate an adequacy in mathematics, in which he performs at grade level. This seems an excellent place to afford him more feelings of success. He could be paired with a child who has great difficulty in mathematics so that he could be helpful and improve his own self-image. Since his visual perceptions are adequate and his general information level is at grade level, he evidently has interests and is absorbing information from his environment. His interests should be discovered, and learning activities with visual emphasis could be launched from these interests. Praise for small successes should be enthusiastic and direct. Approximations of assignments should be accepted and validated in the same way. "Sandwich praise," a kind of praise often used by teachers and parents, which places the compliment between two requirements or criticisms—"You should try to be neater. The work is good. Try not to erase so much next time"—should be avoided. Details are unimportant in the beginning and should be ignored if the learning activity has been completed and understood.

Since Bobby will make little progress academically until he learns to control his behavior and to attend, both of these areas must be remediated. A behavioral system might be set up to modify his disruptive activities and help him work toward a goal of self-control. He probably would need a token economy initially; hopefully, as his self-image improves, it could change to a social reward system—something that would bolster pride in accomplishment. Any behavior that reflects a change toward better social adjustment must receive immediate and enthusiastic reinforcement.

Academic work that Bobby can handle and that seems pleasant, such as dot-to-dot mathematics and phonic activities, maze puzzles, film loops for viewing and writing about, and programed reading materials, might help Bobby to lengthen his attention span. A token economy of behavior modification might be helpful here too.

Although a teacher can use behavior modification, a humanistic approach, and emotional first aid on the spot with each disruptive action that Bobby demonstrates, these will not be adequate interventions to treat his basic problems. He is in need of every supporting service available. If possible, he should be referred for counseling both at school and at a mental health center. A social worker could help in the home, giving Bobby's mother support in mediating the neighborhood situation. Bobby could also receive valuable therapy from a "Big brother" program, filling his need for a male image or model.

Of primary importance for all professionals who are helping Bobby, is the establishment of rapport and a relationship of trust with him—becoming real friends. His anger, frustrations, and verbal and physical aggressions must not be accepted; however, he must be recognized as a person while inappropriate behaviors are changed. Acceptable alternative behaviors should be suggested, and at the same time impending aggressive behavior should be prevented if possible. Rules should be clearly defined; Bobby should be reminded of the rules occasionally and supported even when he breaks them.

The class as a whole will be well aware of Bobby's problems from his behavior, and they can be a reservoir of support or of frustration for him. Sessions in Magic Circle (a discussion technique) could be helpful in stimulating emotional growth and in understanding feelings surrounding Bobby's situation. The ability of individuals to know and respect their own and others' feelings, the ability to recognize their own and others' energy and how individuals do and do not control this energy, and the consequences of these feelings and energies can all be explored in Magic Circle. Bobby would need to interact with the group in these sessions and, hopefully, would eventually respond to the motivations evident in these activities. The other children will also be made aware of how Bobby manipulates their own feelings and will become less vulnerable to his attempts to lure them into deviant behaviors.

Behavior counting would seem to be mandatory, regardless of the therapeutic approach undertaken, to determine the effects of the intervention. In addition to this monitoring process, close communication must be maintained with the total staff and with the home and community.

At the same time efforts to alleviate emotional and behavioral disorders are undertaken, Bobby's academic shortcomings must be considered and defined, and specific teaching methods must be prescribed. A unit approach developed around Bobby's interests could be used with a small group and Bobby. Assignments could be based on a contract system, which should have several requirements for success. Completion of approximations of assignments should have immediate rewards, based on accomplishment not obedience. The terms of the contract should be specific, positive, and fair, and should be used systematically for all members of the group. To help Bobby perform well contract activities should be short and could include puppet plays, listening and viewing activities, and discussion.

A suggestion has been previously made for activities in mathematics—that of Bobby being responsible for helping a less able student. If this should prove to be unsuccessful, either in the peer relationship aspect or in the aspect of evident progress, programed materials and behavior modification may have to be used to help Bobby participate in activities that will be worthwhile to him.

Since Bobby's auditory perceptual problem is evident in the Illinois Test of Psycholinguistic Abilities, care would be necessary to ensure that he understands verbal directions, and actions should accompany all instructions. Bobby should be brought to the attention of the specialist in learning disabilities for concentrated remediation or compensation of his apparent learning disability. Classroom procedures might include listening activities, with accompanying visual materials to help him compensate for the disability.

A child generally responds to someone who cares—perhaps not immediately and perhaps never with complete freedom—but enough to begin a relationship that involves understanding, acceptance, and validation. Bobby could surely use a positive relationship with his teacher. Perhaps a male teacher, one who wants to teach Bobby for positive reasons, would be helpful in building understanding, acceptance, and a more healthy self-image.

SUMMARY

This chapter presents a synthesis of the various theoretical positions that have been discussed in the first six chapters. Three case studies are outlined and discussed exten-sively to show how the various theories can be useful in evaluation, placement, and pro-graming for children in conflict.

BIBLIOGRAPHY AND SUGGESTED READINGS

Birnbrauer, J., and Lawler, J.: Token reinforcement for learning, Mental Retardation 2:275-279, 1964.

Glasser, W.: Reality therapy, New York, 1965, Harper & Row, Publishers.

Levin, G., and Simmons, J.: Response to praise by emotionally disturbed boys, Psychological Reports 11:10, 1962.

Menninger Clinic Children's Division Staff: Disturbed children, San Francisco, 1969, Jossey-Bass, Inc., Publishers.

Peter, L.: Prescriptive teaching, New York, 1965, McGraw-Hill Book Co.

Rhodes, W.: A community participation analysis of emotional disturbance, Exceptional Children 36:309-314, 1970.

SECTION THREE

Putting theory into practice

CHAPTER 8

Mainstreaming and the educational team

The concept of mainstreaming, like so many trends in special education, is not a new concept but rather a new emphasis on selective integration of handicapped children into the mainstream of education. Mainstreaming has only recently become a popular word in the vocabulary of teachers, specialists, and parents, but already questions and concerns are being expressed (Gullotta, 1974; Jordon, 1974; Martin, 1974; Payne and Murray, 1974; Smith and Arkans, 1974) by those who are concerned with appropriate implementation of the concept. The concerns being raised are generally not in opposition to the idea of mainstreaming per se but with the process or the intent with which mainstreaming is being implemented.

Smith and Arkans have attempted to show that the special class is definitely needed—probably to a greater extent now than ever before. This assumption is based on the action of several states that have established time lines for the integration of handicapped children into the public school system. Smith and Arkans outline several conclusions to support the need for more special classes in education.

1. State laws are mandating education for all of their retarded children.

2. The number of severely retarded in a given community is increasing as more community-based resources become available.

3. A regular class teacher cannot be expected to meet the needs of twenty to forty children when several have severe handicaps, for example, physical, emotional, educational, and social handicaps.

Although these assumptions are aimed specifically at the population of severely and profoundly mentally retarded individuals, the factors are essentially the same for severely emotionally disturbed individuals.

Martin (1974) reiterates his position on mainstreaming but in the process cautions those who would dash pell-mell in naive ways to mainstream children. Martin raises questions and offers several useful suggestions regarding mainstreaming.

1. What are the attitudes, fears, and anxieties of those who must teach handicapped children and those who will associate closely with them—parents, teachers, principals, peers, and teacher aides?

2. Training for regular teachers needs to be concerned with attitudes as well as with skills.

3. Logistical problems, for example, children coming and going from classes at un-

119

usual times, using different materials, and having separate budgets from which to work, all can have an upsetting effect on the school system.

4. Evaluation, including the effectiveness of mainstreaming on emotional and social aspects of children, needs to be routinely carried out.

5. Mainstreaming has a mythical quality, a faddish attraction that must not cause educators to avoid the truth.

Although most professionals seem to favor a concept of mainstreaming, the number of recent articles that are cautioning practitioners regarding the concept has precipitated a distinct uneasiness. Classroom teachers who are being asked to accommodate children with severe handicaps are generally indicating a great deal of concern. Any suggestion of being opposed to mainstreaming is like being against apple pie and motherhood; however, evidence of successful integration efforts with handicapped children are equivocal at the present time. At a recent meeting of Council for Exceptional Children's Invisible College on Mainstreaming several important concerns were discussed. These concerns are summarized by Jordan (1974: 31-33).

1. First of all, children are children. They have similar needs; they develop similarly. The problems or the handicaps children have must be dealt with on an individual needs basis.

2. Parents of these children also have needs which the public school system has a responsibility to deal with.

3. The public education system has an obligation to all children, which must be fulfilled in a responsible and responsive manner.

4. There are many processes being implemented all over the country dealing with mainstreaming. These approaches seem to have many common facets and these common facets have been dealt with by the faculty.

5. It's clear to everyone that educational change is, for all of us, a way of life. It must be carefully planned in order to be directed so it will lead into constructive service. Yet we know little about the phenomenon called change. It often occurs without our knowing why, without our assistance, and sometimes in spite of us. Most of us know even less about the power which determines, generates, and guides change.

In addition to the five statements regarding the philosophy of mainstreaming, the twelve participants offered many positive guidelines for the mainstreaming process. These include the following:

1. Mainstreaming helps in the more meaningful involvement of large numbers of parents in school activities.

2. A school tends to become a more child centered community when mainstreaming is implemented.

3. Instruction is individualized for more regular class pupils when mainstreaming occurs.

4. Progressive inclusion is a process which provides a workable approach to the accomplishment of mainstreaming.

5. A team approach to assessment, program planning, and review is superior to anything else we know, especially when that team includes persons with key responsibilities for what is going to happen later—persons such as the parents, the referring teacher, the educational diagnostician, the special education teachers, and the principal. Local school terms also should have substantial responsibility and authority and have ready access to another team of systemwide scope.

6. Trade-off is an established part of the dynamic relationship between regular and special education teachers. It results in help for all children who need some particular kind of attention, whether identified as belonging in special education programs or not.

7. Open spaced school arrangements were felt by some to be conducive to more successful mainstreaming.

8. The board of education and the school system staff must be committed to the adopted policy. They then operate as a power base and as enablers.

9. Program implementation should begin slowly and carefully. Principals and teachers should be patiently moved along each step of the way showing positive results with a few beacon light cases, wherever possible, and providing specific help to teachers on the problems that teachers consider important.

10. Mainstreaming may be difficult but it certainly is possible. More importantly, it's desirable and perhaps imperative for the sake of all of us, not just the children.

11. This group voiced a real concern that the whole story be told. Mainstreaming should not be offered as a panacea. Instead, the dynamics of idea development should be presented.

12. It is important in telling the whole story that mainstreaming be presented as something that is not yet fully proven to be the most appropriate way of organizing for instruction. Of course, in that sense it is not any more fully proven than any other way of supplying special education.

13. Society has a mainstream into which not all are allowed to merge on their own terms. This problem has yet to be resolved. For example, is the special education resource room just an instance of tokenism regarding exceptional children?

Beery (1972) has listed nine questions that he believes schools must answer as they wrestle with the concept of appropriate pupil placement in special education. Appropriate mainstreaming models will have answers that are affirmative on most of his nine questions.

1. Does the model recognize and provide for a *continuum* of programs for children who are experiencing difficulty? Some people are taking what I regard to be an unrealistic view that *no* children should ever be removed from regular classrooms. In my opinion, we will always need a wide variety of educational environments available to children, ranging from all-day, self-contained special education classrooms to individualized "regular" classrooms in which specialists may come into the classroom but pupils are never "pulled out" for remedial purposes.

2. Does the model consciously work towards and actually accomplish reduction of "pull-out" programs? Some profess to, but it doesn't seem to happen.

3. Does the model call for specialists to work in regular classrooms as much as possible?

4. Does the model encourage regular classroom personnel to use special classrooms and equipment?

5. Does the model concentrate on assisting classroom teachers to increase personalization and individualization for *all* children in the classroom?

6. Does the model provide for an *on-going*, meaningful staff-development program which is oriented toward *practicum* and seminar work among staff? Does the staff-development program focus on individualization and have classroom and resource personnel working together?

7. Does the model involve the principal in such a way that he or she is intimately involved as educational leader in the staff-development and special education programs?

8. Is cross-fertilization between schools within and/or across district lines encouraged so that teachers are observing other classrooms—exchanging ideas and moral support?

9. Are interrelationships between the school and local colleges encouraged so that interns and professors are working *in* the school?

Beery's list is not intended to be all inclusive. Additions or deletions may be made as needed to meet individual differences. His view of mainstreaming is more than having normal children sit next to handicapped children; it is a system of human interaction that encourages interrelationships among everyone concerned with the continuous growth of children.

The issues that have been raised regarding mainstreaming for exceptional children must obviously be raised in regard to children in conflict. Although most children in conflict have been and will continue to be educated in regular classes, there are some who will need more intensive psychoeducational intervention. The extent to which this support can be given will undoubtedly underscore successes and failures in the integration process. There are indications that massive efforts must be made if educators are to integrate behaviorally disordered children into regular classes for much of a school day (Martin, 1974).

It is understandable that some distrust, disillusionment, and fears are presently being expressed by teachers who are being asked to work with children whose behavior is significantly different from what is considered acceptable in the classroom. With adequate support these anxieties often can be allayed. This support must be more than giving the classroom teacher new skills to deal with deviance, more than a new gimmick or shortcuts to success. Support means *working together* for the benefit of all children.

Beery (1972) proposes that most school staffs have the capability to meet the needs of exceptional children if they pool their resources effectively. To do this the teacher must be working in a stimulating, cooperative, and enjoyable environment. Beery calls this a "growth environment." Instead of this growth environment, specialists are often confronted with isolation, indifference, and even punitive action.

Before professionals in special education point an accusing finger too vigorously at their unaccepting colleagues in education, they ought to survey the situation from another perspective. Many special education programs were founded on the premise that regular classroom teachers were not doing an adequate job educating all children, that they probably could not do a good job under their present conditions, and that specialists had many of the answers to the problems presented by exceptional children. Training programs also contributed to the problem by training only for regular classroom duties or only for special duties. Over a period of years regular classroom teachers became specialists in teaching normal children, whereas other specialists were prepared to work only with exceptional children. The cleavage in training and expectations was widened by special privileges granted to specialists such as decreased duties and/or an increased stipend for working with special education children. In recent years the frustration has mounted, with increasing funding for special programs while regular classroom funding was held at a lesser growth rate.

It is indeed unfortunate that such a situation was able to develop among professionals dedicated to the same goal of helping children. The first steps for changing the present situation have begun to take place. Common salary schedules are being adopted when educational requirements are similar and when extra time is not required. Whenever possible children are left in the regular classroom with the specialists working closely with the classroom teacher. Cooperation is replacing isolation.

Beery (1973) has detailed one method of developing a cooperative effort for teaching exceptional children. The project is called Catalyst and is designed for maximum pupil, teacher, and principal growth. The growth process is based on democratic processes with all staff sharing in the action. Initial response to this system is extremely encouraging to those who suport the concept of integration. The Catalyst method provides the stimulus for each school within a district to develop its own unique formula for main-streaming exceptional children. The Catalyst concept provides for each attendance unit to differ in its approach, attitude, and implementation of mainstreaming. Consultants are utilized only as stimulators, not as guides. The school staff develops its own potential for expertise in a shared environment with goals established by the entire staff for their school and their children.

In the early stages of program development the "team" concept was one of the more popular ways of handling the problems presented by children in conflict. The proposal that follows is based on the team concept with some notable changes stimulated, to a large degree, by Beery's work in mainstreaming.

THE EDUCATIONAL TEAM

The educational team is suggested as one alternative for providing teachers with the support they need in the development of an educational program for all children in the classroom. The educational team is similar to the diagnostic or staffing team concept in that it represents a group effort in problem solving. At this point, however, much of the similarity ends. Table 7 compares the basic conceptualization of the two systems.

Each of these roles will be discussed in more detail to outline the specifics of the educational team concept.

1. Leadership is determined by role, ability, and interest. The traditional staffing team

Table 7. Comparison of the staffing team and educational team

Traditional staffing team	Educational team
1. Leadership of team by position	1. Leadership determined by role, ability, and interest
2. Membership often determined by professional position	2. Membership determined by interest in and working with the child
3. Membership is static	3. Membership varies with needs
4. Staff all children into and out of special programs	4. Team not responsible for staffing children
5. Team direction often determined by team leader	5. Team direction generally a democratic process
6. Emphasis on evaluation (pre-post evaluation)	6. Emphasis on evaluation programing, and follow-up

is often headed (by state regulation in many states) by the school psychologist, the director of special services, or other professionals because of the position they hold within the school district. Leadership by position often leads to a hierarchy of power so that members do not share on equal terms in discussion and decision making.

2. *Membership is determined by the interest in and working with the child.* A flexible membership that is based on interest in the child and working with the child or family helps to ensure a stronger commitment to the child. Generally the membership will be limited to those who are associated with a single school. Professionals are not excluded from membership. For example, the director of special education might be a team member on all the teams in a district only if he is actively involved with all exceptional children. A psychologist would only be a member of teams from the schools he or she serves and then only with those with whom he or she interacts. The same would be true for nurses, social workers, and teachers. In other words, the team's basic structure would generally come from only one school, with each school having its own educational team or teams as needed. By this method much flexibility could be achieved. Expertise that is present in every school building would be encouraged to grow rather than be stymied by the traditional concept that expertise comes from outside the school. Under this structure, membership would generally be considerably different from that in the staffing team. Membership might include the custodian, bus driver, art teacher, minister, and the child's parent. Teachers who work with the child would be included, as would the principal, psychologist, and psychiatrist who is actively involved with the child. Professionals who are not actively working with the child could contribute their diagnostic findings to the team but would otherwise not be involved in team proceedings.

Many teams have operated under relationships that were antagonistic at best. Team members had no common goals, they shared little of professional importance, and they "set the teachers up" for failure. It might be like a Republican caucus collaborating to select political candidates for the Democratic primary. Both parties are, hopefully, working for better government. This analogy seems farfetched but actually represents what has occurred when professionals are assigned to diagnostic teams on the basis of position rather than involvement. An example of the lack of understanding that can occur when a direct relationship is not maintained with the child follows. At the end of our weekly staff meeting the psychiatrist (who was also the team leader) made a revealing faux pas. As he gathered his materials he said, "Ah! Now I know who we were talking about today. I have had her mother in therapy." Unfortunately, even after an hour of staffing (the third he had participated in concerning this girl), he did not have the right child in mind. One thing can be said for this team and for this psychiatrist. Had the psychiatrist been working directly with the child, this lack of communication would not have developed. Whereas his honesty was admirable, the situation raises serious questions as to the value of his contributions to the team. It is generally believed that the quality of decision making will be superior if made by those who are both interested in and working with a child.

3. *Membership varies with needs.* This principle helps to ensure that team members will do more than meet and share ignorance. Expertise that is needed could be sought out by the team to help in solving specific problems. The key factor would be *what is needed for each child.* For example, one child might have a severe vision problem in addition to emotional problems. A person, hopefully from within the district, with expertise in helping low vision children could be consulted and perhaps added to the team. This person would not only participate in discussions concerning the child but would work with the child and/or support the classroom teacher or resource teacher as needed.

Generally more than one team would be functional within a given school. Table 8 shows how this could be arranged.

Table 8. Educational team membership

Jon	Sheri	David
Mr. C. (regular teacher)	Mr. W. (homeroom supervisor)	Ms. W. (regular teacher)
Ms. E. (resource teacher)	Mr. J. (bus driver)	Ms. T. (school psychologist)
Mr. L. (parent)	Ms. P. (school cook)	Tom (peer)
Mr. V. (custodian)	Ms. T. (school psychologist)	
	Sheri	
	Dr. M. (psychiatrist)	

From these three examples one can see the variety of persons who could become members on a given team. The number of team members should range from three to seven to maintain a workable group size.

4. Educational team is not responsible for staffing children. Many states specify the competencies that must be present on a staffing team that makes placement decisions. Generally the educational team would not serve in this capacity, although theoretically it could satisfy this function if its membership were appropriate to state staffing guidelines. Membership on the team should generally not be altered just to provide for staffing role, since this could destroy the major reason for the team's existence. The staffing team was often the result of a need to staff children and was never intended to serve as an ongoing support for classroom intervention. The educational team is not designed to replace the staffing team, only to complement its function.

5. Team direction is generally a democratic process. Leadership of an education team is generally emergent rather than appointed or decided by rank. Some groups have been able to function without a specified leadership person; however, this is a decision of the group. During the course of helping a child, various team members can take leadership roles depending on the needs of the child, the situation, the relative ability of each member to lead, and a willingness to play a leadership role.

6. There is an emphasis on programing. The general emphasis of the educational team is on programing for children in conflict rather than evaluation and placement, which are often responsibilities of the staffing

team. Whereas some ongoing evaluation and adjustments in placement would be considerations for the educational team, they are not a major function. This is a working team, interested in detail, and supportive of any techniques that will ultimately help the child.

Educational team philosophy

The philosophy that sustains the educational team is simple: *Schools have within their walls sufficient expertise to solve most of the educational and behavioral problems that need to be solved.* The process of shared growth will provide staff with the opportunity to grow in their ability to provide for the needs of all children. The practice of providing "experts" and specialists to solve problems within a school has often undermined the confidence of teachers, staff, and parents to solve their own problems. This has developed, to a large extent, because of a ready supply of professionals (special education teachers, remedial reading specialists, psychologists, speech therapists, etc.), who were willing and in some cases anxious to tell teachers how to deal with a given child. In many school districts children in conflict were actually removed from the regular classroom so that they could "benefit" from total immersion in a special class. We can hardly blame teachers if they exhibit a reluctance to become involved in efforts to maintain a child in their classroom when only a year earlier they were asked to refer this child for special class placement.

The educational team should be an informal arrangement that falls somewhere on the continuum between the formal staffing team and the informal coffee lounge discussions about children. Guidelines for the team need to be established so that members know their position within the school framework. Team members need to be aware of any constraints on their decision-making power. Whether or not the team can exclude a child from school, reassign the child to another class, call in parents, consult with the school psychologist, or use alternative techniques to effect change, all need to be

---

EDUCATIONAL TEAM

PERSONAL DATA FORM

Student's Name   Ron B.   Date 11-1-74

Date of Birth   11   3   62
           Month Day Year   Sex   M

Teacher   Ms. V.

Name of Parent or Guardian   Mr. B.

Address   217 Levis Rd.   Telephone 351-1891

Emergency Contact Person Mr. D.   Telephone 352-6093

Medical Doctor Dr. L.   Telephone 356-7096

Miscellaneous Information:

Need information from master file for conference –
to be held in 3 wks –

Fig. 8-1

carefully "spelled out" in advance or wasted effort will undoubtedly result.

Establishing an educational team

The educational team should be established as a result of needs to help children grow. If a school is working effectively with all children, there is no need for this system. However, if its use could help to solve educational problems, there are several guidelines helpful for implementing the concept.

1. The team should outline the major con-

EDUCATIONAL TEAM GUIDE

Name __Ron B.__   Date __11-26-74__

Team Members	Working Relationship to Student
(1) Ms. V.	Home room teacher
(2) Ms. S.	Reading Specialist
(3) Mr. B.	Ron's father
(4) Ms. S.	Bus Driver
(5) Ms. L.	Music teacher
(6) Mr. J.	School psychologist
(7) Mr. J.	Resource teacher

Major Concerns of Team Members   (In Hierarchy)

(1) Ron's foul mouth

(2) Fighting behavior

(3) Doesn't finish school work

(4) Talks back

(5) Doesn't listen

(6)

Fig. 8-2

cerns or problems that they believe need to be modified before a child can grow educationally and socially. This is generally done individually by each team member after observing, counting, and charting deviant behaviors.

2. From the total list of concerns the team should identify one or two problem areas as starting points. These can be decided upon by (a) selecting only a serious problem that concerns all team members, (b) selecting a behavior that is observable, (c) selecting

---

EDUCATIONAL TEAM GUIDE (Con't.)

Intervention Procedure

(1) Teacher & psychologist will visit with Ron re. swearing & fighting
(2) Reward appropriate language — Ignore foul lang.
(3) Set up contract for appropriate lang. — Reinforcement will be free time in gym.
(4) Lay off academic pressures

Responsibilities of Team Members

(1) Mr. J. & Ms. U. outline contingency plan
(2) Ms. S. plan Re. program for bus
(3) Mr. T. outline schedule of Re.
(4) Mr. J. Contact M.D. for info.

Results
Classroom & bus behavior improved — Art a disaster

Recommendations
Take Ron out of art for 2 wks. — Visit with art teacher
Continue all other plans.

Fig. 8-2, cont'd

a behavior that will likely respond to change, and (d) selecting a behavior that will likely have a positive spread effect to other behaviors.

3. The team should discuss alternative

measures for changing the selected behavior and decide on the simplest measure that also offers reasonable odds for success.

4. The team should evaluate the success of intervention by comparing baseline data

---

EDUCATIONAL TEAM BACKGROUND INFORMATION FORM

Name **Ron B.**   Age **12 - 0**

	Date	Information	Source
Behavioral	10-73	Fighting daily – Terrible language	Ms. F.
	10-73	WRAT: Rdg. 3-8 ; math 5-0	ms. F.
	10-74	Iowa Test: Rdg. 3-9; math 5-1	ms. V.
		Fighting in school & on bus – Swearing – Doing nothing in school	ms. V.
Psychological	1-70	PPVT M.A. 8-5	mr. J.
	1-72	Durrell – Oral 2-5 ; Silent 2-4 ; Listening 3-0	ms. S.
	10-73	WISC Functioning in ave. range	mr. T.
	11-74	Behavior Count (swearing 15 per hr.; fighting 5 per wk.; 1/4 work turned in)	ms. V.
Sociol./Ecological	8-71	3 children (Boy 14; girl 2) Mother abandoned	Father
	9-71	Children placed in foster home	S. W.
	3-72	Father remarried (children returned home) Two step daughters –	Father
	9-74	Father reports need for school support	
Biophysical	10-74	Complete physical (No report)	Sch. Nurse
	11-74	Ron having fainting spells	Father
Needed	11-74	Follow-up report on fainting	Team
	11-74	Observe to see what Ron works for	
	11-74	Evaluation of home situation – Ck. with Doctor to get medical report	

Fig. 8-3

with present functioning level. Team efforts should be redirected as necessary.

The educational team concept represents a renewed faith in the local attendance unit and new hope for meaningful teacher involvement. Although it recognizes the role of mental health professionals, it clearly establishes the teacher's role as a bona fide change agent and a contributor to team efforts to meet the needs of each child in an economical, efficient, and effective manner.

System of data collection

As educational teams are formed, they will need to develop a viable system of data collection (Figs. 8-1 to 8-3). Individual child folders often contain excellent data for use by the team, but they generally are not presented in a format that is readily usable. In the following pages I have outlined components of a data collection system that have been found to be functional for classroom use. They are offered as an outline guide to assist professionals to condense the more comprehensive data generally found in individual folders, as a quick reference, and as a means of keeping up-to-date records with a minimum of time expenditure. They should generally serve only as a guide to the more personalized needs of an individual school or teacher.

Developing a meaningful individual record for each child receiving attention from the educational team can have positive effects on the staff as well as the child.

1. It encourages staff to review the specifics of a case in detail.

2. Sharing information often encourages positive attitudes to develop rather than negative feelings.

3. Outlining information from the folder helps to put all of the available information into perspective.

4. Reviewing folders can point out information gaps to the team.

5. Developing individual folders gives the teacher a classroom record to use for ongoing record keeping.

Chapter 9 will outline specific skills, techniques, and materials for use with children in conflict. These are selected to provide a wide variety of alternatives, regardless of the administrative structure under which the teacher is functioning.

SUMMARY

The educational team is proposed as one viable alternative for meeting the needs of various mainstreaming proposals. Discussions of mainstreaming by participants of CEC's Invisible College on Mainstreaming and Keith Beery support the need for positive communication and decision making that is unencumbered and objective.

The educational team offers several advantages to the traditional staffing team. It encourages teacher participation, membership because of interest and involvement, and democratic decision making.

In addition to presenting an outline for efficient and effective administration of programing, a system of data collection is presented, including a personal data form, team guide, and background information form.

BIBLIOGRAPHY AND SUGGESTED READINGS

Beery, K: Models for mainstreaming, San Rafael, Calif., 1972, Dimensions Publishing Co.

Beery, K.: Catalyst profiles and faces (experimental edition), San Rafael, Calif., 1973, Dimensions Publishing Co.

Christoplos, F.: Keeping exceptional children in regular classes, Exceptional Children **39:**569-572, 1973.

Christoplos, F., and Renz, P.: A critical examination of special education programs, Journal of Special Education **3:**371-379, 1969.

Dunn, L.: Special education for the mildly retarded—is much of it justifiable? Exceptional Children **35:** 5-22, 1968.

Glavin, J., Quay, H., Annesley, F., and Werry, J.: An experimental resource room for behavior problem children, Exceptional Children **38:**131-137, 1971.

Gullotta, T.: Teacher attitudes toward the moderately disturbed child, Exceptional Children **41:**49-50, 1974.

Jones, R.: Labels and stigma in special education, Exceptional Children **38:**553-564, 1972.

Jones, R.: Student views of special placement and their own special classes: a clarification, Exceptional Children **41:**22-29, 1974.

Jordan, J.: Invisible college on mainstreaming addresses critical factors in implementing programs, Exceptional Children **41:**31-33, 1974.

Kirk, S., and Weiner, B., editors: Behavioral research on exceptional children, Washington, D. C., 1963, Council for Exceptional Children.

Martin, E.: Individualism and behaviorism as future trends in educating handicapped children, Exceptional Children 38:517-524, 1972.

Martin, E.: Some thoughts on mainstreaming, Exceptional Children 41:150-153, 1974.

Payne, R., and Murray, C.: Principals' attitudes toward integration of the handicapped, Exceptional Children 41:123-125, 1974.

Shotel, J., Iano, R., and McGettigan, J.: Teacher attitudes associated with the integration of handicapped children, Exceptional Children 38:677-683, 1972.

Smith, J., and Arkans, J.: Now more than ever: a case for the special class, Exceptional Children 40:497-502, 1974.

Valletutti, P.: Integration vs. segregation: a useless dialectic, Journal of Special Education 3:405-408, 1969.

CHAPTER 9

Specific methods for behavior change

This chapter is designed to meet the needs of teachers who are on the "firing line" with children in conflict. The first part will center around techniques to be used with the child in the regular classroom situation. Individual techniques and ideas are presented so that teachers might be able to identify the types of children with whom they are involved and then be able to determine some individual or group technique to remedy the problem. These are basically surface-oriented techniques that would be appropriate as a "first-aid" method of dealing with the child's problems. They are not intended to be in-depth interventions that will do away with behaviors that need more intensive interaction on the part of the teacher. Although the lists are somewhat extensive, there are obviously many other techniques that would be equally satisfactory with various behavioral concerns. The ideas presented are only intended to be "pump primers," which will undoubtedly stimulate additional ideas by the teacher.

Deviance will be divided into four basic behavioral patterns. This is done only for convenience and to provide the reader with some basic structure from which to generate alternatives. It should not be assumed that deviant behaviors come in neat packages with a label attached. In most cases behavior deviations will cross all barriers of established "behavioral types." A variety of techniques for behavior change are presented to the teacher. Hopefully this will lead to a selection process based on need rather than pat answers to preconceived problems.

The four basic behavioral types are acting-out behaviors, withdrawing behaviors, defensive behaviors, and disorganized behaviors.

Behavior management techniques will be presented in the following manner: (1) deviant behaviors will be outlined; (2) alternative solutions will be proposed; and (3) methods that have generally failed to produce desired outcomes will be discussed.

ACTING-OUT BEHAVIORS

The behaviors presented represent teacher descriptions of acting-out behaviors. Most are observable behaviors that tend to occur in clusters rather than in isolation.

1. Talks out in class without regard for others
2. Does not attend to classroom directions
3. Often does not listen
4. Exhibits out-of-seat behavior
5. Touches or pushes others in an irritating fashion
6. Is easily distracted
7. Aggressive in behavior toward others, both physically and verbally
8. Slams doors
9. Talks back to the teacher and other authority figures

10. Abuses other children
11. Is disruptive in the classroom
12. Child is out of control
13. Often has temper tantrums
14. Makes loud clicking noises; yells in the classroom or in the hallway
15. Swears
16. Runs around the room, talks, does not work
17. Exhibits argumentative behavior
18. Hurts other children
19. Refuses to cooperate
20. Is stubborn and disrespectful
21. Is always goofing around
22. Interrupts everyone
23. Harasses other children
24. Exhibits rowdiness
25. Is unable to control anger
26. Must always be first in line
27. Fights
28. Refuses to work

It has been said that children in conflict drive many teachers to an early retirement. If a teacher is unable to cope with the child's behavior, the result is an unhappy situation with poor teaching and little learning rather than the desired situation with good teaching and much learning. In meetings with teachers regarding the needs of children in conflict one often sees teachers who have given up on children. A comment that teachers make all too frequently is "I have tried everything." An inquiry of what techniques have been tried often reveals that the teacher has really tried little in the way of techniques designed to cope with the problem but has used techniques designed to avoid the problem, for example, placing the child in the front or in the back of the classroom, rather than to get at the source of the problem.

The alternative solutions that will be presented are not intended to be a panacea for teachers but rather to give some techniques and materials that might be used to help with problem children and also to help support mental health processes in "normal" children. The teacher's mental health is also a concern. Hopefully the stresses that can be allayed will pay dividends in teacher effectiveness with all children.

In the initial stages of working with acting-out children it is important to show them as clearly as possible what their behavior is like. Children must gain insight that the behavior

is inappropriate. This can be done in several ways.

1. The child might view his behavior on a video tape recorder.

2. The child might count his own behaviors.

3. Another child can monitor the child's inappropriate behavior so that he can get an impartial interpretation from a peer.

4. The teacher could count the child's inappropriate behaviors.

Once behavior is counted, the teacher and child should have a conference at which the teacher can explain how he or she feels about the child's behavior. The child can also relate to the teacher his interpretation of the behavior. At times this will be sufficient to encourage children to change their behavior. Often children exhibit inappropriate behavior of an acting-out variety so that they can get attention or be able to move around the classroom to meet their own physiological and psychological needs. The teacher should recognize this need and provide acceptable outlets for the child. Some of these outlets can include alternative learning activities or parallel learning activities.

As children grow older, the list of acceptable reinforcers generally becomes smaller for the teacher. Hopefully, most young people will have their acting-out behavior under control by the time they attend high school. For those who do not, reinforcement of a higher intensity is often needed. Such things as free activity time, earning academic credit, and free time to work on paying jobs have proved to be effective with high school children (Ullmann and Krasner, 1965; Woody, 1969).

For reinforcement programs to be immediately effective with young adults there must have been a pattern of reinforcement effectiveness established at an earlier age. The young adult who has been able to manipulate the environment effectively for several years will be much more difficult to manage than a student whose behaviors have responded to reinforcement in the past (MacMillan, 1973).

Before teachers begin any system of behavior change they must consider several important questions concerning their approach to teaching.

1. Is the classroom atmosphere conducive to learning?

2. Is the material relevant and interesting for each child?

3. Is each child working at a success level?

These questions and any others of particular interest to the teacher must be answered in the affirmative before beginning work to modify the specific behaviors of identified children. Behavior management cannot replace a positive classroom atmosphere, appropriate classroom materials, and innovative techniques that stimulate a positive interaction between teacher and student.

Alternative solutions

Planned ignoring. Ignoring is one of the most often used methods of modifying inappropriate behaviors. This technique has been used with mild talk-out behaviors, with attention-getting behaviors such as hand waving, and sometimes with out-of-seat behavior. The older child who attempts to manipulate or alienate teachers through behaviors that are in conflict with the value system of adults can often be changed through ignoring. Teachers have found that ignoring some behaviors will do more to change the behavior than attending to it with verbal reprimands or other forms of punishment.

Some acting-out behaviors that are potentially dangerous to the child cannot be ignored. For example, the young child who runs from the playground into the street must be attended to, since ignoring might cause serious harm to the child. The same is true for an older student who is behaving inappropriately in his automobile around the school grounds. Ignoring the potentially dangerous behavior may prove to be harmful to both the student and other children in the vicinity of the school.

Behaviors that provide their own reinforcement value often do not respond to planned ignoring. For example, hitting behaviors, slamming doors, fighting, harassing others, hurting behaviors, stealing, and swearing all seem to have reinforcing properties of their own. The teacher will have to decide which behaviors can and cannot be ignored and which will likely respond to planned ignoring.

Reinforcement. A second approach in changing acting-out behavior is to capitalize on the need of the student to play a leadership role. This can often be done by assigning the student extra duties such as coming in before and after school to perform tasks for the teacher. This seems to work with both young children and older students. However, an appropriate level of activity needs to be established for different age levels. The younger child might clean off the chalkboards before school or help the teacher to take down decorations from the bulletin board after school. These would generally be inappropriate activities for most older students. For them, activities such as helping the coach clean out the locker room, preparing materials in the office, putting chalk lines on the athletic fields, or helping in the nurse's office have been used as positive reinforcers.

Counterconditioning. A third technique for changing acting-out behavior is to encourage a behavior in the classroom that is in conflict with acting-out behavior. For the younger child this might be as simple as reinforcing behaviors that require the child to work at his seat quietly or to be otherwise actively engaged in a behavior that cannot be done at the same time that acting-out behaviors occur. The child who is busy working at arithmetic cannot fight with the child across the aisle. This can also work effectively with older children. Various organizations at the high school level, athletic teams, and musical groups can all productively involve the student so that acting-out behaviors have less time in which to occur. The student is also getting appropriate attention at these times so that the need for inappropriate attention is often unnecessary.

Self-analysis. Another method for changing acting-out behavior is to use a video tape recording so that children can see their own behavior. This appears to be particularly effective with younger children. Although this is a somewhat cumbersome system, it is worth while if behavior change results.

An office. Setting up an office or study carrel for children who cannot otherwise keep their behavior under control can be helpful. This is not a place where students are sent as punishment but a place that allows them freedom from distracting stimuli present in the classroom. In extreme cases, a child may desire to remain in the isolated setting for an entire period; however, a few minutes is generally sufficient.

Counseling. The techniques that have been discussed in Chapter 4 should be considered viable alternatives for intervention in acting-out behaviors. Life space interviewing, mirroring feelings, listening, and accepting the child while rejecting behaviors all represent usable examples.

Contingency management. Contracting, or contingency management, is an excellent technique for use with acting-out children. With this technique the child and teacher contract for an amount of work that must be completed before the student can earn free time to do what he wants or to have special privileges in the classroom. This technique seems to work with both younger and older children, provided the reinforcer established is appropriate to the age level. Contingency management can be used with an individual, with a small group, or with an entire class.

Satiation. Satiation means allowing inappropriate behavior to continue or insisting that it continue until the inappropriate behavior is satiated or is unlikely to return. Many teachers have used satiation as a way of stopping inappropriate behavior with younger children. This might include saying inappropriate words over and over, writing inappropriate words over and over, or filling a wastebasket full of spitballs. With older children this technique has been used in similar ways. One example was used by a teacher who "allowed" a group of boys to continue chewing tobacco when they wanted to leave the room to spit it out. This resulted in mild nausea and at least temporary satiation for tobacco.

Teaching technique. The classroom teacher should strive to establish a classroom structure that is unambiguous, simple, and to the point. Often unclear directions lead students to a frustration level that promotes acting-out behavior.

1. Giving clear, concise directions. Establishing directions that are straightforward, simple, and given one at a time in a clear understandable fashion are better than directions that are unclear, ambiguous, and given over and over for clarification. Repeating directions for clarity also leads to inattentiveness, since listening is of little value if directions are going to be repeated several times.

2. Limiting assignments. Many children are overwhelmed by the amount of work that teachers give to them at one time. Work should be presented in assignment formats that the child can tolerate. One apparent way to cut down on the amount of an assignment is to divide the paper in thirds with a colored pencil. The child is asked to work down to the red line before having it checked, then work to the blue line, and finally work to the end. Cutting the paper in half with scissors and allowing the child to do the first half and, on completion, do the second half is another way to accomplish this same goal. Children in conflict often have a tendency to give up too easily when assignments appear so overwhelming that failure is certain.

3. Providing for physical movement. Children can be given appropriate reasons to leave their seats to work off some excess energy. No adult would be able to tolerate sitting in seats for as long as some students are expected to sit. The child should be given the opportunity to move about the classroom for meaningful purposes. If the teacher does not do this, the acting-out child will find excuses to move around the classroom. Allowing the child to come to the teacher's desk when the assignment is completed, having centers or work areas to which the child can move as needed, and establishing learning activities that require physical involvement or movement can all promote an atmosphere in which the child does not feel "tied" to his desk.

Seating variables. Often the acting-out child can be seated near the teacher, where touch control and visual contact can be maintained. In this way the teacher can physically touch the child on occasion to reinforce appropriate work and to give the child the necessary assurance to be able to maintain appropriate behaviors. Children who are acting out often get attention by being told to sit down, to be still, and to leave someone alone. The teacher should use nonverbal cues as much as possible to modify the child's behavior. Taking the child back to his seat without saying anything can often be effective. The teacher should try to avoid verbal cues that are often highly reinforcing to the child.

Running from the classroom is a behavior often attributed to impulsive, acting-out children. To avoid the inevitable problems that develop from running behavior the teacher should arrange the classroom to minimize this possibility. Establishing a work station near the door will allow the teacher to be near the door much of the time. Once the child has turned his back on the teacher and has left the room, it is extremely difficult, if not impossible, to get him back to the classroom without a confrontation. Putting a child in an embarrassing position in front of several students will undoubtedly force the child to save face by running away from the situation.

Presenting a low profile. The ability to teach acting-out children successfully depends, to a great extent, on the teacher's attitudes toward teaching and children. The teacher's ability to relate to children in a low-keyed but resolute approach will do much to quiet an acting-out child and will help to maintain tranquillity within the classroom.

Encouraging children to monitor themselves. If acting-out children are somewhat cooperative during better moments, the teacher can work out a way for them to keep a record of their own behavior progress. The teacher should have the child try to increase the amount of time spent on appropriate behavior by a system of record keeping. The child should monitor only one behavior at a time, since a behavior change will likely have a positive effect on other inappropriate behaviors. The child does not have to change all the behaviors at one time.

Relaxation exercises. For the younger child relaxation exercises are often helpful. For an older child, activities that can wear off some excess energies, such as athletic events, can be helpful. A punching bag, a blocking dummy that can be hit and kicked, or a dart board can all be helpful in alleviating hostility and pent-up anxiety in the student.

Minimizing rules. The acting-out child often tries to manipulate the rules that are set. Rules that are necessary should be few in number, simple, and consistently administered. Consequences to rule breaking should be clearly set so that ambiguity of interpretation is minimal. The acting-out child should not be threatened. If the teacher intends to punish the child, he should be punished. If the teacher intends not to allow the child to do something, he should not be allowed to do it. But the teacher should not harass, not threaten, and not accuse the child of inappropriate behavior.

Reinforcing appropriate behaviors. When the student is acting appropriately, the teacher should be attentive to this good behavior. It should not be ignored. Sometimes teachers believe that a student who is acting appropriately should not have his "chain pulled" so that they ignore appropriate behavior when it does occur. If teachers are going to ignore inappropriate behavior, there is no reason for the child to exhibit appropriate behavior.

Students who are in conflict with the system often dislike to be reinforced in public. A quiet word away from the other students, a smile, or a nod can often be very appropriate for an older student, where a verbal reinforcer could be extremely punishing if overheard by other students. The teacher should discuss the acting-out child's problems in private either at the child's desk, in a quiet area of the classroom, or away from other students. Students should not be given the reinforcement of discussion or arguing a point in front of all the other students. Communication that is nonverbal in nature can be understood by the student so that

Fig. 9-1. A buddy system can be an effective tool for controlling behavior and providing a leadership role for another child. This helping relationship can often grow into a friendship.

the teacher does not have to verbalize all feelings.

Encouraging peer reinforcement and ignoring. Students are excellent modifiers of behavior. At certain age levels peers are the best reinforcers for both appropriate and inappropriate behaviors. Getting other students to reward appropriate behavior and to ignore inappropriate behavior will go a long way in changing an acting-out child's behavior.

Assignment to a buddy. The buddy system is particularly effective for new children in class (Fig. 9-1). A buddy can give a new child a feeling of being welcome and can also give needed responsibility to a child who is playing the helping role.

Providing success. Success brings success, especially with children who have failed so often. This means success in school as well as success in behavioral tasks.

Reducing auditory and visual stimulation. Acting-out children often cannot cope with visual and/or auditory stimulation without becoming "involved" in the action. Using visual and auditory barriers between these children and activity areas of the class can be helpful.

Consistency. Acting-out children need to know where the teacher stands on various issues. They need to know that the teacher will behave the same today, tomorrow, and next week.

Methods that have generally failed

Teachers can do well to make a list of teacher behaviors that have failed to change acting-out behaviors so that they can be avoided. A partial list might include the following:

1. Using force
2. Ridiculing the behavior
3. Taking away privileges
4. Forcing a child to admit lies or errors
5. Punishing the child
6. Demanding a confession of guilt
7. Confrontation over issues
8. Asking the child why he acts out
9. Comparing the child's behavior to other children's behavior

WITHDRAWING BEHAVIORS

The withdrawing child is often inconspicuous in the classroom and therefore can be ignored by the teacher. The following behaviors are examples that might lead the teacher to believe that the child is withdrawing from the reality of the classroom:

1. Not responding when spoken to
2. Thumb-sucking, chewing on pencils, or chewing on clothing

3. Failure to talk even though the skill to talk is properly developed
4. Rocking or other self-stimulating behavior
5. Attending more to animals or toys than to people
6. Sitting and playing alone when other children are nearby.

Alternative solutions

Encouraging parallel activities. Withdrawn children should not be forced to interact with other children. Often the best that a teacher can hope for is parallel activity. From parallel play the child can often be involved slowly into a more active role.

Encouraging activity with the environment
1. Art activities—clay, water, fingerpainting, drawing, and manipulation of materials
2. Role playing with puppets
3. Hiking, wading in water, and climbing activities
4. Music therapy—drums, piano, and shakers

Guaranteeing success. By using short experiences of an appropriate level of difficulty the teacher can often encourage involvement. A quiet manner, along with understanding and an accepting attitude, will also encourage participation.

Pets in the classroom. The younger child can often relate to pets in the classroom before relationships with people are possible. Allowing the withdrawn child to care for pets is an excellent technique for involving the child in a meaningful activity.

Group projects. The older child can often be involved in group projects so that individual abilities are diluted among others. The child who would cringe with fear at the thought of singing a solo can sometimes feel secure by singing in a group.

Establishing guidelines for behavior. Establishing some guidelines for behavior will often allow withdrawn children greater freedom in their relationship with that limited environment. Withdrawn children need a time and a place within the school environment to be alone during the day. This gives them an opportunity to withdraw when they really need to withdraw and be alone.

Allowing physical involvement to replace verbal involvement. The teacher should not force participation, especially when oral language is involved. Involvement should center around physical involvement rather than verbal involvement, at least in the beginning states. The child might hold the chart for the group, hand the teacher materials to put on the chart, or point to pictures that others name. In this way the child is involved, if only peripherally.

Empathizing with the child. When contact can be made, the teacher should empathize with the child. The teacher might explain about his or her own problems in becoming involved with certain school activities. Some of the things the teacher did to overcome this lack of involvement can be offered. Often the child will begin to realize that other people have felt the same way he is feeling.

Informal conversation. Informal conversation groups among children can be encouraged so that the child can become involved in small talk before being encouraged to interact in a more formal atmosphere. Any participation by the child should be encouraged. However, the teacher must not rush children into involvement for which they are unprepared. Withdrawn children are suspicious of being pushed too quickly and thus being embarrassed by a situation in which they cannot succeed.

Methods that have generally failed

Methods that have generally failed when used with withdrawing children include the following:
1. Forcing the child to become involved
2. Embarrassing the child
3. Ignoring the behavior
4. Asking the child why he does not want to take part
5. Comparing the child to other children

DEFENSIVE BEHAVIORS

Defensive behaviors are behaviors that allow children to protect themselves from failure, from embarrassment, and from the truth and to take the focus from themselves. Defensive behaviors are necessary and appropriate for children at various times. They are dangerous for children when it becomes a way of life rather than a way of handling isolated problems. If children lie when the truth would be easier, their defensiveness is "getting in the way."

Following are several rather typical behaviors that indicate a defensive behavior pattern:

1. Unwillingness to accept assignments
2. Forgetting or not doing homework
3. Avoidance behaviors in the classroom
4. Losing things such as papers, homework, clothes, etc.
5. Exhibiting an I-don't-care attitude when faced with failure
6. Crying behavior and frustration
7. Manipulation behavior to the situation
8. Saying the water is too cold in the swimming pool to avoid going into the water
9. Lack of responsibility and attending in achieving in school
10. Compulsive eating
11. Tattling behavior
12. Asking questions after being given an assignment
13. A child saying, "I'm too tired to work" or "I can't remember"
14. Out-of-seat behavior
15. Wasting time with a pencil or a ruler
16. Playing with objects in school
17. Missing school
18. Becoming ill at specific times during the day
19. Wetting pants to avoid something in the classroom
20. Crying
21. Practical jokes
22. Coming in late for class
23. Running away from school
24. Messy work, particularly in writing
25. Cheating
26. Daydreaming
27. Sleeping during class
28. Giving unreasonable answers
29. Lying

Alternative solutions

Since defensive behaviors are often an indication that the child is afraid to become involved because of the fear of failure, the fear of not measuring up to himself or others, or a fear of embarrassment, it is important that the teacher involve the child at a success level. A few ideas that have worked with children with defensive behaviors follow.

Being truthful with children. Adults often force children to become defensive by their line of questioning and skeptical attitude. If a teacher knows that a child did something wrong, the teacher should not ask the child if he or she did it; for example, if a teacher sees a child take a dollar from another child's desk, the teacher should not ask, "Did you take some money?" Rather, the teacher might tell the child, "I saw you take the dollar. What shall we do about it?"

Planned ignoring. Defensive behaviors can manifest themselves in a variety of ways. Planned ignoring of defensive behaviors is appropriate when allowing the behavior to continue for a brief period will not cause serious problems.

Reinforcement. When children approach problems with realistic behavior, they should be reinforced appropriately. A teacher must be extremely alert in such cases so that proper reinforcement is given. Children who use a variety of defensive behaviors are often difficult to reinforce because teachers fail to observe appropriate behaviors that are exhibited.

Using nonverbal responses. Nonverbal responses often effect greater change than verbal responses. Children become so familiar with verbalization that they often ignore it.

Giving the child something to look forward to. The child who is continually late or who does not come to school can be helped by anticipated events. All children need something to hope for. Small surprises or something special for tomorrow can often encourage children to be on time or to come to school when they might otherwise be absent.

Giving choices. Children who fear work are sometimes afraid of the work the teacher gives them. If choices can be made, the fear is often allayed. The teacher can give parallel choices so that similar learning takes place regardless of the choice made.

Assuring success. The best antidote for defensive behaviors is realistic success. It will take many success experiences to change defensive behaviors. Often success experiences in one area of the child's life will spread to other areas.

Other alternatives. Other teacher alternatives outlined for acting-out and withdrawal behaviors are also useful here. It has been suggested that acting-out and withdrawing behaviors are in fact both defensive behaviors.

Methods that have generally failed

Methods that have generally failed when used with children who behave defensively include the following:
1. Telling the child he is trying to avoid work, school, or reality
2. Taking away privileges
3. Comparing behavior to other children's behavior
4. Threatening the child
5. Punishment
6. Telling the child you are aware of his gimmicks
7. Suspending a child for a few days if the child skips school
8. Taking the child out of activities he likes to do

DISORGANIZED BEHAVIORS

Children who exhibit severe disorganization will generally not be placed in a regular classroom. In fact it is questionable whether disorganized children will even be maintained in a special class in the public school except in a one-to-one relationship with the teacher. These children might be confused in terms of time, place, and their education placement. They might not have speech skills and often will not relate to people. Although significant progress has been made with these children on a one-to-one basis, the prognosis for mainstreaming or part-time placement in a regular classroom is problematical at best. Emphasis in a special class will generally be on (1) building interpersonal relationships, (2) communication, (3) developing work habits, and (4) self-maintenance of self-care skills.

The teacher who works with disorganized children should certainly be in contact and have collaboration with other professionals such as the school psychologist, psychiatrist, pediatrician, and social worker who might lend professional support. In addition, the teacher needs ongoing classroom support from the school staff, including enough aide support for one-to-one interaction with these children.

REINFORCEMENT GENERALLY ACCEPTABLE IN SCHOOL

Much can be said for teachers' use of reinforcement in the classroom regardless of the educational approach being used. Most children are more productive if rewarded appropriately rather than ignored when they exhibit correct behaviors. Teachers generally have a ready supply of highly reinforcing activities at their disposal. The age of the children, their individual needs, and the relationship established between the teacher and students will determine the reinforcement value for each of these activities.

1. Having good citizen sign on the desk
2. Access to quiet play area
3. Access to art area
4. Helping to clean the teacher's desk
5. Access to science area with slides, fossils, terrarium, aquarium, microscope, etc.
6. Monitoring classroom activities
7. Working on a bulletin board
8. Helping to correct work of others
9. Helping to dispense reinforcers to other children
10. Being in charge of sharing time
11. Erasing the chalkboard
12. Sweeping floors
13. Washing desks
14. Cleaning the aquarium
15. Coming early in the morning to help get the room ready
16. Cutting paper
17. Being errand boy or girl
18. Answering the door
19. Taking messages
20. Answering the telephone
21. Working in the office
22. Cleaning erasers
23. Writing daily lesson plans on the chalkboard
24. Watering plants
25. Tutoring a less able child
26. Collecting papers
27. Getting out gym equipment
28. Passing out books
29. Taking roll
30. Acting as line leader
31. Leading the morning pledge of the flag
32. Leading songs
33. Choosing stories to be read in class
34. Being captain of a team
35. Pronouncing the spelling words
36. Choosing a new seat in the room
37. Helping in the school office

38. Visiting in another classroom
39. Going to lunch at recess or home
40. Being allowed to move to another activity
41. Being allowed to read the directions to other children
42. Helping in the cafeteria
43. Assisting the custodian
44. Using colored chalk
45. Using a typewriter
46. Running the ditto machine
47. Stapling papers together
48. Feeding the fish or animals
49. Giving a message over the intercom
50. Writing and directing a play
51. Picking up litter on the school grounds
52. Holding the door during a fire drill
53. Serving as secretary for class meetings
54. Raising or lowering the flag
55. Emptying the wastebasket
56. Carrying the wastebasket while other children clean out their desks
57. Operating a slide, filmstrip, movie projector, etc.
58. Recording his or her own behavior on a graph
59. Correcting papers
60. Teaching another child
61. Playing checkers, chess, cards, or other table games
62. Choosing a game to play
63. Working with clay
64. Doing "special," "the hardest," or "impossible" teacher-made arithmetic problems
65. Reading the newspaper
66. Listening to the radio with an earplug
67. Arm wrestling
68. Learning a "magic" trick
69. Lighting or blowing out a candle
70. Going to the library
71. Helping the librarian
72. Making or flying a kite
73. Popping corn
74. Making a puppet
75. Carrying the ball or bat to recess
76. Visiting with the principal
77. Doing a science experiment
78. Telling the teacher when it is time to go to lunch
79. Sharpening the teacher's pencils
80. Opening the teacher's mail
81. Sitting next to the teacher at lunch
82. Doing crossword puzzles or mathematics puzzles
83. Weighing or measuring various objects in the classroom
84. Adjusting the window shades

These reinforcers and numerous others are available to most teachers. Reinforcers like candy, money, and trinkets are generally less acceptable to other teachers and parents and probably should be avoided if the child will show adequate growth through the use of more socially acceptable reinforcers.

SUMMARY

In this chapter four behavioral types are presented. These include acting-out behaviors, withdrawing behaviors, defensive behaviors, and disorganized behaviors. For each of these behavioral categories deviant behaviors are outlined, alternative solutions are proposed, and methods that have generally failed to produce desirable outcomes are discussed. The proposals made are for behaviors that generally can be dealt with in the regular classroom. Behaviors that are unlikely to respond to surface treatment are indicated.

Most children exhibit one or more of these behavioral types at some time during their lifetime. Children who exhibit one deviant behavior will generally exhibit more, since deviance does not come in any prepackaged, categorized entity. The classroom teacher has an enormous array of reinforcers available within the classroom, a listing of which is given.

BIBLIOGRAPHY AND SUGGESTED READINGS

Blanco, R.: Prescriptions for children with learning and adjustive problems, Springfield, Ill., 1972, Charles C Thomas, Publisher.

Haring, N., and Phillips, E.: Educating emotionally disturbed children, New York, 1962, McGraw-Hill Book Co.

Hewett, F.: The emotionally disturbed child in the classroom, Boston, 1968, Allyn & Bacon, Inc.

MacMillan, D.: Behavior modification in education, New York, 1973, The Macmillan Co.

Ullmann, L., and Krasner, L.: Case studies in behavior modification, New York, 1965, Holt, Rinehart & Winston, Inc.

Wallace, G., and Kaufman, J.: Teaching children with learning problems, Columbus, Ohio, 1973, Charles E. Merrill Publishing Co.

Whelan, R., and Haring, N.: Modification and maintenance of behavior through systematic application of consequences, Exceptional Children **32:**281-289, 1966.

Woody, R.: Behavioral problem children in the schools, New York, 1969, Appleton-Century-Crofts.

CHAPTER 10

Teaching materials

Good materials will not, in themselves, make a good program; however, it is difficult to have a strong educational program without appropriate supportive materials. In reviewing materials for children in conflict one finds a noticeable lack in the affective areas. The materials that are available are fairly new and lack "track records," although some show considerable promise. The published materials reviewed were selected for the following reasons: (1) they are being used or show promise of being useful; (2) they are designed to be used in the affective domain; and (3) they cover age ranges from preschool to the high school level.

When available, the following information is provided: (1) title of material, (2) author, (3) publisher, (4) date of publication, and (5) level. The materials are presented according to chronological age appropriateness, with materials for younger children presented first.

PUBLISHED MATERIALS

Child's Series on Psychologically Relevant Themes

Author: Joan Fassler
Publisher: Videorecord Corporation of America
Date of publication: 1971
Level: Preschool and elementary grades

Child's Series on Psychologically Relevant Themes is a videorecord program that is based on bibliotherapy (helping children to solve their problems through identification with literary characters who have similar problems). The series contains six video cassettes, ranging in length from 6 to 8 minutes, thus holding the attention of younger children. Each cassette contains a beautifully illustrated story, which is narrated by a child; this aids in the identification process necessary for bibliotherapy to be effective.

The teacher's guide contains a brief synopsis of each story, discussion questions, and relevant activities that correspond to each story. The stories in the videorecord program are as follows:

The Man of the House. A little boy, David, takes over his father's role and becomes the protector of his mother while his father is away. He is happy when his father returns because he loves and needs him, but he is a little bit sad because he is no longer "the man of the house."

Don't Worry Dear. Jenny was a little girl who wet her bed, sucked her thumb, stuttered, and cared for her stuffed animal, Barky, as if he were real. The boys

My personal thanks to Mary Straw, Robin Israelski, and Ira Israelski for their contributions to researching and reviewing published materials for this book. I also wish to thank Dr. Sandra Boland for her invaluable advice regarding publishers, materials, and format.

.. down the street laughed at Jenny when she stuttered. Her mother was upset but said, "Don't worry dear, when you get bigger you won't talk like that." One day Jenny's aunts came to visit and told her mother to put bitter medicine on her thumb, but she disregarded their advice and said, "Don't worry dear, when you get bigger you won't feel like sucking your thumb anymore." And she didn't.

A Boy With a Problem. Johnny had a problem; it upset him so much he could not eat, do his school work, or sleep. He even had a stomachache. Johnny took his problem to the doctor, his teacher, and his mother; they all gave him advice before he told them what his problem was. His problem persisted until his friend Peter came to call. Peter was a good listener and allowed Johnny to tell him his whole problem. Johnny slept that night and felt much better.

All Alone With Daddy. Ellen is enjoying her stay with her father while her mother is away visiting. When her mother returns, she becomes jealous and resentful of her. Later she realizes that if she grows up to be just like her mother she may marry a man like her father. And she did.

One Little Girl. Laurie, a little girl, is "slow in school," and she has problems with reading and mathematics. Laurie is unhappy because people refer to her as a "slow child." She discovers that if she concentrates on what she does well instead of complaining about the things she does not do well, she will be happy.

Grandpa Died Today. David's grandfather died. They had been very close; they had talked about special things and played ball together. The story deals with David's struggle to understand his grandfather's death, and his reactions to this sad situation.

Videorecords express the psychodynamic viewpoint; many of the stories provide excellent introductory material for discussing relevant topics (death, accepting one's deficits, coping with a problem). Strong emphasis is placed on the Oedipus and Electra complexes (in *All Alone With Daddy* and *The Man of the House*).

First Things

Author: Joseph C. Grannis (concept development and curriculum design) and Virginia Schone (script for filmstrips)
Publisher: Guidance Associates of Pleasantville, New York
Date of publication: 1970
Level: Primary grades

First Things is designed to introduce the primary grade child to the basic concepts in both the physical and social environment. The program aims at helping the child to understand himself better as an individual and as a member of a group. It helps the child to identify with and recognize the various interactions that occur within groups. *First Things* increases the child's awareness of the effect of these interactions on the individual and helps the child to see how expectations influence interactions. The program deals with five themes: (1) *Who do you think you are?* (2) *Guess who's in a group!* (3) *What happens between people?* (4) *You got mad: Are you glad?* and (5) *What do you expect of others?* Each theme is accompanied by two or three sound filmstrips, which are designed to be motivational. The manual suggests activities to follow each filmstrip that are designed to get the child involved with the theme, to interest him in collecting and examining data about himself and his relationships with others. The activities revolve around observation, classification, sociodrama, and experimentation. The manual states the objectives of each theme, the concepts discussed, and the generalizations that can be drawn from each theme. Suggestions for facilitating discussion are also given to aid the teacher.

The themes of the *First Things* program are interrelated. *Who do you think you are?* deals with the idea that an individual is a combination of facts and figures, actions, and feelings. *Guess who's in a group!* deals with what a group is, the different types of groups, how being part of a group affects people, and the norms of different groups. The concepts dealt with in *What happens between people?* are interactions (both physical and symbolic), goals, and conflicts. *You got mad: Are you glad?* explores the causes, effects, and ways in which hostility is expressed, as well as the ways that conflict can be handled and resolved. *What do you expect of others?* considers the ideas of expectation and prejudgments, how things live up to people's expectations, and the need to be open to people who are different before making prejudgments.

First Things fosters conceptual thinking and can serve to increase the child's listening vocabulary. Ideas and concepts are presented clearly, and the incidents used to present the themes on the filmstrips are easy for the young child to identify with, that is, moving, meeting new friends, being excluded from a group, etc.

DUSO D-1 (Developing Understanding of Self and Others)

Author: Don Dinkmeyer
Publisher: American Guidance Service, Inc.
Date of publication: 1970
Level: Kindergarten and lower primary grades

The *DUSO D-1* program is designed to be used by the teacher or elementary school counselor to help the primary grade child to understand social and emotional behavior. The *DUSO D-1* activities "make extensive use of a listening, inquiry, experiential, and discussion approach to learning." Listening activities rarely extend for more than 5 minutes, reflecting the consideration given to the short attention span of the young child. The program helps the child to build a vocabulary; strong focus is put on teaching the child words that can be used to express feelings; the program also focuses on the dynamic relationship between feelings, goals, and behaviors, and helps the child to learn how to express himself freely.

The *DUSO D-1* program revolves around eight unit themes, each containing four or five cycle themes. The program is designed for use over a full academic year. The eight unit themes follow:

Understanding and Accepting Self is introduced by presenting the following rules of group discussion: (1) raise your hand, (2) listen carefully, (3) don't clam up, (4) stick to the point, and (5) think together. The major emphasis of this unit is to help the child to develop a realistic self-concept, to be aware of both his strengths and liabilities, and to build on his strengths.

Understanding Feelings focuses on helping the child to understand and express both positive and negative feelings. Activities evolve around the ideas of sharing, being sensitive to the feelings of others, and building friendships.

Understanding Others emphasizes helping the child to understand what working in a group entails (cooperation and responsibility), and the benefits inherent in working together.

Understanding Independence focuses on helping the child to see the benefits of doing things for himself, on

doing the best he can, and on the importance of evaluating the consequences of one's actions.

Understanding Goals and Purposeful Behavior helps the child to devise a systematic, appropriate, realistic approach to work. Emphasis is placed on evaluating the whole job, seeing its component parts, establishing an appropriate plan of action, and proceeding efficiently.

Understanding Mastery, Competence, and Resourcefulness focuses on helping the child realistically to understand his capacities. The idea that competency and achievement are results of both desire and ability is stressed.

Understanding Emotional Maturity helps the child to investigate both effective and ineffective ways of dealing with stress and change. The activities focus on the ineffectiveness of worrying, crying, throwing temper tantrums, impatience, anger, etc.

Understanding Choice and Consequences helps the child to understand that feelings, values, and behaviors are interrelated. It stresses the need to make value judgments, to hold to beliefs under group pressure, and to accept the consequences of his choice.

The *DUSO D-1* program is packaged in a convenient metal carrying case, and all the components are bound or packaged in vinyl folders. The kit contains the following:

1. A manual, which includes the rationale and objectives of the program, the stated purpose of each activity, and clear directions for conducting the program. Discussion activities, supplementary activities, and reading are also included.

2. Two storybooks, which contain forty-one stories and 200 beautiful colored illustrations. The stories are designed to introduce each cycle theme and to motivate discussion.

3. Thirty-three full-colored posters, which state the main idea of each cycle story.

4. Thirty-three puppet and thirty-three role-playing cards to provide the child with opportunities to dramatize real-life situations connected with the cycle themes.

5. Seven puppets (Fig. 10-1).

6. Puppet props, which help the children to create the desired setting for their puppet shows.

7. Group discussion cards, which present the five rules for group discussion.

The *DUSO D-1* program is excellent. Most characters are animals or Duso's underwater friends, which adds to the delight of the children. The discussion, role playing, and puppet activities allow the children to become

Fig. 10-1. The use of puppets in class discussions can spark lively interactions. This class is using materials from the *DUSO* kit.

involved with the topics and allow their creativity to be expressed.

Focus on Self-Development,
Stage two: Responding

Authors: Judith L. Anderson and Patrica Miner
Publisher: Science Research Associates, Inc.
Date of publication: 1971
Level: Elementary grades

Focus on Self-Development is an audiovisual guidance program for the elementary grades. The program is designed to be used by the classroom teacher. Its purpose is to get the child to think and act about himself, others, and his environment in an intelligent fashion. The program is based on nineteen units: three on environmental influences, six on the personal self, eight on the social self, and an introductory and summary unit. The units and their objectives are as follows:

1. Self-concept: helps the child to realize he responds differently in different situations
2. Interests: the child becomes aware of social, emotional, and intellectual aspects of himself
3. Abilities: helps the child to explore his interests
4. Limitations: the child comes to understand his abilities and limitations
5. Goals: helps the child to find his goals and to understand how he may approach them
6. Concerns: discusses the death of a dog and how to deal with such problems

7. Responsibility: describes what responsibility is and what it entails
8. Physical environment: the child becomes aware of how his environment affects him
9. Cultural differences: the child learns to accept and understand people with different backgrounds
10. Social influences: provides awareness of how attitudes toward others affect personal interaction with the individual
11. Communication: discusses what it means to communicate
12. Honesty: child becomes aware of the effects honesty and dishonesty have on others
13. Companionship: discusses the concepts of friendship
14. Acceptance and rejection: helps the child to deal with rejection
15. Respect: discusses respect and the lack of it and how it affects others
16. Trust: discusses the effects of trust or the lack of it on others
17. Loyalty: the child explores what it means to be loyal
18. Competition and cooperation: discusses winning and losing in relation to the competitive spirit
19. Summary: the child is asked to reflect on the year's work and to determine how his behavior has changed

The materials included in the program are as follows:

1. The teacher's guide, which presents the purposes, content, and components of the program. Suggestions are given to help the

teacher introduce the various units. Questions for discussions and a list of supplementary materials are enclosed. The appendix of the teacher's guide gives suggestions on group techniques, including principles of guidance, how to set up a role-playing activity, role of the teacher, and working with feelings.

2. *The Me I Know* is a workbook that allows the child to express his personal feelings about the concepts presented in the units. (The workbook is regarded as the child's property, and he should not be required to show his work or lack of it to the teacher.)

3. Filmstrips. Six of the themes' activities revolve around filmstrips with accompanying sound tracks.

4. Story records. All themes not introduced by a filmstrip utilize story records to present the themes.

5. Photoboards. Twenty-two sided photoboards and a displaying easel to stimulate discussions and role-playing activities are included.

Focus on Self-Development is a total counseling program that will produce desirable results when used by the creative teacher.

Bill Martin's Freedom Books

Author: Bill Martin, Jr.
Publisher: Bowmar Publishing Corp.
Date of publication: 1970
Level: Fifth to twelfth grades

The *Freedom Books* are designed to be used with fifth through twelfth grade children as a social studies program. (However, it appears to be usable with fifth through ninth graders because of the simplicity of the text and the nature of many of the recommended activities.) The *Freedom Books* depart from the usual textbook format, which stresses reading ability, memorization, the development of study habits, and emphasize the building of conceptual abilities. The themes of these books revolve around the author's desire to "help children keep faith in the American Dream." The subject matter is mostly nationalistic, and the program is designed to inspire creative, analytical thinking about the problems that confront people.

The author describes the purpose of the books as follows: "The first purpose of the Freedom Books is delight," the second is creative involvement, the third is analytical investigation, and the fourth is to help the child organize personal and social meaning.

The books are beautifully illustrated, using a multiplicity of techniques. The story lines are short and written in poetic verse. In most of the books the story line is contained in the illustrations, and in some of the books it departs from the left-right progression across the page. This style can make reading more joyous but also limits the use of this program. Children who have learning problems in reading, figure-ground discrimination, or visual perceptual problems might have a difficult time using these books as readers. The program, in addition to the books and teacher's manual, includes a tape or record for each book. On the tape the author reads or sings the story line, provides musical accompaniment for the children to read by, discusses his ideas about the theme of the story, has a discussion with the illustrator of the book, and in some instances sings songs or reads poems and/or stories related to the theme of the book. The use of these tapes creates a language model for the children and helps them to see how effectively words can be used to express thoughts and feelings. As a result of the repetitive nature of verse, many words become part of the child's vocabulary almost unconsciously. Many new words are introduced in a nonchalant manner in the tape discussions as well.

The entire program is designed and presented in a delightful fashion. Even the teacher's manual is designed creatively. It includes the purposes of the program, the stories, and suggestions for creative involvement and discussions. Dance and dramatization make up a large part of the program, the stories, and suggestions for interaction with the themes of these books. The creative presentation of this material and its focus on creative, analytical thinking aid in motivating the uninterested child.

Each book deals with a specific theme.

I Am Freedom's Child emphasizes the need for a positive self-concept and the acceptance and appreciation of differences among people. *Gentle, Gentle Thursday* points out that everyone needs time for themselves, a gentle Thursday, to be a contributing member of society. It stresses the need for people to be in touch with their personal feelings and desires and to reflect on the demands others are putting on them. *I Reach Out To the Morning* deals with the individual's reactions to things and people that are strange and different and stresses the need for the individual to accept and not be frightened by the differences encountered. *Freedom's Apple Tree* evolves around the idea that every individual is an important component in the make up of a free society. The theme of *America, I Know You* deals with the idea that "America is a collection of beliefs, happenings and circumstances of times conflicting that need to be understood." Poor Old Uncle Sam stresses the importance of believing in the value system of America. *It's America For Me* points out that protest is part of America and that the diversity of opinions contributes to making America a land of personal freedom. *Once There Were Bluebirds* focuses on the beauty of nature and on the fact that this beauty is being threatened by pollution. *Spoiled Tomatoes* also deals with the theme of pollution, showing how pollution can shift the balance of nature. The last book in the series, *Adam's Balm*, is concerned with the threat of the atomic bomb and deals with the ideas behind nuclear disarmament.

The Adventures of the Lollipop Dragon

Publisher: Society for Visual Education, Inc.
Date of publication: 1970
Level: Primary grades

The Adventures of the Lollipop Dragon is a sound filmstrip program for the primary grade child. Six filmstrips portray stories that focus on the concepts of sharing, working together, littering, caring for personal property, taking turns, and being kind to animals. The first filmstrip introduces the Lollipop Dragon, who is the main character of the program. The program is designed to motivate discussion and interest in the concepts that are presented, and it can be utilized in the classroom media center or for individualized instruction.

The kit contains (1) a teacher's guide, which states the objectives of the program and scripts that correspond to the cassette recordings of the stories; (2) a coloring book, which is analogous to the first filmstrip, *How the Lollipop Dragon Got His Name;* (3) filmstrips; and (4) cassettes or records.

The Lollipop Dragon appears to have great appeal to young children. The filmstrips are beautiful illustrations of a small kingdom where lollipops are made. The morals of the stories often appear to be overemphasized, but this does not detract from the child's enjoyment of the program.

DUSO D-2 (Developing Understanding of Self and Others)

Author: Don Dinkmeyer
Publisher: American Guidance Service, Inc.
Date of publication: 1973
Level: Upper primary and fourth grades (ages 7 to 10 years)

The *DUSO D-2* program is designed to be used by teachers and elementary school counselors as a developmental guidance program. The program is designed to be used through a full school year. It is based on eight major themes, each divided into four or five cycles or subthemes. Each cycle is designed for a week's use and makes use of inquiry, experiential, and discussion approaches to learning. The eight major themes follow:

Towards Self-Identity: Developing Self-Awareness and a Positive Self-Concept
Towards Friendship: Understanding Peers
Towards Responsible Interdependence: Understanding Growth from Self-Centeredness to Social Interest
Towards Self-Reliance: Understanding Personal Responsibility
Towards Resourcefulness and Purposefulness: Understanding Personal Motivation
Towards Competence: Understanding Accomplishments
Towards Emotional Stability: Understanding Stress
Towards Responsible Choice Making: Understanding Values

The general objectives around which these themes revolve are developing understanding about the value of a good self-concept and of interpersonal relationships; the teleological aspects of human behavior (in both cognitive and affective domains); the dynamic interrelationship of ideas, feelings, beliefs, and behaviors that enable people to express feelings accurately; and understanding the components of achievement.

The *DUSO D-2* materials are well organized and are contained in a convenient metal carrying case. They include the following:

1. The manual, which presents the general format for the *DUSO D-2* program. Each cycle includes a story, a problem situation, a role-playing activity, a discussion picture, a career awareness activity, and supplementary activities and readings. Guidelines for the presentation of these activities are in the manual.

2. Eight self and social development activity cards, which are designed to be used early in the program and are aimed at helping children become better informed about themselves and others through involvement and activities that stress communication.

3. Seventeen records or five cassettes which contain dramatizations of stories and songs that correspond to the cycles. These are designed for high motivation.

4. Thirty-three colored posters, which review the themes of each story, are included in a vinyl folder, which can be used as a display easel.

5. Thirty-three role-playing activity cards.

6. Thirty-three puppet activity cards, which are designed to give children the opportunity to dramatize situations that are related to the cycle themes.

7. Eight puppets for role playing.

8. Thirty-three career awareness cards, which are designed to relate cycle themes to career awareness and exploration.

9. Thirty-three discussion pictures (and an introduction card), which are related to cycles and themes. They are designed to stimulate discussion about feelings, attitudes, values, and purposes the child perceives and interprets.

10. Six discussion guide cards, which are presented in the introductory lesson. They are designed to stimulate discussion and are recommended for use throughout the program. The activity cards are packaged in vinyl folders, and each day's activity is printed on a separate card. This makes the kit more manageable during use.

The instructions for use of the various components of the program are very explicit; however, because of the expressive, open nature of the activities, the teacher must be adept in carrying on discussions and motivating productive participation. The *DUSO D-2* program is an excellent tool for helping children to understand themselves and others better, and if used by a skilled teacher, it can be of great benefit to the child in conflict.

Dimensions of Personality

Author: Walter Limbacher
Publisher: George A. Pflaum Publisher, Inc., and Standard Reference Works Publishing Co.
Date of publication: 1969
Level: Fourth to sixth grades

Dimensions of Personality is a graded program in affective education. It is intended for use in the elementary grades, junior high school, and high school. Materials for fourth, fifth, and sixth grade students were written by Walter Limbacher. The George A. Pflaum Publisher, Inc., has expanded the program to include the primary, junior high, and senior high levels.

Dimensions of Personality considers the whole child—his emotional and his intellectual capacities. It is hoped that through this program children will come to understand their physical, intellectual, and emotional growth better. The program fosters interaction. Pictures, cartoons, text, "What's your opinion?" questions, activities—all seek to involve the children by provoking lively discussion and individual insight.

Special editions have been designed to provide teachers with classroom activities that they can use to initiate goal-oriented group responses. These activities are devised to open communication so that children can identify with the message of the text.

A brief review of the fourth grade text gives an indication of the total thrust of the program. It is titled *Here I Am*. Individual topics include the following:

1. Are there two different kinds of "feeling awful"?
2. Are being awake and aware the same?
3. The five senses and what consciousness means
4. Recognizing and accepting differences in others

One activity at this level is especially fun for the children. They are asked to trace each other's body outlines on large sheets of butcher-type paper. Each child then fills in his or her own image with paint, crayon, etc. If possible, the finished products are hung where all can view them. Such an activity could well spark a unit entitled, *The Body I've Inherited*.

Teachers who have used these materials report that the enthusiasm of the children was high. Their enjoyment served as a challenge to consider additional ways to make their education a satisfying and rewarding experience.

(Contact) Maturity: Growing Up Strong

Author: Editors of *Scholastic Scope*
Publisher: Scholastic Book Services
Date of publication: Copyright 1968; updated printing July, 1972
Level: Eighth to tenth grades reading on a fourth to sixth grade level

This program is designed to stimulate student interest in learning, reading, thinking, and expressing their thoughts and feelings and to help the student read, speak, and write better. The program is designed primarily for use in a student-centered classroom in which the teacher functions as a catalyst. The program provides means for involving inattentive, passive, withdrawn children. It allows children to reflect on themselves and their social interactions with others while enhancing their expressive skills.

1. A teacher's guide containing suggestions for activities and presentation of the materials

2. An anthology containing short stories, poems, plays, letters, comments, and questions, which are designed to motivate the reader to investigate his own feelings about what was read

3. A logbook of activities corresponding to the readings and providing an opportunity of subjective expression

4. Posters corresponding to the chapters in the anthology and logbook activities

This program can be used as a language arts program for the unmotivated child. It offers useful guidelines in the promotion of self-evaluative skills by way of role playing, discussion, and drawing and writing activities. The subject matter in the anthology deals primarily in the affective domain while interest in reading and learning is nurtured. The creative teacher will find this program an effective and productive tool.

Target Behavior

Author: Roger Kroth
Publisher: Select-Ed, Inc.
Date of publication: 1973
Level: Can be adapted for use at all ages

The *Target Behavior* kit is a diagnostic tool; it aims at selecting behavioral objectives that will improve the child's self-concept. This is accomplished by recording data of how the child perceives himself (real self) and how the child would like to see himself (ideal self). The kit includes two sets of twenty-five behavior cards; one set corresponds to classroom behavior and the other to home behavior. The child is presented with one set of cards and is asked to arrange them on the target behavior board under the column that best describes him (the real sort). The board is divided into the following nine columns: (1) most like me, (2) very much like me, (3) like me, (4) a little like me, (5) undecided, (6) a little unlike me, (7) unlike me, (8) very much unlike me, and (9) most unlike me. The columns are arranged in a normal distribution, allowing for just one response at either end of the distribution; the median response (undecided) allows for the placement of five behavior cards. This arrangement forces the child to be discreet in placement of the cards. When the child has completed this task, the number of the column in which each behavior card was placed is recorded. The cards are then removed from the board, and the child is asked to arrange them to show how he would like to be (the ideal sort). These responses are recorded, and the differences between the real sort and the ideal sort are calculated. These differences are then squared. Any squared difference of sixteen points or more constitutes a significant discrepancy. These discrepancies are treated as target behaviors for modification. A formula is provided to show the correlation between the real and the ideal sortings. The higher the correlation the better will be the child's adjustment. The manual also suggests administering a post test to check the effectiveness of the behavior modification program.

Teachers can adapt *Target Behaviors* to any grade level by designing their own behavior cards that are appropriate for their students. This kit is a useful synthesis of the behavioral and self-concept theories. Its simple design makes administration easy for the teacher or parent. The behavioral objectives are those aspects that the child would like to obtain, thus making modification both motivating and relevant to the child.

The Coping With Series

Authors: Shirley Schwartzrock and C. Gilbert Wrenn
Publisher: American Guidance Service, Inc.
Date of publication: 1973
Level: Junior high and high school

The Coping With Series comprise a set of informative, nonjudgmental books that focus on the interest, concerns, and frustrations of today's adolescents. The books are designed to stimulate thought and discussion on the related themes covered in the books. The set consists of twenty-three books and a teacher's manual. The teacher's manual contains objective procedures and activities for the presentation of the books, and it also contains a teacher and student bibliography.

The books and their themes are as follows:

Facts and Fantasies About Drugs, which is a report of laws, uses, abuses, and effects of stimulants, glue, marijuana, LSD, heroin, and other hard drugs

Facts and Fantasies About Alcohol, which deals with how young people become acquainted with alcohol, its effects, and misconceptions about it

Facts and Fantasies About Smoking, which presents motivational factors concerning the risk and effects of smoking

The Mind Benders, which discusses the motivational determinants of drug abuse, an actual account of an ex-addict, and problems people have who use drugs

Some Common Crutches, which examines the dynamics involved in the use of crutches in alleviating emotional problems

Food as a Crutch, which examines the dynamics involved in the use of food crutches in alleviating emotional problems

Alcohol as a Crutch, which conveys the physical, emotional, and social effects of alcohol dependency

Living With Differences, which deals with understanding and accepting differences in religion, age, nationality, and race

You Always Communicate Something, which examines the conscious and unconscious effects on communication and how to communicate effectively

Understanding the Law of Our Land, which describes what laws are, how they are changed, civil disobedience, and the arrest of a drug pusher

Easing the Scene, which examines the effect of one's self-concept in social interaction with others

In Front of the Table and Behind It, which describes the function, rules, participation, and leadership of group dynamics

Can You Talk With Someone Else? which discusses the need, importance, and method of effective communication with others

To Like and Be Liked, which conveys the importance, problems, and suggestions for improving relationships with others

My Life, What Shall I Do With It? which pertains to the importance of making well-thought out decisions in planning for the future

Do I Know the "Me" Others See? which examines the importance of realizing self-worth and objectively assessing one's strong and weak points

Crises Youth Face Today, which explores problems that arise out of an inability to adapt to a rapidly changing world

Changing Roles of Men and Women, which takes the position that society's attitudes toward members of the opposite sex are changing as the entire social order of society changes

Coping With Cliques, which discusses the various types of cliques and the problems associated with being excluded from and being a member of a clique

I'd Rather Do It Myself If You Don't Mind, which deals with considerations one contemplates when making decisions

Living With Loneliness, which illustrates the feelings of loneliness and ways to deal with them

Parents Can Be A Problem, which discusses conflicting values of parents and teen-agers, problems with communication and special problems that parents may have (alcoholism, divorce, being overly permissive and overly restrictive)

Grades, What's So Important About Them Anyway? which examines the importance of grades and their effects on the child

Each book contains illustrations, stories, and factual information to develop further understanding of its theme. The great variety of themes presented in *The Coping With Series* makes them extremely adaptable to the needs of the pupil, and they can be of great value in stimulating thought and discussion in the classroom.

ADAPTED MATERIALS

Since formal materials for children in conflict are in short supply, teachers must call on their own ability to adapt standard materials

Fig. 10-2. These boys are taking turns releasing their aggression on each other with soft bats. This is a fun way to release frustration in an acceptable manner.

for use with individual children. A few of the materials that have been adapted by teachers are described briefly. These are presented with the hope of stimulating teachers to use similar materials and to develop others.

Punching bag. Children sometimes need to express themselves with inanimate objects. An old tackling dummy or other soft but durable object can be used for this purpose. The bag should be constructed so as to take abuse without breaking, even when kicked. The bag should remain stationary so that it will not "return" blows dealt by the child, which might cause more frustration.

Dart board. A dart board can provide a great deal of tension release. The child can put a picture of the teacher, a parent, or another child on the board as a target.

Soft bats. Several varieties of soft bats are available for use with children (Fig. 10-2). These provide a safe tool for swinging, throwing, or even striking another person. An angry, aggressive child can express hostility in an acceptable manner with these soft bats, whereas the withdrawn child is provided with a safe outlet for expression of feelings.

Tape recorder. The teacher of children in conflict must rely on a variety of educational techniques for delivery of information (Fig. 10-3). The tape recorder is one of the most useful. It can provide a nonthreatening tool for individualizing instruction, self-expression, and reinforcement. Recorders should be simple to operate and durable so that children can handle them.

Mats. Soft mats are useful in the classroom for protection of children during games, in self-expression activities, and in physical activities such as tumbling and wrestling.

Individualized materials. Academic materials that are available in a variety of delivery formats and at several levels are essential for children who have emotional problems. These might include programed materials, materials that utilize more than one sense simultaneously, or materials that appeal to a wide variety of interests.

Materials for therapeutic play. A variety of materials are needed to develop individual skills. These might include rackets for lawn

Fig. 10-3. Teaching machines are available to teachers in a variety of types and price ranges. These machines can help a teacher to individualize instruction so that she can interact on a one-to-one basis with children.

Fig. 10-4. Large desks with plenty of space for one and sometimes two active children provide a roomy atmosphere for work. Enclosing these areas provides a measure of privacy.

tennis, table-tennis paddles and balls, fly rods, basketball goals, handball equipment, and a place to swim, ice skate, hike, and fish. Much of this equipment can be rented when ownership is impossible.

Quiet areas for study. Children in conflict often need a quiet area in which to work (Fig. 10-4). This area can provide children with the security they need when they feel out-of-sorts with the world or with a place relatively free of external stimuli when things become too much for the child to tolerate. A quiet area or office can be constructed from dividers that extend from the floor to above eye level. Generally these carrels should be individual, but some teachers have placed two carrels facing one another to save material and space.

Large shatter-proof mirror. Many activities can center around a mirror to build self-image, a realistic view of the image one is presenting to others, and for practical activities such as grooming.

Individual diaries for children. Allowing children to keep individual diaries (if they wish to do so) can be a cathartic activity. Children must be free to say whatever they want to say without fear of teacher snooping and/or reprisals.

In addition to these adapted materials the teacher should have ready access to the following teaching essentials:

Art supplies
Bulletin boards for displays
Chalkboards
Pencil sharpener
Shades to darken room
Lounge area for quiet reading (can be used in reinforcement)
Clock and 30-minute kitchen timers
Carpeting, at least in one section of the classroom
Telephone or other intercommunication system
Storage cabinets for materials, at least one drawer with a lock

Typewriter
Book shelves
Small conference tables for group work
Sink and running water, bathroom in primary classrooms
Time-out facility that can be shared with one other classroom
Large student desks with elbow room
Audiovisual materials including 16 millimeter projector, overhead projector, slide projector, phonograph, and cassette tape recorder and player
Portable chalkboard to use with small groups
Adequate lighting and ventilation
Stapler and other teacher desk supplies

Publishers that market educational materials are listed in Appendix C.

SUMMARY

There appears to be a noticeable lack of materials that support the affective domain. The materials that are available generally are designed to be used with normal children to help support mental health development. Formal materials reviewed indicate promise with emotionally disturbed children. In addition to the materials developed especially for the affective domain, there are many other materials that can be adapted for use with these children. Several of these materials are discussed with specific uses proposed.

CHAPTER 11

Change agents: teachers, parents, ancillary personnel

Change agents are those individuals who actively involve themselves in changing the behavior of children. Three major groups will be discussed: teachers, parents, and ancillary personnel. These are the people who make a system work, who orchestrate the modification process, and who bring about a lasting change to children in conflict. Without their shared expertise change is only a hollow ritual—without reason, form, or direction. None of these groups is more important than others; each has its own job to do which, at that moment, is the most critical factor for the child. Teachers and parents will receive more critical review because of the emphasis of this text and because of their commitment (in time spent) with children.

A CENTRAL FOCUS OF CHANGE—THE TEACHER

Competent teachers are helpful to all children, but for children with "built-in" problems the teacher is critical to change. The specific competencies needed, preservice and in-service training and skills of regular and special teachers will be discussed at some length in this section.

Regular classroom teacher

The front line of any educational offensive must be anchored by classroom teachers who are interested in the education of all children. Education specialists have, at various times, undermined these professionals by suggesting that only average children could be educated effectively in their classrooms. Unintentionally they have been made "special educators" for the average child. In efforts to develop better special education programs education specialists have segregated, separated, and splintered the efforts of regular teachers to the extend that fragmentation of teaching and learning was inevitable.

As education specialists slowly begin changing their emphasis from isolation to encouraging cooperation between regular and special teachers, there will likely develop fears of maintaining role identification and defenses against change. Regular classroom teachers who have been asked to refer children in conflict so that specialists could intercede are now being asked to maintain these children in regular classrooms. This all-or-nothing attitude held by some special educators appears disquieting for teachers, who must wonder what is coming next. Most special educators believe that all children in conflict cannot be maintained in the regular classroom and are seeking a continuum of services for these children that will allow each child to function as closely as possible to reality.

Teacher competencies

There is no comprehensive guide available to suggest just which traits are best for regular classroom teachers who interact with children in conflict. Several characteristics or teacher behaviors appear to be significant, as determined by a study of classrooms where successful integration is taking place. These include the following behaviors:

1. Group management. One of the most important skills of regular classroom teachers includes group management techniques (Fig. 11-1). Several components of classroom management behaviors have been delineated; however, it is debatable whether these skills can be taught. A variety of management skills are necessary, including both small and large groups and individual interaction. In viewing classrooms in a variety of educational set-tings, classroom management appears to be one of the more serious weaknesses of classroom teachers. When classroom management techniques of a teacher are weak, the addition of children in conflict to the classroom will often create chaos for the entire class.

It is difficult for training institutions to prepare teachers to manage an entire classroom because preservice stations often do not allow classroom management to be placed totally in the hands of untested teachers. It is important for practicum students to be placed with strong supervising teachers who can "allow" students some failure and still maintain a positive control over classroom activities.

2. Reluctance to give up. When classroom teachers are bombarded with new expectations almost daily, it is inviting to "give up" on problem children. There has been little encouragement to do otherwise. In selecting placement sites for children in conflict education specialists should consider teachers who are not easily discouraged by lack of observable growth in children.

3. Security in teaching ability. The regular classroom teacher must be secure in the

Fig. 11-1. Group management skills are a "must" for teachers of children in conflict. This teacher makes "attending" important and management an easy task.

ability to teach while working as part of a team. This requires an ability to give and take without feeling threatened by the specialists with whom the teacher interacts or being threatening to other team members.

4. Willingness to teach through strengths. The regular classroom teacher will generally try to circumvent problem behaviors whenever possible. This requires the teacher to work through each child's strengths to reach stated goals. Looking for the causes of deviant behavior is often an attractive pasttime but a luxury not afforded the regular classroom teacher.

5. Ability to motivate students. Much student activity in the regular classroom is of necessity self-directed with routine follow-up by the teacher. The ability to motivate self-direction with many students is essential if any individualization is to occur with other children.

6. Willingness to give more of self. The classroom teacher who wants to teach children in conflict must be willing to pay the price required. This price often includes extra time in preparation, meetings with educational teams, conferences with parents, and interactions with the resource specialist. Many of these responsibilities will need to be met after school hours and at night. These children are demanding. Change sometimes occurs between 9:00 A.M. and 3:30 P.M., but it often requires longer hours and some inconvenience to the teacher's normal routine.

The special teacher

The skills required of the special teacher are essentially the same as those required of good regular classroom teachers. The implementation of these skills does present some different problems, however. Various studies of teacher competencies needed for special classes have largely related to teachers who work in isolation from the regular class (Mackie et al., 1957; Bullock and Whelan, 1971). From initial observations of programs in operation, state certification guidelines, and training program guidelines it appears that special skills are necessary for resource specialists who work with children in con-

flict. These include the following competencies:

1. Flexibility. The special resource teacher must interact with several teachers during each school day and communicate with the educational team on a regular basis. This requires a flexible teaching style and a willingness to adjust to a variety of teaching systems or styles of regular classroom teachers. The specialist cannot and should not change the regular classroom to fit a prescribed mold but instead must often adapt techniques to fit the needs of each classroom unit.

2. Ability to share expertise. Professionals who possess special skills have often protected those skills as though sharing might be dangerous. The resource specialist must break with tradition and share expertise with the regular classroom teacher so that cooperation and growth take place. This sharing of skills will encourage the classroom teacher to communicate more fully with the specialist, which should result in more efficient educational programing for all children.

3. Understanding of techniques for relieving conflict in the regular classroom. The resource specialist must provide assistance and innovative leadership in approaching recurrent problems facing classroom teachers. Regular class teachers can get into a rut working with behavior problem children. The specialist must be a catalyst for fresh ideas while sustaining the teacher's confidence to manage the classroom learning situation.

4. Ability to unify. The resource specialist must be willing and capable of coordinating information from various members of the educational team into a workable plan or program. This requires a low-key but stable approach that lends support to all members and threatens as few as possible. The child in conflict often exhibits behavior that causes tensions within the classroom and among adults trying to help the child.

5. Willingness to share the glory of success with others. Experience indicates that the ability to give credit for success to the classroom teacher and other members of the educational team pays high dividends in future cooperation and success. Conversely,

taking much of the glory of pupil growth often assures the specialist of poor cooperation and failure. It is not unusual to find teachers with fewer curriculum skills who are able to work more effectively in a cooperative setting than a teacher with greater skill development. Situations have been observed in which the teacher seemed to become less effective in human relations as teaching skills were developed. Specialists need to develop the knack of saying, "I don't have the answer," "Can you help me?" and "Let's work it out together." Asking for help and giving credit to others may be among the most important skills a specialist can develop.

Aside from the general competencies listed for special teachers there are many specific skills that are generally taken for granted. These might include an understanding of exceptional children, the ability to remediate academic weaknesses, an understanding of curriculum and methods used in the regular class, and a desire to learn from others. Many administrators believe that similar competencies are needed by those who act as resource specialists, itinerant teachers, and special class teachers. Although there are similarities in role expectations, there are basic differences that must be considered. With more integration, the specialist must work more closely with classroom teachers—an expectation that requires greater skill in areas of human relations and professional interaction. The teacher who works in an isolated setting of a special class needs to be self-motivating, innovative, and capable of functioning with much less professional support. University training programs have been taking a close look at the product that they prepare, trying to supply public schools with well-trained specialists who have the versatility to fit into the pattern of various school districts. Preservice does have many limitations, one of them being the inability to prepare students who can work successfully in all role expectations.

One of the most difficult tasks for school districts is to define clearly the kind of educational programs they want to implement for children in conflict. An early study that compared various programs for emotionally disturbed individuals supports this claim (Morse et al., 1964). The science of changing human behavior is surely an inexact science, as is human behavior itself. To bring some order to this inexact process education specialists must "carve out" some logical goals to help guide their efforts.

Maintaining the teacher's mental health

Teachers are sometimes placed in situations in which no alternatives to failure exist. Some children are so out of touch with reality during part or all of the school day that an adult needs to be with them almost constantly. In addition, teachers need to have interaction and support from "people who count." In a regular classroom the teacher often receives reinforcement from children, from parents, and from ongoing success in the classroom. These reinforcements are often unavailable to special teachers who are working with children in conflict. Reinforcement is often replaced by punishment, which is adroitly administered by children, parents, and even other teachers. Several notions for maintaining the mental health of the teacher will be considered.

1. Adequate preparation. There seems to be no alternative to adequate preservice for teachers. The turnover or dropout rate of teachers who begin teaching children in conflict before they are fully trained is far too high. Being responsible for the educational program of seriously troubled children is no place to gain teaching competence any more than jumping into ten feet of water is an appropriate way to learn swimming skills.

2. Adult support. Conscientious teachers need the support of significant adults if a high level of teaching efficiency is to be maintained. This support must be based on an understanding of program goals and how these goals are being met. The therapeutic team can lend significant support to the classroom teacher, since their interest is verified by interaction with the child.

3. Human beings first. Teachers who work with children in conflict are people first and

Fig. 11-2. Patience can be exhibited in a variety of ways. This teacher has decided to relax and allow the child to learn in a relaxed atmosphere.

teachers only as a choice of occupation. As people they should engage in stimulating and rewarding activities outside the school room. Working with children who take rather than give requires the teacher to be renewed constantly. Hobbies, sports, and free time just to relax are all possible renewal activities. A teacher needs to face each new day fully recovered from the problems that were faced the day before.

4. Awareness of self. There is no mold of mental health from which teachers should be cut. The fact that teachers exhibit a variety of feelings is actually a strengthening feature of special programs. Each teacher has special strengths and weaknesses of which he or she should be aware. No teacher will enjoy all pupils equally well or be effective with all personality types. As long as this awareness exists, effective programing can be maintained through proper pupil placement. The teacher must feel comfortable in admitting a dislike for particular children if acceptable matching of pupils and teachers is to be assured. It is difficult to describe specific personality patterns that seem to work best with children in conflict. Teachers who appeared to be slightly neurotic and/or compulsive have often been observed to do an outstanding job in the classroom with troubled children.

5. Patience. Teachers who have not taught children in conflict have a difficult adjustment to make in terms of the time it takes to change behaviors (Fig. 11-2). When children are first screened for special programs, they are often 9 to 11 years of age. These children did not develop problem behavior overnight. Children often feel comfortable with their deviance and will resist change, even if the change is toward more acceptable behavior. Under the best conditions this takes time; two steps forward and one step back is often acceptable progress. The teacher who is unable to notice tiny gains or who must compare growth by what is considered "normal" will often become extremely discouraged.

6. Therapy for the teacher. It has been suggested that teachers of disturbed children need to receive some form of therapy (Long and Newman, 1971). Although teachers need therapy at the same rate as all other professionals, those who work with children in conflict often need some additional emotional first aid. It was suggested earlier that this can be gained through interaction with the educational team. Long and Newman suggest that a human wailing wall is often needed to help the special teacher. A sympathetic ear needs to be more than just someone to listen; it must be the ear of an informed person who

knows the situation and is able to be supportive to the teacher.

Through the years many young and talented teachers have left the special education training program at the University of Northern Colorado to enter a new teaching career. These have been mostly experienced teachers who have already been successful in the classroom. Although most of them have adjusted to the role and expectations of specialists, there have been some notable exceptions. Following are some complaints that often have led to disenchantment and finally to a change in career teaching goals.

1. Some blame the principal. "Our principal doesn't understand special education and what we are trying to do. He acts as though he is afraid of us, never coming near the classroom. We are treated as outcasts (our classroom is where the storage room once was, next to the furnace). We have invited our principal into the classroom, but he is always too busy to come. I can accept the fact that he is busy, but I get the message that he wants to be left alone."

2. Others blame the staff. "The teachers act as though I caused the kids to act the way they do. It's not our kids but your kids. When I try to integrate a child in one of their classes, they do it as a favor to me, not to help the child. One teacher told me she would help me any way she could, but not to send Greg back to her classroom. I want to be part of the staff, but I am always made to feel different."

3. The "system" is blamed by some. "We have a complete special education program in our school, all in my classroom. I'm supposed to be teaching children who are emotionally disturbed, but I teach every conceivable problem. Some of my kids are retarded, some have serious sensory problems, and last week they brought me a physically handicapped child. My room is the dumping ground for all of the kids no one else wants. I'm supposed to work with children for a part of the day and have part of each day to work with teachers, but I have nearly twice as many kids as state regulations allow. When I do a good job, I get reinforced by getting more kids. Some have not been properly evaluated when I get them. I'm supposed to be on the evaluation team, and I haven't been called for a meeting for over a month."

4. Parents are sometimes blamed. "The parents of my kids are completely oblivious as to what I'm trying to accomplish. They won't come to school, they won't answer my notes, and they won't invite me to visit their homes. I don't know what they are interested in, but it certainly isn't their kids."

Other problem situations that are often mentioned by discouraged teachers include too many children, no time allowed for planning, inadequate salaries, extra demands made on teachers such as supervising school activities, selling tickets, and lack of supportive personnel. The problems enumerated by special teachers are common to regular classroom teachers as well.

There is no standardized mental health approach for schools to follow. The educational team, described earlier, offers a positive outlet for teachers who interact with other professionals around the needs of children in their classes. This concept could be enlarged to create a focus of discussion for an entire school. Most schools appear to have the professional competence to promote healthy environments for their members. Often this competence has been allowed to become dormant or has been used ineffectively. Teachers and administrators can take the first step by developing a system that is open to discussion, to innovation, and to appropriate change. In cases of serious morale problems professional assistance might be needed to get some positive direction.

PARENTS OF CHILDREN IN CONFLICT

The role of parents in program redevelopment is an essential one. Often their presence and support determines district decisions in terms of financing new programs, hiring additional staff, and other important fiscal matters. The continual involvement of parents seems to be essential, both as change agents and in program development efforts.

Most teachers believe that parents of children in conflict are worthy of much program emphasis; many colleges offer one or more courses that emphasize the counseling aspects of working with parents; and nearly every school system encourages its staff to interact with parents. What is the net result of this emphasis? Special programs for handicapped children have expanded in both number and scope, with many children receiving educational services. This growth cannot be attributed totally to interaction with parents, but this is certainly one positive indicator of parental support. Programs that have capitalized on parental involvement report positive dividends in increased parental support, community acceptance, and successful intervention with children.

Overall, however, it appears that efforts with parents of children in conflict have been inadequate. Teachers still blame parents for inadequacies that appear to have been caused by several factors, teachers and schools included. Teachers generally have had only a one-way relationship with parents, with little sharing of ideas.

Roles of parents in the deviance of their children

A review of recent literature shows that information about parents of children in conflict is noticeably lacking. There are many "how to do it books" on child rearing but few good research efforts to determine if parents of deviant children are different from parents of normal children.

Much of the literature blames parents for the way their children act. This blaming is seldom in the form of a direct attack on parents but is a subtle undermining of parents' positions through suggestions of poor home life, inappropriate child-rearing practices, and deviant parent attitudes.

Teachers and other professionals who interact with children are often heard blaming parents for the problems that children exhibit. One sometimes hears things like: "What can you expect of John? Do you know his father?" or "Jennie's mother is working, and you know what that means," or "Didn't you know Bobby's mother and dad are divorced?" or "David's mother and father were killed in an automobile accident when he was 4 years old." All of these statements suggest that teachers believe that good parents and wholesome family life are important to the development of healthy personalities in children.

In her book on emotionally disturbed children, Despert (1965) devoted one section to the family of disturbed children. In a highly emotional narrative she is critical of parents and society on several issues.

1. This is the age of the vitamin pill, scientific formula, and worship of children, but one essential seems to be lacking in our mothers—love. Despert attributes much of the mother's problems to changes in society that have affected her role: smaller families, a mobile society, and a disappearance of the extended family. Despert (1965:248) states that "Instinctive motherliness is being smothered in the material wealth of modern life."

2. The thing that mothers really need cannot be taught—her feelings which can help to guide her behavior with children. Too much attention has been paid to those who have prepared "cookbooks" for motherhood. The young mother feels trapped by her role. She responds to this frustration by overindulgence in her children on the one hand and punishment on the other.

3. A mother has little time or energy to adjust to the role of motherhood if she must rush off to a job each day. In addition, the children must often come home to an empty house or a babysitter. At times the mother must leave home before the father is ready to leave. Despert believes that the confusion of this arrangement can gradually grow into unsolvable problems within the home.

4. A role confusion has developed because of pressures toward a career and a knowledge that it is difficult to be a mother and career person at the same time. Advertisements portray a modern kitchen as a place that all but prepares dinners and does the dishes. Young girls often come to marriage totally unprepared for the tasks that await them.

5. The care of the baby has been one area where mothers have given up much of their natural feelings for the conveniences of mod-

ern life. Breastfeeding is given as a notable example. Despert believes that mothers and babies have suffered because mothers are so concerned over giving the baby what he needs that no time is left to pay attention to what the baby wants.

6. Discipline is difficult for the mother because of the guilt of being absent. In addition, she does not get to know her child intimately enough for adequate discipline.

7. Emotional disturbance in the child is often related to inadequate mothers, to those who are alcoholics, psychotics, and drug addicts.

8. Children have not had the opportunity "to be a part of the family" and thereby learn the process of decision making and the resulting emotional growth. Despert believes that children learn the role of healthy family relationships from their mothers and fathers, not from books.

Despert takes what many might believe to be a regressive position; however, she represents a professional opinion (professor of child psychiatry, teacher, and consultant) that should demand the attention of educators. She refuses to be overwhelmed—a modernism that robs parents and children of their humanism.

Review of selected studies

One of the early attempts to study parent-child relationships was made by Adler (1926), who believed that childhood neurosis resulted from parental overindulgence, pampering, and overprotectiveness. Adler's contention was supported by Levy (1943), who found that many emotional abnormalities were caused by maternal overindulgence. Glidewell (1961) summarized the studies of maternal attitudes as having contributed several important pieces of information, including a loss of socialization caused by (1) extremes of control (overcontrol as opposed to indulgence) and autonomy (ignoring as opposed to overprotecting); (2) extremes of acceptance and rejection; (3) variables of confident spontaneity in the acceptance of the maternal role; (4) the capacity of the mother to find real satisfaction with dependent chil-

dren; and (5) the lack of consistency in the first four dimensions.

In a report by the Joint Commission on Mental Health Noshpitz (1973) suggests that much uncertainty surrounds the relationship of parents to the mental illness of their children. Some believe that the cause is due to parental mishandling, others believe that the causes are unknown, whereas many believe that inborn congenital problems are to blame. Noshpitz believes that many problems are caused by the reluctance of teachers, pediatricians, and friends of the family to recommend therapy for children in need of help. Instead they continue to recommend therapy for parents.

Most of the research on child rearing is centered around the role of the mother. This emphasis appears to overlook several important role factors.

1. The sex role provided by fathers seems to be critical for boys and girls. This is particularly important, since women generally dominate the lives of young children.

2. Fathers often play a role of helping children set limits that are realistic. Limit setting is particularly important early in life until the child can develop internal controls.

3. Fathers equalize the fantasy and wish fulfillment of mothers by their attachment to reality (Noshpitz, 1973).

In an early study of atypical development of children, Rank (1949) found three factors to be important in a child's early life: (1) a serious disturbance in the early relationship between the mother and child, (2) a serious disturbance in the early relationship between the father and child, and (3) traumatic events that affect the child. All of these factors relate to the importance of parent-child relationships in developing emotional health.

Although the research presented indicates that parents play an important role in the formation of emotional health, there is no solid evidence that parents of emotionally disturbed children follow a behavioral pattern from which deviance of their children can be reliably predicted. It appears that when deviance is caused by inappropriate parental behavior, it results from an unhealthy interaction between parents and children rather than from any particular behavioral trait of the parents.

The teacher's role

Karnes et al. (1974) have outlined several assumptions regarding families of handicapped children that appear to have much validity for teachers and parents of children in conflict. These assumptions are summarized as follows:

1. Families are interested in their children and would like to improve their interaction with their children.

2. Families can be helped to improve their interaction skills.

3. Parents can work in a classroom setting in which their own child is a member.

4. Families will find time to become involved with children if their involvement is meaningful.

5. Family members will learn to interact appropriately when their training is to the point and when direct application is possible.

6. Families are easiest to involve when there is a close "match" between their goals and values and those of school personnel.

7. When there is a large discrepancy in the "match," a greater flexibility will be required of the program.

8. Families will become involved in direct proportion to their ability to participate in decision making.

9. Families will involve themselves most when they are getting positive feedback.

10. Families will involve themselves more when they receive genuine interest as individuals from professionals.

11. Involvement is greatest when trained personnel are working with the family.

12. Families will involve themselves when their involvement is individualized.

13. Families will become more involved if they can pass their information on to others.

14. More positive attitudes will be developed when involvement is successful.

15. Families will need less staff help as they develop skills.

16. Families may develop the skills necessary to be helpful to other families.

This list outlines many of the activities that school personnel should keep in mind as they involve parents in the educational programs of their children.

Activities with parents can be effective and rewarding for teachers, children, and parents. Teachers who have the skills and interest in parent interaction should use their ability to promote a cooperative relationship between the home and school. Those who do not have the skills should learn the skills or rely on another teacher, a social worker, or a school nurse with this competency.

Teachers generally will not have the answers for parents; however, through a sharing of ideas with other educational team members, acceptable solutions to problems can often be achieved and growth can result.

ANCILLARY PERSONNEL

Although teachers and parents generally spend a greater number of hours with children in conflict than do ancillary personnel, the involvement of this latter group is critical in a holistic approach. The role played by each of these personnel will vary according to the approach; for example, the social worker's role will generally be different in a behavioral program than in a psychodynamic one. The role descriptions that follow are typical of those employed in schools but not to the exclusion of other alternatives.

School psychologist

The psychologist may serve as a consultant to teachers or other staff, may do individual psychological evaluations, and may work with individual children or small groups. In addition, the school psychologist acts as a liaison to families and community agencies and lends support to in-service activities for the school staff. In states that require individual intelligence testing the psychologist is generally responsible for providing this service.

Counselor

The guidance counselor is generally involved in screening, evaluation, and placement procedures as well as working in a counseling capacity. Often the school counselor has primary responsibility for communications with the home, consultation during crisis situations, and small group counseling. The counselor must work closely with the psychologist and teachers to ensure a productive educational environment.

Social worker

School social workers are skilled in interview and case work techniques, which are extremely important to schools. The liaison between school and home is often fragmented without social work support. In addition to home-school relations the social worker often serves as a contact person with local mental health agencies, physicians, and other community-based specialists. The skilled social worker can offer much insight into school-based operations through collaboration with professionals from various community agencies such as law offices, the courts, and detention centers.

Psychometrist

Some states recognize the psychometrist as the primary person responsible for coordination of screening and testing services— activities generally delegated to the school psychologist. A more limited role can increase the efficiency and free psychologists for concentrated interaction with teachers and students.

Clinical consultants

Child psychologists, psychiatrists, and pediatricians are the major clinical consultants to the school. They are of service as consultants, in private practice with children and families and as supportive personnel to teachers. Teachers who have developed positive relationships with these clinicians have found their support and information invaluable.

Vocational rehabilitation counselors

Rehabilitation counselors offer services to emotionally disturbed individuals that often are unavailable through other sources, including evaluation for work and training programs, job-related counseling, and job placement. These services are generally available only to older students who are nearing work age.

Art, music, and recreational therapists

Art, music, and recreational specialists have definite skills in their respective areas that are beneficial to children in conflict. Each of them uses components from their skill area that have therapeutic value. Specialists of this type are still relatively rare in both public school and clinical situations.

GUIDELINES FOR PROGRAM REDEVELOPMENT

The following guidelines are offered for those who wish to establish new programs or redevelop those already functioning.

1. Establishing administrative support
   a. Legislative action has put a great deal of weight behind those who wish to provide programs for all handicapped children, including the emotionally disturbed. This legislative posture was started during the Eisenhower administration and has continued since that time.
   b. Available financial support should be explored as an incentive to those who begin programs to serve handicapped children.
   c. Administrative routes must be found to gain building level support for children in conflict if programs are to be successful. The principal can often be as effective as the teacher in the outcome of a given program.
2. Priorities
   a. It is necessary to decide on the population to be served (ages, severity, etc.).
   b. A procedure should be developed for referral, screening, and evaluation, etc.
   c. The location and role of special programs should be determined.
   d. Needed staff and materials that are presently unavailable should be acquired.
   e. The continuum of services to be provided should be outlined.
   f. The budget necessary to fund the needed services must be determined.
3. Developing an educational strategy
   a. Emphasis should be made to keep children as close to the regular classroom as feasible.
   b. Individual programing should be the goal whenever possible.
   c. A team approach should be encouraged in addition to reliance on individual problem solving.
   d. Alternative programs should be provided for those who cannot function in the mainstream.

e. Contracts should be made with external agencies for ancillary services not available within the schools.
4. Provision of in-service training
   a. Goals of the in-service program should be outlined.
   b. Trainers for the in-service program should be selected.
   c. Delivery alternatives should be negotiated.
   d. The in-service training must be provided.
   e. The results of training should be evaluated.
5. Alternatives to in-service training
   a. "Professional leaves" for renewal of skills (e.g., classroom visitation, sabbatical leaves).
   b. Grade level and school staff meetings.
   c. Extension courses from colleges.
   d. Consultants (e.g., textbook and equipment companies, colleges).
   e. Workshops.
   f. Professional conventions.
   g. Professional library.
   h. District, state, and regional newsletters.

SUMMARY

Several key personnel must be effective agents of change for children in conflict. The special teacher needs to have a certain flexibility and ability to share expertise with other professionals, an understanding of techniques in relieving conflicts in a regular classroom, an ability to unify, and a willingness to share the glory of success with others.

Teachers must not only be psychologically healthy on entry to the classroom but be able to maintain their mental health. Adequate preparation, adult support, self-awareness, and patience are a few of the important steps in remaining healthy. Custodians, bus drivers, and parents would be logical team members.

The vital role of parents is outlined. As agents of change, parents offer teachers some of the stronger co-workers if allowed to participate in the change process. A posture of cooperation rather than a posture of confrontation is all that is needed in many cases to stimulate this change.

Parents of emotionally disturbed children have been the subject of many studies to discover their unique qualities. Most of these appear to be weakened because they are focused only on the mothers of disturbed children. The disturbance of children appears

to result from an inappropriate interaction that develops between parents and the child rather than any specific behavioral type.

Ancillary personnel are discussed in relation to both the teacher and the child. These include the psychologist, counselor, social worker, art and music therapists, and other specialists who often are supportive to the educational endeavors of teachers.

Finally, guidelines for program redevelopment were discussed, including the establishment of administrative support, priorities, developing an educational strategy, and in-service training.

BIBLIOGRAPHY AND SUGGESTED READINGS

Adler, A.: The neurotic constitution: outlines of a comparative individualistic psychology and psychotherapy, New York, 1926, Dodd, Mead & Co.

Despert, L.: The emotionally disturbed child: an inquiry into family patterns, Garden City, N.Y., 1965, Anchor Books, Imprint of Doubleday & Co., Inc.

Glidewell, J.: Parental attitudes and child behavior, Springfield, Ill., 1961, Charles C Thomas, Publisher.

Glueck, S., and Glueck, E.: Unraveling juvenile delinquency, New York, 1950, The Commonwealth Fund.

Karnes, M., Zehrbach, R., and Teska, J.: Involving families of handicapped children. In Kelly, T., Lyndall, L., and Dykes, M., editors: School and community resources for the behaviorally handicapped, New York, 1974, MSS Information Corp.

Levy, D.: Maternal overprotection, New York, 1943, Columbia University Press.

Long, N., and Newman, R.: The teacher and his mental health. In Long, N., Morse, W., and Newman, R., editors: Conflict in the classroom, Belmont, Calif., 1971, Wadsworth Publishing Co., Inc.

Mackie, R., Kvaraceus, W., and Williams, H.: Teachers of children who are socially and emotionally handicapped, Washington, D.C., 1957, Government Printing Office.

Morse, W., Cutter, R., and Fink, A.: Public school classes for the emotionally handicapped: a research analysis, Washington, D.C., 1964, The Council for Exceptional Children.

Noshpitz, J., editor: Report of the Committee on Clinical Issues. In Lustman, S.: The mental health of children: services, research, and manpower, New York, 1973, Harper & Row, Publishers.

Peter, L.: Prescriptive teaching, New York, 1965, McGraw-Hill Book Co.

Rank, B.: Adaptation of the psychoanalytic technique for the treatment of young children with atypical development, American Journal of Orthopsychiatry **19:** 130-139, 1949.

CHAPTER 12

Program development: present and future

Programing for children in conflict appears to be in the midst of change. Many states are in the process of developing, or have already enacted, legislative guidelines for schools that establish a time line for implementing programs for all handicapped children. To assess the present status of programing and certification procedures, I sent a questionnaire to fifty states, Puerto Rico, and Washington, D. C. Information forms were completed and returned from all except two of the states for a total number of fifty of fifty-two respondents. A copy of the questionnaire used in the study is shown in Appendix G.

FINDINGS AND CONCLUSIONS OF STATE SURVEY

1. Forty-one respondents reported that state regulations were in force regarding the education of emotionally disturbed children. The remainder of the respondents indicated that special certification was not required.

Conclusion: Most states have certification requirements for teachers who are preparing to teach emotionally disturbed children.

2. Thirty-two respondents reported that certification could be gained at the baccalaureate level. The remainder indicated that

hours beyond this level were required for full certification. No states required a master's degree for initial certification.

Conclusion: The majority of states allow certification without graduate credits.

3. Twenty-six states certify applicants on the recommendation of colleges or universities, whereas fifteen states indicated that certification was determined by the state. Nine respondents indicated their endorsements were competency based. Since several respondents indicated an interest in the work of other states in competency-based programs, I have chosen to list those which indicated competency-based certification. They are California, Florida, Idaho, Nebraska, New Hampshire, New Mexico, New York, North Carolina, and Ohio. Persons interested in competency-based certification can contact these states for details of their certification procedures. Addresses for these agencies are included in Appendix B.

Conclusion: The majority of state agencies certify applicants on the recommendation of colleges and universities who have approved programs. Although several states indicate that they have competency-based certification programs, their responses suggest that the competencies are not "spelled out" in behavior terms but are determined by course title or approved college programs that are competency based.

4. Thirty respondents indicated that they honor certification from other states; however, several of these placed conditions on their response. Eleven respondents said that they did not honor certification from other states.

Conclusion: Most states honor certification in the education of emotionally disturbed children from one or more states. Most of these have some limitation on this policy. The student should check with individual states to be certain of their position in this regard.

5. Twenty-nine respondents indicated that a combination of program emphasis is allowed under certification guidelines. Six respondents said that a psychological approach was emphasized, and six respondents indicated that a behavioral emphasis was required. Other areas received one or fewer responses.

Conclusion: Certification agents reports indicate that no particular program emphasis is fostered in this area. Most states use a combination of two or more strategies with the psychological and behavioral approach most often mentioned as the preferred combination.

6. Thirty-one states reported that temporary certification was available. Grace periods for completion of certification requirements ranged from 1 year to an indefinite time period, with most respondents indicating from 1 to 3 years. Ten states reported that they did not have plans for temporary certification.

Conclusion: A majority of the states have provisions for temporary certification.

7. Thirteen states indicated that they have sufficient numbers of certified teachers for emotionally disturbed children, whereas twenty-six states reported an insufficient number was available.

Conclusion: More than one half of the states report a need for more certified teachers of emotionally disturbed children.

In addition to the numerical data, several impressions were generated by the nature of the responses to the questionnaire and comments that were volunteered by respondents:

1. States are in a period of reappraisal and reorganization of certification requirements.

2. There are still many jobs available for those (a) who are willing to work in rural and inner-city areas and (b) who are fully qualified to work with disturbed children.

3. State certification requirements allow for much flexibility in program philosophy.

4. State certification agents are interested in what other states are doing and extremely responsive to questions regarding their programs.

THE FUTURE

It is always interesting to look to the future and predict what the next decade will bring. This is particularly true at a time when delivery systems in special education appear to be undergoing such drastic changes. Although these predictions are based on the trends and facts of the present, they actually represent "guestimates" of the future rather than what is "hoped for" or what will actually occur.

1. In the next 10 years a point will be reached where many children who cannot function adequately will be placed in regular classrooms. There likely will be a return to some special classes and to resource rooms to supplement regular classes.

2. Behavior modification techniques will decline in popularity and become one of several theoretical approaches used in the school. Requirements for accountability will encourage evaluation techniques that were developed through the behavioral orientation.

3. There will be a return to a team approach, with teachers playing a vital role in team efforts.

4. Teacher unions will take on a more aggressive role in determining professional responsibility to children in conflict.

5. Labeling will continue, but it will be an "in house" process rather than a public posture.

6. Institutional placement will decrease as

schools provide day classes for severely disturbed children. Foster placement and group homes on a smaller scale will likely replace larger state institutions.

7. Economic conditions will force a reassessment of delivery systems so that consumers can get the most for their educational dollar.

8. A greater emphasis will be placed on the role of the family as change agents.

9. Educational programs will rely more heavily on the expertise available within each individual school system, with consultants from outside used only sparingly.

10. Regular classroom teachers will begin to differentiate more precisely the behavioral expectations for individual children. Those capable of appropriate behavior will be held more responsible, whereas those incapable of appropriate behavior will be held accountable at their individual performance level.

11. Classroom teachers will have a greater professional voice in decisions that affect screening, placement, and programing for children as well as competencies for their own certification.

SUMMARY

This chapter reports the findings of a state survey that I conducted. Responses were received from fifty respondents out of fifty-two questioned. The study indicates an active and continuing interest in the education of emotionally disturbed children. The future of disturbed children appears to be bright from a teaching viewpoint, with most state directors indicating that more teachers need to be trained to meet the demands of schools in their respective states.

BIBLIOGRAPHY AND SUGGESTED READING

Rhodes, W.C., and Sagor, M.: A study of child variance: the future, Ann Arbor, Mich., 1974, The University of Michigan Press.

Appendixes

Agencies that support children in conflict

Many services are available for emotionally disturbed, socially maladjusted, and behaviorally disordered children. Whereas agencies will be listed as being either local or national in scope, national groups will often have local chapters that can be consulted for information.

1. Local organizations
   a. Family counselors
   b. Family service agencies
   c. Local information and referral agencies or the yellow pages of telephone books
   d. Mental health clinics
   e. Pastoral counseling services
   f. Public schools
   g. Vocational rehabilitation counseling

2. National organizations

   American Society for Mentally Ill Children
   177 Broad St.
   Staten Island, N.Y. 10304

   Association for Children with Learning Disabilities
   2200 Brownsville Rd.
   Pittsburgh, Pa. 15210

   Child Study Association of America
   9 E. 89th St.
   New York, N. Y. 10028

   Council for Exceptional Children
   1411 South Jefferson Davis Hwy., Suite 900
   Arlington, Va. 22202

   National Association for Mental Health, Inc.
   1800 N. Kent St.
   Arlington, Va. 22209

   National Committee Against Mental Illness
   405 Lexington Ave.
   New York, N. Y. 10017

   National Education Association
   New York Regional Office
   1271 Avenue of the Americas
   New York, N. Y. 10020

   National Society for Autistic Children
   621 Central Ave.
   Albany, N. Y. 12206

   Society for Children with Emotional Disturbances
   1504 Stillwell Ave.
   Bronx, N. Y. 10461

   National Institute of Mental Health
   Bethesda, Md. 20014

   The Institute for Training and Research in Child
      Mental Health
   120 W. 57th St.
   New York, N. Y. 10019

Teacher certification agencies

Teachers who are interested in certification in special education can obtain information by writing to the appropriate state department of certification. These state agencies are also helpful in career planning in general education.

Coordinator of Teacher Education and Certification
State Department of Education
Montgomery, Ala. 36104

State of Alaska
Department of Education
Alaska Office Building
Pouch F. Juneau, Alaska 99801

State Department of Public Instruction
Room 27, Capitol Building
Phoenix, Ariz. 85007

State of Arkansas
Department of Education
State Education Building
Little Rock, Ark. 72201

Commission for Teacher Preparation and Licensing
1020 O St., Room 222
Sacramento, Calif. 95814

State Department of Education
State Office Building
Denver, Colo. 80203

State of Connecticut
Department of Education
P. O. Box 2219
Hartford, Conn. 06115

State Department of Public Instruction
Dover, Del. 19901

District of Columbia Public Schools
415 12th St., N. W.
Washington, D. C. 20004

Department of Education
Floyd T. Christian, Commissioner
Tallahassee, Fla. 32304

State Department of Education
Office of Instructional Services
Teacher Certification Service
State Office Building
Atlanta, Ga. 30334

Office of Personnel Services
State Department of Education
P. O. Box 2360
Honolulu, Hawaii 96804

Department of Education
State of Idaho
Len B. Jordan Office Building
Boise, Idaho 83720

State Teacher Certification Board
212 E. Monroe St.
Springfield, Ill. 62706

Division of Teacher Education and Certification
Room 230 State House
Indianapolis, Ind. 46204

Department of Public Instruction
Grimes State Office Building
Des Moines, Iowa 50319

Kansas State Department of Education
Kansas State Education Building
120 E. 10th St.
Topeka, Kan. 66612

Division of Teacher Education and Certification
State Department of Education
Frankfort, Ky. 40601

State of Louisiana
Department of Education
P. O. Box 44064
Baton Rouge, La. 70704

Division of Professional Services
State Department of Education
Augusta, Me. 04330

Maryland State Department of Education
P. O. Box 8717
BWI Airport
Baltimore, Md. 21240

The Commonwealth of Massachusetts
Department of Education
182 Tremont St.
Boston, Mass. 02111

Michigan Department of Education
Special Education Services
Box 420
Lansing, Mich. 48902

State of Minnesota
Department of Education
Capitol Square
550 Cedar St.
St. Paul, Minn. 55101

State of Mississippi
Department of Education
P. O. Box 771
Jackson, Miss. 39205

State Department of Education
Division of Public Schools
P. O. Box 480
Jefferson City, Mo. 65101

Superintendent of Public Instruction
State Department of Public Instruction
Helena, Mont. 59601

State of Nebraska
Department of Education
233 S. 10th St.
Lincoln, Neb. 68508

Nevada Department of Education
Carson City, Nev. 89701

Director, Teacher Education and Professional Standards
State House Annex, Room 410
Concord, N. H. 03301

Department of Education
Division of Field Services
Bureau of Teacher Education and Academic Credentials
Trenton, N. J. 08625

State of New Mexico
Department of Education
Education Building
Santa Fe, N. M. 87501

The University of the State of New York
The State Education Department
99 Washington Ave.
Albany, N. Y. 12210

State of North Carolina
Department of Public Instruction
Raleigh, N. C. 27611

Department of Public Instruction
Bismarck, N. D. 58501

Division of Teacher Education and Certification
1012 State Office Building
Columbus, Ohio 43215

State Department of Education
Oklahoma City, Okla. 73105

Teacher Standards and Practices Commission
942 Lancaster Dr., Ne.
Salem, Ore. 97310

Commonwealth of Pennsylvania
Department of Education
Box 911
Harrisburg, Pa. 17126

Commonwealth of Puerto Rico
Department of Education
Hato Rey, P. R. 00919

State of Rhode Island and Providence Plantations
Department of Education
199 Promenade St.
Providence, R. I. 02908

State Department of Education
Rutledge Office Building
Columbia, S. C. 29201

Department of Education and Cultural Affairs
Division of Elementary and Secondary Education
State Capitol Building
Pierre, S. D. 57501

Department of Education
Teacher Education and Certification
125 Cordell Hull Building
Nashville, Tenn. 37219

Texas Education Agency
201 E. Eleventh St.
Austin, Tex. 78701

Utah State Board of Education
1400 University Club Building
136 E. South Temple St.
Salt Lake City, Utah 86111

Vermont Department of Education
Montpelier, Vt. 05602

Commonwealth of Virginia
State Department of Education
Richmond, Va. 23216

Superintendent of Public Instruction
Old Capitol Building
Olympia, Wash. 98504

State of West Virginia
State Superintendent of Schools
Department of Education
Charleston, W. Va. 25305

State Superintendent
Department of Public Instruction
126 Langdon St.
Madison, Wis. 53702

Pupil Services
Casper-Midwest Schools
c/o Willard School
129 North Elk
Casper, Wyo. 82601

Films and video tape recordings that discuss children in conflict

The following films and video tape recordings are available for those who interact with children in conflict. They may be appropriate for teacher and parent groups and for in-service training as well as for college classes. A brief outline of each film is presented.

16 mm films

A Time For Georgia (b & w; 14 minutes)
Captioned Films for the Deaf
624 E. Walnut St., Suite 223
Indianapolis, Ind. 46204

A pre-school workshop is the setting of this film, which shows children who are experiencing social, emotional, and learning disabilities. The film focuses on Georgia, a 4-year-old who exhibits autistic behaviors.
Audience: College or professional level persons interested in early identification and placement of handicapped children.

Activity Group Therapy (b & w; 56 minutes)
Center for Mass Communication of Columbia University Press
440 W. 110th St.
New York, N. Y. 10025

Activity group therapy was developed using hidden cameras over a 2-year period. The film shows emotionally disturbed boys aged 10 and 11 years during various therapy situations.
Audience: Child care workers, clinicians, and teachers.

Aggressive Child (b & w; 28 minutes)
McGraw-Hill Films
330 West Hill Films
New York, N. Y. 10036

The film shows Phillip, an intelligent 6-year-old, whose disruptive behavior stimulates the authorities to suggest psychiatric help to the parents.
Audience: Professionals and parents. Film shows real patients in a therapeutic situation.

Angry Boy (b & w; 33 minutes)
McGraw-Hill Book Co.
330 West 42nd St.
New York, N. Y. 10036

This film shows a traditional team approach of a mental health clinic as they interact with a 10-year-old boy who has been caught stealing.
Audience: Mental health workers and teachers.

Autism's Lonely Children (b & w; 20 minutes)
Audio-Visual Center
Indiana University
Bloomington, Ind. 47405

This film investigates the problem of the autistic child within the neuropsychiatric school at the University of California at Los Angeles. It shows the isolation of autism and how it is helped by the use of a "learning box."
Audience: College and professional persons interested in severe emotional problems.

Battered Child (b & w; 58 minutes)
Audio-Visual Center
Indiana University
Bloomington, Ind. 47405

This is a documentary of child abuse by a team of professionals at the University of Colorado. In the film
the team discusses the cause and effects of child
abuse.
Audience: Teachers, parents, child care workers, and
medical personnel.

Beach Interview (b & w; 27 minutes)
Wediko Films
267 W. 25th St.
New York, N. Y. 10001

This film shows the use of life space interview techniques with two boys who demand to leave camp
while they are upset by camp events.
Audience: Professionals interested in the use of life
space interview techniques with disturbed children.

*Behavior Modification: Teaching Language to Psychotic
Children* (color; 42 minutes)
Film Library
Prentice-Hall, Inc.
Englewood Cliffs, N. J. 07632

This film is based on the work of Ivar Lovaas at the
University of California at Los Angeles. It shows reinforcement and stimulus fading techniques that are
used in language development with psychotic children.
Audience: Professionals interested in language development and behavior modification with psychotic children.

Boy With a Knife (b & w; 19 minutes)
International Films Bureau
332 S. Michigan Ave.
Chicago, Ill. 60608

A gang of boys are headed for problems with the law
when a group worker is able to reach them. The
film is a reenactment of a case story from the films
of a Los Angeles youth service agency.
Audience: Teachers, social workers, and others working
with delinquent youth.

Boys in Conflict (b & w; 72 minutes)
Wediko Films
267 W. 25th St.
New York, N. Y. 10001

This is a feature-length film that covers one camp counselor's day-to-day experiences with nine boys who are
experiencing emotional and behavioral problems. It
is an overview of an entire summer camp experience.
Audience: Professionals interested in working with disturbed boys; it is excellent for discussion purposes.

Broken Bridge (color; 35 minutes)
Time-Life Films, Inc.
43 W. 16th St.
New York, N. Y. 10011

This film shows actual therapy sessions with autistic
children by Irene Kassoria. Over a period of 6 months
Dr. Kassoria is able to penetrate the walls that im-
prison these children. Using a three-step technique,
she (1) teaches imitation, (2) teaches children to answer questions, and (3) finally teaches techniques for
asking questions.
Audience: Professionals, college students, and others
interested in child care.

Bruce (b & w; 26 minutes)
Wediko Films
267 W. 25th St.
New York, N. Y. 10001

Bruce is a 13-year-old boy who is unable to control
his impulses. He is in constant conflict with those
around him. This is filmed in a summer camp setting.
Audience: Professionals who are interested in disturbed
boys in a summer camp setting should find this film
excellent for discussion purposes.

Child Behind the Wall (b & w; 30 minutes)
SK & F Services Department
Smith, Kline and French Laboratories
1500 Spring Garden St.
Philadelphia, Pa. 19101

This is a filmed documentary of an emotionally disturbed
child undergoing treatment at the child study center
of the Institute of Pennsylvania Hospital, Philadelphia.
Audience: Teachers, parents, and others interested
in the emotionally disturbed child. It provides an
excellent overview for public understanding of problems of disturbance.

Children in the Hospital (b & w; 44 minutes)
International Film Bureau, Inc.
332 S. Michigan Ave.
Chicago, Ill. 60604

The film records the spontaneous activity of children in
the wards of Boston City Hospital. It illustrates the
emotional responses of children 4 to 8 years of age
to the stress of hospitalization, illness, and separation
from parents.
Audience: Child care workers who want to learn about
childhood reaction to stress.

Delinquent Child (color; 32 minutes)
Wyeth Film Library
P. O. Box 8299
Philadelphia, Pa. 19101

This film shows the experiences of a delinquent girl, who is also disturbed, in an institutional setting. The film shows a therapeutic program, including medical management and adjunctive therapy.
Audience: Professional child care workers interested in delinquent children.

Discipline and Self-Control (b & w; 25 minutes)
Duart Film Laboratories
245 W. 55th St.
New York, N. Y. 10019

The film discusses the problems of discipline and how teachers can develop control in a friendly atmosphere. The dangers of too much and too little control are pointed out.
Audience: Teachers interested in working with children in conflict.

Early Treatment of the Mentally Ill (b & w; 29 minutes)
Audio-Visual Center
Indiana University
Bloomington, Ind. 47405

This film outlines the history of insanity through the Middle Ages, including the healing techniques used by Romans and Greeks.
Audience: Adults interested in the history of mental illness.

Girl in Danger (b & w; 28 minutes)
McGraw-Hill Book Co.
330 W. 42nd St.
New York, N. Y. 10036

This film shows the problems of a teen-age girl as she becomes entangled in various emotional conflicts, running away, stealing, and breaking the rules. Efforts to help her to develop emotional maturity and responsibility are shown.
Audience: Teachers, counselors, and other child care workers.

One to Grow On series
National Institute of Mental Health Film Collection
National Audiovisual Center (GSA)
Washington, D. C. 20409

He Comes From Another Room (color; 28 minutes)

This film discusses the integration process of Chris and David, two of seven children from a special class. It outlines the process of mainstreaming with support from various school staff and ancillary personnel.
Audience: School staffs interested in mainstreaming.

Other films in the series include the following color films:

Act II—Lindsey
Sarah
A Pretty Good Class for a Monday

These three films are all set in a high school and can be described as problem films with the participants providing solutions to the problem situations.

Individuals
A Teacher in Reflection
Learning Strategies

These three films are all set in an elementary school and present problems and propose solutions to the viewer.
Audience: All of these films are intended for those who are interested in the mental health of children in the classroom.

Jamie: A Behavioral Approach to Family Intervention (b & w; 15 minutes)
Neuropsychiatric Institute
MRCPP Media Unit, Room 78-208
760 Westwood Plaza
Los Angeles, Calif. 90024

This film shows how parents of a disturbed child can receive help from a behavioral approach. Behavior therapy is used with a 5-year-old child, and discussions with parents are shown. It is an excellent film for parent interaction.
Audience: Parents, child care workers, and teachers.

Jennifer is a Lady (b & w; 26 minutes)
New York University Film Library
26 Washington Pl.
New York, N. Y. 10003

This film shows teaching techniques used with autistic children who are attending a preschooler's workshop.
Audience: Teachers and other professionals interested in language development with disturbed preschool children.

Johnny (b & w; 32 minutes)
Wediko Films
267 W. 25th St.
New York, N. Y. 10001

This film shows Johnny, a 9-year-old boy, as he tries to gain control over his feelings and find more appropriate ways to communicate. It is a highly controversial film, which adds to its teaching potential through discussion.
Audience: Excellent film for discussion among professionals interested in emotionally disturbed boys.

Madison Plan (color; 28 minutes)
Santa Monica Project
1723 4th St.
Santa Monica, Calif. 90401

This film is a follow-up of the Santa Monica Project, which shows how various exceptionalities can be handled in a larger group setting.
Audience: Teachers.

No Two Kids Are Alike (color; 28 minutes)
Captioned Films for the Deaf
624 E. Walnut St., Suite 223
Indianapolis, Ind. 46204

This film suggests ways of helping parents maintain control of emotionally disturbed children so that gains made in school will not be undone at home. It stresses individual differences of children who are handicapped.
Audience: Parents and teachers.

One Hour a Week (color; 15 minutes)
Captioned Films for the Deaf
624 E. Walnut St., Suite 223
Indianapolis, Ind. 46204

This film shows the program at the League School for Seriously Disturbed Children, which trains mothers to deal with special problems of their disturbed children. The program is designed to help parents who want to keep their disturbed child at home rather than in an institution.
Audience: Parents of disturbed children and teachers.

Peer Conducted Behavior Modification (b & w; 30 minutes)
Neuropsychiatric Institute
MRCPP Media Unit, Room 78-208
760 Westwood Plaza
Los Angeles, Calif. 90024

This film illustrates a unique approach to dealing with a disturbed child through peer interaction. Parents are shown how the child's peers and their parents can be mobilized to help modify behavior problems.
Audience: Parents and teachers interested in the role of parents and peers in behavior modification.

Point of View: A Comparison of Play-Centered Therapy and Behavior Modification (color; 20 minutes)
Captioned Films for the Deaf
624 E. Walnut St.
Indianapolis, Ind. 46204

This film compares and explores the differences between two approaches to therapy.
Audience: Professionals working with handicapped children.

Prior and Present Experience (b & w; 30 minutes)
Audio-Visual Center
Indiana University
Bloomington, Ind. 47401

This film demonstrates the need for teachers to consider the background differences between themselves and those they teach. These differences are pointed out as a result of a field trip to the museum.
Audience: College level students and professionals in education.

Problem Children (b & w; 20 minutes)
SWS Films
744 N. Fuller Ave.
Hollywood, Calif. 90046

This film shows how two boys, one acting out and aggressive and the other withdrawn, can be helped in school.
Audience: Teachers interested in a variety of behavioral problems.

Randy (b & w; 27 minutes)
Wediko Films
267 W. 25th St.
New York, N. Y. 10001

This film shows Randy, one of the more seriously disturbed children at Camp Wediko. Randy, aged 11 years, is shown being helped by four different counselors.
Audience: Professionals interested in severely disturbed boys.

Referred for Underachievement (b & w; 35 minutes)
Center for Mass Communication of Columbia University Press
440 W. 110th St.
New York, N. Y. 10025

Leo, a 12-year-old child, is referred for underachievement and because of his unsatisfactory performance to the Child Psychiatric Unit of Massachusetts General Hospital.
Audience: Adults interested in family interviewing.

Rewards and Reinforcements (b & w; 26 minutes)
Audio-Visual Center
Indiana University
Bloomington, Ind. 47401

This film demonstrates the principles of operant conditioning in teaching economically underprivileged children. Reinforcers include candy, money, clothes, and other material objects.
Audience: Professionals interested in operant conditioning with economically deprived children.

Santa Monica Project (color; 28 minutes)
Santa Monica Project
1723 4th St.
Santa Monica, Calif. 90401

The film outlines the behavior modification techniques used in the project during a contrived setting.
Audience: Those interested in educational intervention with behaviorally disordered children.

School (b & w; 30 minutes)
Grove Press, Inc.
80 University Pl.
New York, N. Y. 10003

This film shows the educational approach used during the filming of *Warrendale*. Footage for this film was also produced during the shooting of the film *Warrendale*.
Audience: Teachers.

Self-Management of Behavior (b & w; 33 minutes)
Neuropsychiatric Institute
MRCPP Media Unit, Room 78-208
760 Westwood Plaza
Los Angeles, Calif. 90024

This film shows two behavior-problem children, an 11-year-old who is living in a residential treatment program and a 7-year-old who is being treated as an outpatient. The film has commentary by B. F. Skinner and shows self-intervention behavior modification.
Audience: Teachers and child care workers.

Springtime for Hugo (color; 900 feet)
Technifilm, Inc.
919 N. W. 19th Ave.
Portland, Ore. 97209

This film describes a public school program in Parkrose School District, Oregon. Techniques used with emotionally disturbed children are shown.
Audience: Teachers.

Street Corner Research (b & w; 30 minutes)
Center for Mass Communication of Columbia University Press
440 W. 110th St.
New York, N. Y. 10025

A psychologist goes to the street corner to search out clients. The film reports the results of such an encounter.
Audience: Adult audiences interested in social maladjustment and counseling of young adults.

Toddler Management (color; 22 minutes)
Captioned Films for the Deaf
624 E. Walnut St., Suite 223
Indianapolis, Ind. 46204

A demonstration film showing mothers how to cope with oppositional behavior of emotionally disturbed children. Mid-Cumberland Regional Intervention Program at Nashville, Tennessee, is the site of this filming.
Audience: Parents, teachers, and counselors.

The Better Way . . . Learning to Care (color; 16½ minutes)
Aims Instructional Media Services, Inc.
P. O. Box 1010
Hollywood, Calif. 90028

A documentary film showing how a dance teacher sees the self-confidence of troubled girls develop. Las Palmas School for Girls is the scene of this film.

Audience: Professional persons working with young adults; police, teachers, social workers, college students, and those interested in the values of dance as therapy.

The Neglected (b & w; 30 minutes)
International Film Bureau, Inc.
332 S. Michigan Ave.
Chicago, Ill. 60604

This film discusses the neglected child and his family as well as reasons for this neglect and/or abuse. The film suggests ways in which the child protective agencies can change family behavioral patterns that are dangerous and unhealthy.
Audience: Child care workers and teachers.

The Quiet One (b & w; 67 minutes)
McGraw-Hill Book Co.
330 W. 42nd St.
New York, N. Y. 10036

A child who is extremely lonely is shown as he slowly becomes involved in delinquent acts to achieve those things he has been unable to gain in other ways.
Audience: Teachers and mental health workers.

The World Outside (b & w; 31 minutes)
S-L Film Production
5126 Hartwick St.
Los Angeles, Calif. 90041

This award-winning film shows how two severely emotionally disturbed children are helped by skilled therapists to see the world outside.
Audience: Teachers, counselors, and psychologists.

Time's Lost Children (color; 29 minutes)
Audio-Visual Center
Indiana University
Bloomington, Ind. 47401

The private world of the autistic child is reviewed in this film by parents, teachers, and physicians. Parents tell how their children appeared to be normal until they were 2 or 3 years of age.
Audience: Professionals and parents interested in children with autistic behavior and ways to deal with it; it is excellent as an introductory overview of autism.

Troubled Campers (b & w; 18 minutes)
Wediko Films
267 W. 25th St.
New York, N. Y. 10001

This film provides an overview of the problems of disturbed children attending Camp Wediko. It is very useful for discussion purposes.
Audience: Professionals interested in working with disturbed boys.

Warrendale (b & w; 105 minutes)
Grove Press, Inc.
80 University Pl.
New York, N. Y. 10003

This feature-length film is a dramatic portrayal of the emotionally disturbed. The film was made in Canada.
Audience: Anyone interested in emotional disturbance in children.

Who Is This Child (b & w; 30 minutes)
Buffalo Regional SEIMC
New York State Education Department
Media Materials Distribution Center
55 Elk St.
Albany, N. Y. 12224

A case study technique is used to show how the disturbed child can be identified. An autistic child is shown attending a regular public school class, and an acting-out child is shown attending a residential treatment center. It is an excellent overview film.
Audience: Teachers and child care workers interested in definition of emotional disturbance.

Who Shall Help This Child (b & w; 20 minutes)
Buffalo Regional SEIMC
New York State Education Department
Media Materials Distribution Center
55 Elk St.
Albany, N. Y. 12224

This film overviews techniques for helping emotionally disturbed children: residential programs, BOCES programs, resource rooms, teacher mothers, etc.
Audience: Teachers, child care workers, and parents.

Why Vandalism (b & w; 17 minutes)
Encyclopedia Brittanica Corp.
425 N. Michigan Ave.
Chicago, Ill. 60611

This film tries to show the causes that underlie acts of vandalism performed by three boys. In this case the problems are thought to include character traits and environmental factors.
Audience: Teachers and workers with juvenile offenders.

Video tape recordings

In addition to the professional films that are available for teachers there are a number of video tape recordings that have been prepared by the Conceptual Project in Emotional Disturbance. These video tape recordings were prepared through funding from the United States Office of Education and cover a variety of topics and theoretical positions. All tapes are ½-inch EIAJ standard.

1. General introduction
   A Study of Child Variance: Part A, *Theories* (20 minutes)
   A Study of Child Variance: Part B, *Interventions* (34 minutes)
2. Topical interviews
   a. Theories
      Bernard Rimland—*Biogenic* (25 minutes)
      Jay Birnbrauer—*Behavioral* (53 minutes)
      Jane Kessler—*Psychodynamic* (58 minutes)
      Thomas Scheff—*Sociological* (55 minutes)
      Edwin Willems—*Ecological* (57 minutes)
      Herbert Grossman—*Countertheory* (28 minutes)
      Everett Reimer—*Countertheory* (38 minutes)
   b. Interventions
      Alan Cott—*Biogenic* (30 minutes)
      K. Daniel O'Leary—*Behavioral* (30 minutes)
      Jeannine Guindon—*Psychodynamic* (31 minutes)
      Carl Fenichel—*Behavioral/Psychodynamic* (31 minutes)
      LaMar Empey—*Environmental* (20 minutes)
      Humphry Osmond—*Environmental* (31 minutes)
      Peter Marin—*Countertheoretical* (30 minutes)
   c. Care-delivery systems
      Vernon Haubrich—*Education* (30 minutes)
      John Seeley—*Mental Health* (30 minutes)
      Sanford Fox—*Legal/Correctional* (30 minutes)
      Haskell Miller—*Religious* (30 minutes)
      Richard Cloward—*Social Welfare* (30 minutes)
      Sam Keen—*Counter Institutions* (30 minutes)
3. Discussion topics (conference excerpts)
   a. Theories
      Borrowing Across Theories (32 minutes)
   b. Interventions
      Ethical Issues (25 minutes)
      Forms and Effectiveness of Institutions (31 minutes)
      Effective Teaching (20 minutes)
   c. Care-delivery systems
      Bullets and Ballots (18 minutes)
      Special Problems and Needs of Caring Institutions (24 minutes)
      We Begin in the World (28 minutes)
      Defining Deviance (24 minutes)
      Redefining Values (24 minutes)

Ordering video tape recordings
Conceptual Project
ISMRRD
130 S. First St.
Ann Arbor, Mich. 48108

Publishers of professional books, curriculum materials, and equipment for teachers of children in conflict

Publishers are currently developing many new materials for use with children in conflict. The following alphabetical listing was adapted from Gearheart (1973) with additional sources identified by means of a survey of publishers, suppliers, and research bureaus for children in conflict.

Academic Therapy Publications
1539 Fourth St.
San Rafael, Calif. 94901

Acropolis Books
2400 17th St., N. W.
Washington, D. C. 20009

Allied Educational Council
Distribution Center
P. O. Box 78
Galien, Mich. 49113

Allyn & Bacon, Inc.
470 Atlantic Ave.
Boston, Mass. 02210

American Educational Publications
245 Long Hill Rd.
Middletown, Conn. 06457

American Guidance Service, Inc.
Publishers Building
Circle Pines, Minn. 55014

Ann Arbor Publishers
2057 Charlton
Ann Arbor, Mich. 48103

Appleton-Century-Crofts
440 Park Ave., S.
New York, N. Y. 10016

Association for Childhood Education International
3615 Wisconsin Ave., N. W.
Washington, D. C. 20016

Audio-Visual Research
1317 Eighth St., S. E.
Waseca, Minn. 56093

Baggiani & Tewell
4 Spring Hill Court
Chevy Chase, Md. 20015

Basic Books, Inc., Publishers
404 Park Ave., S.
New York, N. Y. 10016

Bell & Howell Co.
7100 McCormick Rd.
Chicago, Ill. 60645

The Bobbs-Merrill Co., Inc.
4300 West 62nd St.
Indianapolis, Ind. 46206

Borg-Warner Educational Systems
7450 N. Natchez Ave.
Niles, Ill. 60648

Bowmar Publishing Corp.
622 Rodier Dr.
Glendale, Calif. 91201

William C. Brown Co., Publishers
135 S. Locust St.
Dubuque, Iowa 52001

Burgess Publishing Co.
4265 6th St.
Minneapolis, Minn. 55415

Chandler Publishing Co.
124 Spear St.
San Francisco, Calif. 94105

Child Study Association of America
9 E. 89th St.
New York, N. Y. 10028

Childcraft Education Corp.
964 Third Ave.
New York, N. Y. 10022

Constructive Playthings
1040 East 85th St.
Kansas City, Mo. 64131

Consulting Psychologists Press, Inc.
577 College Ave.
Palo Alto, Calif. 94306

Continental Press, Inc.
Elizabethtown, Pa. 17022

Control Development, Inc.
3166 Des Plaines Ave.
Des Plaines, Ill. 60018

Council for Exceptional Children
1411 S. Jefferson Davis Highway
Arlington, Va. 22202

Craig Corp. & Industrial Division
921 W. Artesia Blvd.
Compton, Calif. 90220

Creative Playthings
Edinburg Rd.
Cranbury, N. J. 08512

The John Day Co., Inc.
257 Park Ave., S.
New York, N. Y. 10010

Developmental Learning Materials
3505 N. Ashland St.
Chicago, Ill. 60657

Dick Blick, Inc.
P. O. Box 1267-F
Galesburg, Ill. 61401

Dimensions Publishing Co.
Box 4221
San Rafael, Calif. 94903

The Dryden Press, Inc.
901 N. Elm
Hinsdale, Ill. 60521

Educational Activities, Inc.
Freeport, N. Y. 11520

Educational Development Laboratories
284 Pulaski St.
Huntington, N. Y. 11744

Educational Projections Corp.
1911 Pickwick Ave.
Glenview, Ill. 60610

Educational Research Information Center (ERIC)
ERIC Document Reproduction Service
Bell & Howell Co.
1700 Shaw Ave.
Cleveland, Ohio 44112

Educational Service, Inc.
P. O. Box 219
Stevensville, Mich. 49127

Educational Teaching Aids
159 W. Kinzie St.
Chicago, Ill. 60610

Educators Publishing Service, Inc.
75 Moulton St.
Cambridge, Mass. 02138

EduKaid of Ridgewood
1250 E. Ridgewood Ave.
Ridgewood, N. J. 07450

Expression Co.
155 Columbus Circle
Boston, Mass. 02116

Eye Gate House
146-01 Archer Ave.
Jamaica, N. Y. 11435

Fearon Publishers, Inc.
2165 Park Blvd.
Palo Alto, Calif. 94306

Follet Educational Corp.
1010 W. Washington Blvd.
Chicago, Ill. 60607

Gamco Industries, Inc.
P. O. Box 1911
Big Springs, Tex. 79720

Garrard Publishing Co.
1607 N. Market St.
Champaign, Ill. 61820

Ginn & Co.
125 Second Ave.
Waltham, Mass. 02154

Group for the Advancement of Psychiatry
Publications Office
419 Park Ave., S.
New York, N. Y. 10016

Grune & Stratton, Inc.
111 Fifth Ave.
New York, N. Y. 10003

Gryphon Press
220 Montgomery St.
Highland Park, N. J. 08904

Guidance Associates
1526 Gilpin Ave.
Wilmington, Del. 19800

Guidance Associates of Pleasantville, New York
41 Washington Ave.
Pleasantville, N. Y. 10570

E. M. Hale and Co.
1201 S. Hastings Way
Eau Claire, Wis. 54701

Harcourt Brace Jovanovich, Inc.
757 Third Ave.
New York, N. Y. 10017

Harper & Row, Publishers
49 E. 33rd St.
New York, N. Y. 10016

D. C. Heath & Co.
125 Spring St.
Lexington, Mass. 02173

Hoffman Information Systems
5623 Peck Rd.
Arcardia, Calif. 91006

Holt, Rinehart & Winston, Inc.
383 Madison Ave.
New York, N. Y. 10017

Houghton Mifflin Co.
2 Park St.
Boston, Mass. 02107

Ideal School Supply Co.
11000 S. Lavergne St.
Oak Lawn, Ill. 60453

Imperial International Learning Corp.
P. O. Box 548
Kankakee, Ill. 60901

Incentive Products Educational
1902 Coral Way
Miami, Fla. 33145

Instructo Corp.
200 Cedar Hollow Rd.
Paoli, Pa. 19301

Intext Publishing Co.
Scranton, Pa. 18515

The Johns Hopkins Press
Baltimore, Md. 21218

Journal of Learning Disabilities
5 N. Wabash Ave.
Chicago, Ill. 60602

Kenworthy Educational Service, Inc.
P. O. Box 3031
Buffalo, N. Y. 14205

Keystone View Co.
Box D
Meadville, Pa. 16335

Kingsbury Center
2138 Bancroft Pl.
Washington, D. C. 20008

Kismet Publishing Co.
P. O. Box 90
South Miami, Fla. 33143

Knowledge Aid
6633 W. Howard St.
Niles, Ill. 60648

Kutz Corp.
P. O. Box 140
McLean, Va. 22101

Laidlaw Brothers
Thatcher and Madison St.
River Forest, Ill. 60305

Language Research Associates
Box 95
Chicago, Ill. 60637

Lawson Book Co.
9488 Sara St.
Elk Grove, Calif. 95624

Lea & Febiger
600 S. Washington Sq.
Philadelphia, Pa. 19106

Learning Research Associates, Inc.
1501 Broadway St.
New York, N. Y. 10036

Learning Systems Press
P. O. Box 909-E
Rantoul, Ill. 61866

Learning Trends
115 Fifth Ave.
New York, N. Y. 10003

J. B. Lippincott Co.
E. Washington Sq.
Philadelphia, Pa. 19105

Little, Brown & Co.
34 Beacon St.
Boston, Mass. 02106

Litton Instructional Materials, Inc.
1695 W. Crescent Ave.
Anaheim, Calif. 92801

Love Publishing Co.
6635 E. Villanova Pl.
Denver, Colo. 80222

Lyons & Carnahan
407 E. 25th St.
Chicago, Ill. 60616

McGraw-Hill Book Co.
Educational Development Laboratories
284 Pulaski Rd.
Huntington, N. Y. 11743

David McKay Co., Inc.
750 Third Ave.
New York, N. Y. 10017

The Macmillan Co.
866 Third Ave.
New York, N. Y. 10022

Mafex Associates, Inc.
111 Barron Ave.
Johnstown, Pa. 15906

Math Media, Inc.
P. O. Box 345
Danbury, Conn. 06810

Mead Educational Services
245 N. Highland Ave.
Atlanta, Ga. 30307

Media
P. O. Box 1355
Vista, Calif. 92083

Medical Motivation Systems
Research Park, State Rd.
Princeton, N. J. 08540

Mental Health Materials Center
419 Park Ave., S.
New York, N. Y. 10016

Charles E. Merrill Publishing Co.
1300 Alum Creek Dr.
Columbus, Ohio 43216

Milton Bradley Co.
74 Park St.
Springfield, Mass. 01106

The C. V. Mosby Co.
11830 Westline Industrial Dr.
St. Louis, Mo. 63141

MultiMedia Education, Inc.
11 W. 42nd St.
New York, N. Y. 10036

National Association for Mental Health, Inc.
10 Columbus Circle
New York, N. Y. 10019

National Clearinghouse for Mental Health Information
National Institute of Mental Health
Bethesda, Md. 20014

National Department of Health and Welfare
Mental Health Division
Ottawa, Canada

New York Association for Brain Injured Children
95 Madison Ave.
New York, N. Y. 10016

Noble & Noble, Publishers, Inc.
750 Third Ave.
New York, N. Y. 10017

Open Court Publishing Co.
P. O. Box 599
LaSalle, Ill. 61301

Oxford University Press, Inc.
200 Madison Ave.
New York, N. Y. 10016

Peek Publications
164 E. Dana St.
Mountain View, Calif. 94040

Phonovisual Products, Inc.
12216 Parklawn Dr.
Rockville, Md. 20852

Plays for Living
Family Service Association of America
44 E. 23rd St.
New York, N. Y. 10010

Prentice-Hall, Inc.
Englewood Cliffs, N. J. 07632

J. A. Preston Co.
71 Fifth Ave.
New York, N. Y. 10003

Priority Innovations
P. O. Box 792
Skokie, Ill. 60076

Project Life—General Electric
P. O. Box 43
Schenectady, N. Y. 12301

Pruett Publishing Co.
P. O. Box 1560J
Boulder, Colo. 80302

Psychotechnics, Inc.
1900 Pickwick Ave.
Glenview, Ill. 60025

Public Affairs Pamphlets
22 E. 38th St.
New York, N. Y. 10016

Research Press Co.
CFS Box 3327
Champaign, Ill. 61820

Research Relating to Children
Children's Bureau
U. S. Department of Health, Education and Welfare
Washington, D. C. 20201

Response Systems Corp.
Edgemont, Pa. 19028

Rheem Mfg., Califone Division
5922 Bowcroft St.
Los Angeles, Calif. 90016

Scholastic Book Services
906 Sylvan Ave.
Englewood Cliffs, N. J. 07632

Scholastic Magazines, Inc.
50 W. 44th St.
New York, N. Y. 10036

Science Research Associates, Inc.
259 E. Erie St.
Chicago, Ill. 60611

Scott, Foresman & Co.
1900 E. Lake Ave.
Glenview, Ill. 60025

Select-Ed, Inc.
973 Mart Way
Olathe, Kan. 66061

Smith, Kline & French Laboratories
1500 Spring Garden St.
Philadelphia, Pa. 19101

Society for Visual Education, Inc.
1345 W. Diversey Pwy.
Chicago, Ill. 60614

Special Child Publications
4535 Union Bay Pl.
Seattle, Wash. 98105

Speech & Language Materials, Inc.
P. O. Box 721
Tulsa, Okla. 74101

Stanwix House, Inc.
3020 Chartiers Ave.
Pittsburgh, Pa. 15204

Steck-Vaughn Co.
P. O. Box 2028
Austin, Tex. 78767

R. H. Stone Products
18279 Livernois
Detroit, Mich. 48221

Superintendent of Documents
U. S. Government Printing Office
Washington, D. C. 20402

Syracuse University Press
Box 8, University Sta.
Syracuse, N. Y. 13210

Teachers College Press
1234 Amsterdam Ave.
New York, N. Y. 10027

Teachers Publishing Corp.
23 Leroy Ave.
Darien, Conn. 06820

Teaching Resources Corp.
100 Boylston St.
Boston, Mass. 02116

Teaching Technology Corp.
7471 Greenbush Ave.
North Hollywood, Calif. 91609

Charles C Thomas, Publisher
301 E. Lawrence Ave.
Springfield, Ill. 62703

Toplinger Publishing Co., Inc.
200 Park Ave., S.
New York, N. Y. 10003

Tweedy Transparencies
208 Hollywood Ave.
East Orange, N. J. 07018

United Transparencies, Inc.
P. O. Box 688
Binghamton, N. Y. 13902

University of Chicago Press
5750 Ellis Ave.
Chicago, Ill. 60637

University of Illinois Press
Urbana, Ill. 61801

University of Kansas Press
366 Watson
Lawrence, Kan. 66044

Videorecord Corporation of America
180 E. State St.
Westport, Conn. 06880

Webster Division of McGraw-Hill Book Co.
Manchester Rd.
Manchester, Mo. 63011

Henri Wenkart
4 Shady Hill Sq.
Cambridge, Mass. 02138

Western Psychological Services
12031 Wilshire Blvd., Dept. E
Los Angeles, Calif. 90025

John Wiley & Sons, Inc.
605 Third Ave.
New York, N. Y. 10016

Word Making Productions
P. O. Box 1858
Salt Lake City, Utah 84100

Federally sponsored Learning Resource Centers (LRCs)

In 1974 the Bureau of Education for the Handicapped (BEH) awarded contracts to twenty-six regional contractors to form the Learning Resource Center network. Thirteen contracts were awarded to Regional Resource Centers (RRCs) and thirteen to Area Learning Resource Centers (ALRCs). The RRC network is designed to stimulate, reinforce, and guide individual states and local agencies in their efforts to reach the 1980 BEH goal: to provide an appropriate education for every handicapped child.

Whereas coordination between the RRCs and ALRCs is provided in the LRC concept,

specific charges are made to each program area. RRCs are basically responsible for appraisal of and programing for handicapped children, whereas the ALRCs are accountable for the development of materials, media, and educational technology services to those identified as needing special intervention. This could be conceptualized as shown in the accompanying diagram.

To appreciate fully this rather complex system one will need to utilize the services that are available. A listing of LRC contractors by region is provided so that teachers and others interested in the services may

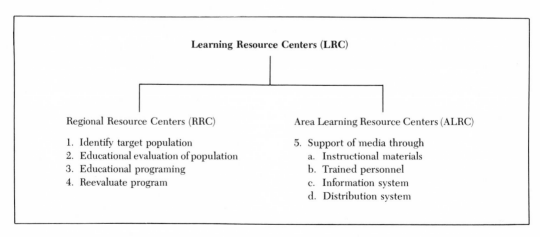

Learning Resource Centers (LRC)

Regional Resource Centers (RRC)

1. Identify target population
2. Educational evaluation of population
3. Educational programing
4. Reevaluate program

Area Learning Resource Centers (ALRC)

5. Support of media through
   a. Instructional materials
   b. Trained personnel
   c. Information system
   d. Distribution system

contact the office in their area for further information.

Learning Resource Center Network

Regional Resource Center	States served
Northwest Regional Resource Center Project Director University of Oregon Clinical Services Building, Third floor Eugene, Ore. 97403	Alaska, Hawaii, Samoa, Guam, Trust Territory, Wash., Idaho, Ore., Mont., Wyo.
California Regional Resource Center Project Director 1031 S. Broadway, Suite 623 Los Angeles, Calif. 90007	Calif.
Southwest Regional Resource Center Project Director 2363 Foot Hill Dr., Suite G Salt Lake City, Utah 84109	Nev., Utah, Colo., Ariz., N. M., B.I.A. Schools
Midwest Regional Resource Center Project Director Drake University 1332 26th St. Des Moines, Iowa 50311	N. D., S. D., Neb., Kan., Okla., Iowa, Mo., Ark.
Texas Regional Resource Center Project Director Texas Education Agency 201 E. 11th St. Austin, Tex. 78701	Tex.
Great Lakes Regional Resource Center Project Director Wisconsin State Department of Public Instruction 126 Langdon St. Madison, Wis. 53702	Minn., Wis., Mich., Ind.
Illinois Regional Resource Center Project Director Peoria Public School District 3202 N. Wisconsin Ave. Peoria, Ill. 61603	Ill.
Ohio Regional Resource Center Project Director Ohio State Department of Education Division of Special Education 933 High St. Worthington, Ohio 43085	Ohio
Northeast Regional Resource Center Project Director 384 Stockton St. Hightstown, N. J. 08520	Me., Vt., N. H., Mass., R. I., Conn., N. J.
New York Regional Resource Center Project Director City University of New York 144 W. 125th St. New York, N. Y. 10027	N. Y.
Pennsylvania Regional Resource Center Project Director 443 S. Gulph Rd. King of Prussia, Pa. 19406	Pa.
Mid-East Regional Resource Center Project Director 1901 Pennsylvania Ave., N. W. Suite 505 Washington, D. C. 20036	Del., D. C., Md., Va., W. Va., Ky., Tenn., N. C.
Southeast Regional Resource Center Project Director Auburn University at Montgomery Montgomery, Ala. 36109	La., Miss., Ala., Ga., S. C., Fla., P. R., Virgin Is.

Coordinating Office for the Regional Resource Centers

CORRC Project
Project Director
Bradley Hall
University of Kentucky
Lexington, Ky. 40506

Area Learning Resource Center	States served
Northwest Area Learning Resource Project Director University of Oregon Clinical Services Building, Third floor Eugene, Ore. 97403	Alaska, Hawaii, Trust Territory, Guam, Samoa, Wash., Ore., Idaho, Mont., Wyo.
California Area Learning Resource Center Project Director 1031 S. Broadway Suite 623 Los Angeles, Calif. 90007	Calif.
Southwest Area Learning Resource Center Project Director New Mexico State University Box 3AW Las Cruces, N. M. 88003	Nev., Utah, Colo., Ariz., N. M., B.I.A. Schools
Midwest Area Learning Resource Center Project Director 114 Second Ave. Coralville, Iowa 52241	N. D., S. D., Iowa, Neb., Kan., Okla., Mo., Ark.
Texas Area Learning Resource Center Project Director Texas Area Learning Resource Center 2613 Wichita St. Austin, Tex. 78701	Tex.
Great Lakes Area Learning Resource Center Project Director Michigan Department of Education P. O. Box 420 Lansing, Mich. 48902	Minn., Wis., Mich., Ind.

Illinois Area Learning Resource Center   Ill.
Project Director
1020 S. Spring St.
Springfield, Ill. 62706

Ohio Area Learning Resource Center   Ohio
Project Director
Ohio Division of Special Education
933 High St.
Worthington, Ohio 43085

Northeast Area Learning Resource Center   Me., Vt., N. H., Mass., Conn., R. I., N. J.
Project Director
384 Stockton St.
Hightstown, N. J. 08520

New York Area Learning Resource Center   N. Y.
Project Director
New York State Education Department
Division for Handicapped Children
55 Elk St., Room 117
Albany, N. Y. 12234

Pennsylvania Area Learning Resource Center   Pa.
Project Director
443 S. Gulph Rd.
King of Prussia, Pa. 19406

Mid-East Area Learning Resource Center   Del., D. C., N. C., Md., Va., W. Va., Ky., Tenn.
Project Director
University of Kentucky
Porter Building, Room 123
Lexington, Ky. 40506

Southeast Learning Resource Center   La., Miss., Ala., Ga., S. C., Fla., P. R., Virgin Is.
Project Director
Auburn University at Montgomery
Montgomery, Ala. 36109

Specialized office
Project Director
Audio-Visual Center
Indiana University
Bloomington, Ind. 47401

The National Center on Educational Media and Materials for the Handicapped
NCEMMH
Project Director
Ohio State University
220 W. 12th Ave.
Columbus, Ohio 43210

APPENDIX F

Directories: Children in conflict

The following listing of directories is available for groups who are seeking information for children in conflict.

General directories

A Selected Guide to Public Agencies concerned with Exceptional Children
CEC Information Center on Exceptional Children
1920 Association Dr.
Reston, Va. 22091

Directory of Easter Seal Services for the Disabled
The National Easter Seal Society for Crippled Children and Adults
2023 W. Ogden Ave.
Chicago, Ill. 60612

Directory for Exceptional Children
Porter Sargent Publisher
11 Beacon St.
Boston, Mass. 02108

Directory of Facilities for the Learning Disabled and Handicapped
Careth Ellingson and James Cass
Harper & Row, Publishers
10 E. 53rd St.
New York, N. Y. 10022

Directory of Half-way Houses for the Mentally Ill and Alcoholic
National Institute of Mental Health
5600 Fishers Lane
Rockville, Md. 20852

Directory of Information and Referral Centers
United Way of America
Alexandria, Va. 22314

Directory of Organizations Interested in the Handicapped
Committee for the Handicapped
People to People Program
1146 16th St., N. W.
Washington, D. C. 20036

Mental Health Directory
National Institute of Mental Health
5600 Fishers Lane
Rockville, Md. 20852

Voluntary Action Centers
National Center for Voluntary Action
1625 Massachusetts Ave., N. W.
Washington, D. C. 20036

Summer camps

Directory of Summer Camps for Children with Learning Disabilities
ACLD
5225 Grace St.
Pittsburgh, Pa. 15236

Easter Seal Directory of Resident Camps for Persons with Special Health Needs
The National Easter Seal Society for Crippled Children and Adults
2023 W. Ogden Ave.
Chicago, Ill. 60612

Guide to Summer Camps and Summer Schools
Porter Sargent Publisher
11 Beacon St.
Boston, Mass. 02108

Alternative schools

Alternatives!
1526 Gravenstein Highway North
Sebastopol, Calif. 97452

New Schools Exchange
2840 Hidden Valley Lane
Santa Barbara, Calif. 93103

Summerhill Society
339 Lafayette St.
New York, N. Y. 10012
or
6063 Harges St.
Los Angeles, Calif. 90034

Private Independent Schools
The Bunting and Lyon Blue Book
Bunting & Lyon, Inc.
238 North Main St.
Wallingford, Conn. 06492

State certification/endorsement survey (emotionally disturbed/ behaviorally disordered)

Check responses most appropriate to your state.

1. Do you have state regulations regarding teacher certification in emotional disturbance?
   a. Yes_____ Legislation number_____
   b. No_____
2. Level at which certification is gained.
   a. B. A._____
   b. B. A. plus _____ hours
   c. M. A._____
3. How is certification determined?
   a. State agency_____
   b. College or university_____
   c. Competency based_____ (please include copy if available)
   d. Other_____ (explain)
4. Does state honor certification from other states?
   a. Yes_____ (which states?)
   b. No_____
5. Major emphasis as determined by certification requirements.
   a. Sociological_____
   b. Psychological_____
   c. Biophysical_____
   d. Behavioral_____
   e. Combination_____ (which?)
   f. Other_____ (explain)
6. Temporary certification available?
   a. Yes_____ (grace period _____ years)
   b. No_____

7. Does your state presently have a sufficient number of endorsed teachers?
   a. Yes_____
   b. No_____
8. Would you like a copy of the results of this study?
   a. Yes_____
   b. No_____

Name_____ Date_____

Return to: Dr. Henry R. Reinert
         Chairman, Department of Special Learning Problems
         University of Northern Colorado
         Greeley, Colo. 80639

Glossary

adjustive resources Resources of an individual child that can be used in solving various problems.

acting-out behavior Inappropriate behavior of an agressive type.

aggressive Exhibiting an outgoing manner, either physically or verbally.

anal-expulsive substage A substage of the anal stage of psychosexual development in which the child derives gratification from the expelling of feces.

anal-retentive substage A substage of the anal stage of psychosexual development in which the child derives gratification from the holding back of feces.

anal stage The stage in psychosexual development lasting from approximately 2 to 4 years of age in which gratification is centered around the anal area of the body and the process of defecation.

anomie The conflict that arises between the approved goals of a society and the means provided by that society to reach those goals.

ancillary personnel Supportive personnel to the professional who holds the major responsibility for a given child.

anticathexis The process by which the ego uses its psychic energy to control the id.

art therapy A therapeutic process using the various visual arts as a vehicle of intervention.

asocial Not social; avoiding contacts and interaction with others.

atypical child Child who varies from the norm of normalcy to a significant degree.

autism Extreme withdrawal from reality and particularly from human relationships.

baseline data The data that are collected before behavioral intervention begins.

behavioral theory A theory that is concerned with outward, observable behavior.

behavior modeling The imitation of others rather than trial and error for behavior and attitude formation; can be used to learn behavior or to induce new behaviors to take the place of undesirable behaviors.

bibliotherapy Use of stories to help children overcome conflicts in their lives.

biochemical diseases Disorders of the body related to its chemical make up.

biochemical factor An element relating to the chemical makeup of the body.

biogenetic disorder A severe behavior disorder that results from the physical-chemical environment.

biogenetic factor An element relating to the inherited makeup of the body.

biophysical theory A theory concerned with the constitutional, genetic, and chemical factors that affect the life of the individual.

catalyst The name of a particular democratic method used for developing a cooperative effort among administrators, teachers, and children to meet the educational needs of exceptional children.

cathexis Use of mental energy to further the needs of the individual.

castration anxiety In Freudian theory an unconscious fear of losing the genital organs, usually as a punishment for sexual desires.

cathartic form of therapy A form of therapy in which the individual talks out problems.

child in conflict The child who manifests behavior that has a deleterious effect on personal or educational development and/or the personal or educational development of peers. Negative effects may vary considerably from one child to another in terms of severity and prognosis.

classical conditioning The process by which a specific stimulus is given the power to elicit a response that it does not normally elicit; same as respondent conditioning.

classroom teacher A teacher whose main responsibility is to teach basic educational skills.

clinical exploitation of life events The process of dealing with a crisis and the events surrounding it in a methodical way, taking as much time as necessary, so that the individual can see the relationships between the beginning, development, and resolution of the conflict.

clinical psychologist One who has studied behavior and the mental processes and who subsequently works in the evaluation and treatment of mental illness.

conformists Those who follow rules.

conformity When used by Merton, means the acceptance of cultural goals and of the institutional means to reach these goals.

conscience In Freudian theory the part of the superego that is morally critical of the behavior, actions, and values of the self.

contiguity theorists A branch of behaviorists who hold that the essential element in learning is the closeness in time and space of stimulus and response.

contingency management Manipulation of the environmental consequences of a behavior to achieve control.

counterconditioning Reinforcement of behaviors that are in conflict with undesirable behaviors.

counter theories Those theories that seek to change established procedures; they do not necessarily have common bonds among themselves.

countertheorist One whose theory utilizes parts of the theories of more established approaches such as the psychoanalytical or behavioral theories but who adds components that change the original theory to a significant degree.

crisis intervention Intervention during a crisis in a child's behavior with the emphasis placed on the crisis situation.

crisis teacher A teacher who is trained in the process of intervening in crisis situations with a child.

defensive behavior A term used by Carl Rogers to designate behavior that is traditionally labeled neurosis.

delinquent A child over the age of 10 years who is legally guilty of breaking the law.

deviant An individual who breaks rules.

diagnosis A careful investigation of the facts in a situation with the purpose of deciding what the difficulty is so that it can be remedied.

diathesis An inherited predisposition.

diathesis stress An inherited predisposition coupled with environmental stimulation.

disorganized behavior A term used by Carl Rogers to designate behavior that is traditionally labeled psychosis.

dizygotic twins Fraternal twins, coming from two separate ova in the mother but at the same time.

director of special education The administrator of a special education program in a school district usually working directly under the superintendent.

dominant genes Those genes that are expressed in the makeup of an individual even though paired with another gene that would have been expressed in a different way.

ecological theory A theory that emphasizes the interaction between an individual and the environment.

educational team Unofficial team designed to help individual children.

ego A system within the individual that mediates between the demands of the id and the constraints of the world in which the individual lives.

ego-ideal In Freudian theory the part of the superego that comprises the aims and goals of the individual with emphasis on what the individual should be and do.

ego pathology Difficulty with language development and with relating to people.

Electra complex The Oedipus complex as it relates to the female.

eliciting stimulus A stimulus that precedes behavior, when used by Merton, and means the acceptance of cultural goals but not of the institutional means to reach these goals.

emotional disintegration A breakdown in the functioning of an individual's feelings or emotions so that they function inadequately or erratically.

emotional first aid on the spot The process of dealing with a crisis and the events surrounding it as quickly as possible to facilitate immediate return to the reality situation.

emotionally disturbed Severe disturbance of emotional processes.

endocrine development The development and functioning of the endocrine glands, mainly the thyroid, adrenal, and pituitary glands; these glands produce chemical substances that help to regulate body functioning.

enuresis Involuntary discharge of urine during sleep.

erotic zones Parts of the individual's body that are vested with sexual feelings.

exhibitionism Extravagant or unusual behavior designed to attract attention.

fixation The halting of psychosexual maturation at a particular point in development.

genetic counseling The process of studying the inherited characteristics of an individual and providing advice concerning probabilities of passing on particular characteristics or genes.

genital stage The stage of psychosexual development from adolescence on in which a person achieves a mature sexual relationship.

gestalt The perceiving of a total object while at the same time observing its component parts and their relationship to each other.

high probability behaviors Behaviors that the individual frequently chooses to do and that can be used as natural reinforcers especially for low probability behaviors.

holistic approach An approach to children in conflict that emphasizes a variety of techniques.

humanistic psychologist A psychologist who has added a component of social theory to psychological models.

hyperactive behavior An excessive amount of physical activity and movement.

id The inherited system of instinctual energy that supplies power for the entire personality.

infantile autism The inability of an infant to relate to people or things outside himself.

institutionalized personality Personality type of an individual who has spent considerable time in an institution and consequently develops mannerisms and ways of relating to the environment that are artificial and strange to other people.

intrapsychic conflicts Conflicts that take place within the individual arising from desires and demands of the various impulses and drives within the individual.

intermittent reinforcement Scheduling reinforcers at intervals rather than for every occurrence of a behavior.

interval reinforcement Scheduling reinforcers to time intervals, for example, one reinforcer for every three minutes.

latency stage The stage of psychosexual development from approximately 6 or 7 years of age to adolescence in which there is a slowing up of or resting from active psychosexual development.

labeling theory A theory which holds that labeling alone is a powerful inducement toward deviance or conformity.

learning disability One or more significant deficits in the essential learning process that requires special educational techniques for its remediation. A child with a learning disability shows a discrepancy between expected and actual achievement, which is not the result of a sensory, motor, intellectual, or emotional handicap or the lack of opportunity to learn.

learning disabled An individual who demonstrates a discrepancy between expected achievement and actual achievement that is not due to a sensory, intellectual, motor, or emotional handicap or to the lack of opportunity to learn.

learning theory A system of basic beliefs concerning what causes learning to take place and by what process it takes place.

libido Psychic energy supplied by the id that allows the total personality system to function; this energy is sexual, fluid, and displaceable.

life space interview A cathartic technique used in crisis intervention in which the teacher talks through with the child the crisis and problem at the time it occurs.

low probability behaviors Behaviors that will tend to disappear if not reinforced; they are behaviors seldom chosen by the individual.

mainstreaming The inclusion of handicapped children in regular classrooms with nonhandicapped children.

maladaptive Exhibiting an inability to adjust to the environment.

medical model A method of approaching questions or problems that seeks out causes.

mentally ill General term that describes a variety of emotional problems.

mentally retarded Describes a person who has subnormal mental development and functioning.

mental health professionals Those professionals who help individuals to integrate themselves satisfactorily both within themselves and in relationship to their environment.

mental hygiene Prevention of mental problems through various techniques designed to preserve mental health.

microcommunity The smaller portion of a community that is the immediate environment of the individual.

milieu therapy Of French derivation, a word used to mean the treatment by environment, generally treatment in an institution or hospital setting.

monozygotic twins Identical twins; those coming from one ovum in the mother.

music therapy Using music to bring out feelings that would otherwise fail to surface.

negative reinforcement The maintenance or increase of a particular behavior caused by a particular stimulus being removed.

Neo-Freudian theorists Freudian theorists who offer a newer view of the original theory established by Sigmund Freud.

neurological impairment Damage to or some deficiency in the nervous system of the body.

neurosis A partial disorganization of the personality.

object cathexis The process of investing psychic energy to satisfy an instinct.

occupational therapy A therapeutic process that uses manual activities to treat emotional problems.

Oedipus phase A stage in the development of the child in which he experiences attachment for the parent of the opposite sex and aggression toward the parent of the same sex; this is usually an unconscious process.

operant conditioning The process of reinforcing desired behavior with reinforcers that will cause the child to repeat the desired behavior again.

oral aggressive stage A substage of the oral stage of psychosexual development in which the child experiences pleasure in biting activities; also known as the oral sadistic stage.

oral dependent stage A substage of the oral stage of psychosexual development in which the child experiences pleasure in sucking activities; also known as the oral erotic stage.

oral stage of development The earliest stage of psychosexual development lasting from birth to about 2 years of age in which gratification is centered around the mouth and mouth functions, such as sucking and biting.

organic brain pathology A physical disorder of the brain resulting in a disorder in normal functioning.

overinhibited Holding back normal self-expression in words, behavior, or emotions.

pathology Abnormal condition in behavior that stems from medical causation.

pediatrician A physician who has specialized training in the development, care, and diseases of children.

perceptual causation Caused by the way in which the individual perceives and interprets the stimuli that are present to him.

perceptually impaired Difficulty in perceiving objects or events as they really are; inability to interpret correctly what is seen, heard, or experienced.

permissiveness The practice of allowing the child to be free to express feelings completely.

phallic stage The stage of psychosexual development from approximately 4 to 6 years of age in which the child is preoccupied with sexual matters, centering around the penis or clitoris; it is in this stage that the child is working out sexual identity.

phenylketonuria (PKU) A metabolic disorder found in infants who are lacking an enzyme that is needed to properly assimilate phenylalanine, an amino acid found in foods containing protein. If untreated, it results in mental retardation.

phobia Uncontrollable fear of a pathological nature.

play therapy Making use of the child's natural world of play for therapeutic purposes.

pleasure principle The reduction or elimination of tension from the individual by the avoidance of pain and striving for gratification.

positive reinforcement The maintenance or increase of a behavior because a particular stimulus is applied.

prelatency stages The oral, anal, and phallic stages of psychosexual development.

prescriptive educational programing Educational programing based on individual educational needs, both psychological and academic.

primary deviance The initial rule breaking done by an individual.

primary socializing system System comprising groups of people in the immediate environment and functioning closest to the individual.

Project Re-Ed A project for the reeducation of emotionally disturbed children in which children are placed in a residential care unit that focuses on the educative process.

projective tests Psychological tests used diagnostically in which the material is so unstructured that the subject's responses will reveal something of his personality and conflicts.

psychiatrist A physician who has specialized training in the diagnosis and treatment of mental illness.

psychic energy Energy supplied by the id that allows the total personality system to function; this energy is sexual, fluid, and displaceable.

psychoanalysis A form of psychotherapy originated by Sigmund Freud in which a patient delves into the unconscious to become aware of the existence of and reasons for deep conflicts. Free association and dream analysis are used.

psychodynamic theory The study of the human person recognizing the role of the unconscious.

psychogenesis Having originated and developed in the psyche or mind.

psychopathic personality The personality makeup of an individual who is unable to learn from experiences and does not experience normal feelings such as love or guilt.

psychopathology The study of mental illness with its causes, symptoms, and development.

psychosexual stages of development In Freudian theory the stages of libidinal maturation from birth to adulthood.

psychosis Severely disorganized behavior and personality.

psychotherapy The treatment of emotional disorders by psychodynamic methods.

pull-out program Taking children out of the regular classroom.

punishment In behavioral theory the removal of a positive reinforcer and the presentation of a negative reinforcer to decrease a specific behavior.

puppetry In this book refers to the use of puppets to encourage communication that might not otherwise develop.

ratio reinforcement Reinforcers scheduled according to a ratio of acts to reinforcers, for example, one reinforcer for every three acts.

reality principle The modification of the pleasure principle by the demands of the external world.

reality rub-in The process of making a child aware of what happened immediately after a crisis situation and what the child's part is in the crisis situation.

rebellion When used by Merton, it means the rejection of both cultural goals and the institutional means to reach these goals and the substitution of new goals and new means.

recessive genes Those genes that are only expressed in the makeup of an individual if they are paired with genes similar to themselves.

reinforcement A method by which a stimulus increases or maintains a specific behavior.

reinforcement theorists A branch of behaviorists who hold that the most important element in learning is what happens immediately after the learning.

reinforcer A stimulus that results in the maintenance or increase of a behavior.

reinforcing stimulus A stimulus that follows a behavior.

resource room A classroom where children with special needs go for a part of the school day to obtain special help in learning areas in which they need it or go at times of the day when they need it; the amount of time varies from a few minutes to the bulk of the day. The specially trained teacher in this room works cooperatively with the regular classroom teacher.

resource teacher When used in reference to children in conflict, a person who is a change agent to help children to establish more appropriate ways of interacting with those in their environment.

respondent conditioning The process by which a specific stimulus is given the power to elicit a response it does not normally elicit; same as classical conditioning.

retreatism The rejection of both cultural goals and the institutional means to reach these goals.

ritualism The rejection of cultural goals but the acceptance of the institutional means to reach these goals.

satiation Allowing a behavior to continue until it stops voluntarily.

schedules of reinforcement The rate at which reinforcers are delivered regardless of the pattern.

schizophrenia A form of psychosis characterized by withdrawal, hallucinations, and avoidance of human relationships.

school psychologist A psychologist who has studied the mental processes and behavior and specialized in how these concepts relate to children in a school setting.

screening The process of selecting a small group of children from a much larger group for a specific purpose, such as for diagnostic evaluation.

secondary deviance Rule breaking that occurs after an individual is perceived as a rule breaker.

self-contained classroom A classroom where children with special needs are assigned for the entire day and where the specially trained teacher has the responsibility for their educational program as well as for the behavior intervention process.

Snellen chart A chart to be hung on a wall that has letters or symbols in graded size and is used to screen out children with visual problems.

societal reaction theory Another term used for labeling theory.

sociological theory A theory of behavior with emphasis on human society, its needs, development, and organization.

sociometrics The measurement of the interaction within a social group.

sociopathic personality The personality makeup of an individual who has an extreme disregard of and hostility for society and in particular for all organized segments of society.

socially maladjusted Refers to an individual who has difficulty dealing with society and groups of people.

socially nearsighted behavior A term used by Fritz Redl to mean the inability of individuals to perceive what they have done toward creating their own problems.

social reinforcers Nonmaterial rewards for desired behavior, such as praise or attention.

social worker An individual who is trained in social work techniques such as case work or group work and who holds an M.S.W. or D.S.W. degree.

Stanford-Binet individual intelligence test An individually administered intelligence test that emphasizes verbal ability. It has norms for individuals from age 2 years through adult.

subconscious Refers to both the preconscious and the unconscious.

superego The norms and values of society that are taught to the child by the parents and significant others and are taken into the child's personality.

symbiotic infantile psychosis The psychosis of an infant in which the parent figure and the infant are both disturbed and dependent on each other and who mutually reinforce the disturbance and dependency in each other.

symptom estrangement The process of letting go of inappropriate behaviors.

tangible reinforcers Material rewards for desired behavior, such as candy or tokens.

teacher counselor A teacher who has specialized training in the teaching of emotionally disturbed children and whose emphasis is shared between educational tasks and dealing with behavior.

therapeutic play Play activities that are structured so that maximum therapeutic benefits can be gained.

therapeutic team A team of individuals who work together cooperatively to plan for and service an individual child who has special needs. The makeup of the team is varied and might include classroom teacher, school psychologist, school nurse, social worker, speech therapist, special education teacher, and psychiatrist.

therapist teacher A teacher who is trained to work with the behaviors of children in conflict while maintaining an educational program for their continuity of learning.

time-out room A room away from the regular classroom where no reinforcement is likely and where a child can go to recoup strengths.

token A small gift that is a symbol of having accomplished something; also used as a symbol to be exchanged for some tangible object.

total care facility An institution where individuals spend 24 hours a day because they cannot be maintained in their home or a home substitute and that attempts to meet basic needs for food, shelter, play, and education as well as social and emotional needs.

touch control The method of physically touching a child to affect the child's behavior and mental outlook.

toxic psychosis A psychosis that results from the effect of chemicals and drugs on the individual. These might be produced by the body or taken into it.

transference The process of transferring feelings and attitudes that an individual has toward important people in his life onto someone else, such as a therapist.

tunnel vision Seeing only the part of the world in the individual's immediate area or interest area without being able to see the wider world surrounding it.

uninhibited Without normal restraints.

unsocialized Being unable to deal adequately with groups of people.

variable reinforcement Random reinforcement after various numbers of acts or varying amounts of time.

visiting teacher A teacher who gives school instruction to students who are unable to attend school for medical reasons.

Author index

Subject index